NEW
ROGET'S
THESAURUS

1995 EDITION

Paradise
Press, Inc.

Miami, Florida

CONTENTS

Synonyms . . .

Are those words which appear under the
alphabetical listing
All have the same meaning

Antonyms . . .

Are those words which appear under the
alphabetical listing in parentheses
All have the opposite or different meanings

Parts Of Speech . . .

Abbreviations:

n - noun
v - verb
adv - adverb
adj - adjective

Cover Design 1995 - Carol-Ann McDonald

Printed in U.S.A. All Rights Reserved.

Copyright © 1995

Paradise Press, Inc.

ISBN #1-884907-05-9

30279

A

abandon-v depart, go, quit, vacate, evacuate, exit, retire, withdraw, remove, (spring, fly, embark, reach, attain, advent, arrive, join, return, land, get to)

abate-v decrease, diminish, lessen, wane, ebb, decline, descend, subside, melt, die away, subtract, decay, (advance, gain strength, grow, add, enlarge, increase, augment)

abdicate-v resign, give up, vacate, retire, renunciate, abjuration, renounce, disclaim, anarchy, relaxation, loosening, remission, (authorize, influence, despotism, command)

abduct-v take, catch, hook, nab, bag, clutch, sequester, distress, capture, extortion, rapacity, receive, evict, (unclench, release, replevin, return, give, restore, render)

aberrant-adj abnormal, stray, exceptional, deviant, diverge, irregularity, variety, exemption, qualification, (illustrate, conform, adapt, follow, conventional, normal)

abet-v aid, help, support, sustain, uphold, further, advance, nurture, cradle, suckle, relief, rescue, (bar, clog, drag, hinder, stop, impede, obstruct, thwart, frustrate)

abhor-v dislike, loathe, hate, detest, abominate, repel, sicken, reluctance, unwillingness, repugnance, animosity, (care for, like, desire, take to, want, need)

abide-v persist, remain, stay, endure, maintain, keep, continue, sustain, uphold, carry on, keep one's course, (desist, cease, discontinue, halt, pause, rest)

ability-n ableness, cogent, competency, validity, skill, adroitness, craft, proficiency, knack, (bungle, fumble, botch, incompetent, raw, green, disability, impotent)

ablaze-adj afire, burning, fiery, shining, bright, heat, caloric, temperature, warmth, spark, fever, bonfire, (cool, cold, icy, dark, obscure, gloomy, somber, lightless)

able-adj ability, competent, efficient, enablement, capable, competent, dexterous, proficient, (incompetent, unskilled, awkward, clumsy, helpless, exhaust)

abnormal-adj unconventional, oddity, rarity, freak, bizarre, aberration, individuality, idiosyncrasy, (normal, conform, regular, usual)

aboard-*adv* inhabit, dwell, reside, stay, lodge, presence, occupancy, attendance, inhabit, moored, roost, (absent, void, vacuum, away, gone, missing, lost, elsewhere)

abode-*n* dwelling, lodging, domicile, residence, address, home, fatherland, quarters, roost, camp, household, native land, inhabit, bivouac, native, cottage, hermitage

abolish-*v* destruction, dissolution, annihilation, nullify, annul, put an end to, tumble, topple, smash, destroy, break, undo, (produce, do, make, construct, form, fabricate)

abominable-*adj* evil, bad, sinister, dreadful, dire, horrid, foul, rotten, offensive, hurt, injure, abuse, maltreat, damnify, (super, excellent, good, best, good as gold)

abortion-*n* failure, fault, miscarriage, blunder, botch, fail, unsuccessful, lost, cast away, wrecked, addle, stillborn, fruitless, lame, (succeed, triumph, gain, attain)

about-*adv* reference, refer, analogy, pertaining, related, connect, associate, near, close, nigh, approximate, around, (disconnected, independent, no relation, irrelevant, remote, far, out of the way)

above-*adv* superior, exceed, transcend, out-do, pass, surpass, top, beat, over, eclipse, precede, ultra, supreme, aloft, overhead, elevated, lofty, upper, (below, underlie, down, ebb, inferior, less, smaller)

abroad-*adv* remote, removed, afar, distant, away, off, yonder, farther, further, beyond, apart, asunder, (earshot, close, near, nigh, bordering, contiguous, adjoining, adjacent, proximate, home, intimate, beside, here)

abrupt-*adj* instantly, sudden, moment, flash, burst, hasty, instantaneously, presto, (eternity, ever, perpetual, flowing, everlasting, continued, evergreen, immortal, undying)

absence-*n* alibi, emptiness, vacuum, void, exemption, hiatus, truant, absent, vacate, withdraw, gone, missing, lost, wanting, omitted, empty, devoid, (presence, occupancy, attendance, fill, pervade, permeate)

absolute-*adj* infinity, greatest, transcend, intense, profound, rank, consummate, supreme, grand, majestic, extreme, towering, perfect, unlimited, stark, complete,

unrestricted, entirely,
entirety, perfection, ideal,
unity, whole, (incomplete,
short, meager, uncertain,
doubt, hesitation, fallible)
absolve-v forgive, pardon,
amnesty, conciliation,
excuse, exonerate,
release, forget, acquit,
discharge, free, liberate,
immune, clear, (revenge,
vengeance, avenge,
vendetta, vindictive)
absorb-v combine, mix,
join, union, unify,
synthesize, incorporate,
fusion, blending, embody,
amalgamate, blend,
merge, fuse, consolidate,
import, (disperse,
disembody, disintegrate,
break up, unravel, evict,
expel)
abstain-v avoid, forbear,
evade, elude, reject,
eschew, shun, do without,
dispense with, do nothing,
wait, refrain, (pursue,
quest, chase, hunt, follow,
engage in, use, consume,
employ, perform, operate,
do, execute)
abstract-adj sole, single,
lone, solitary, desolate, by
itself, epitome, analysis,
digest, brief, summary,
draft, note, excerpt,
synopsis, textbook,
prospectus, (accompanied,
appendage, coexistence,
company)
abuse-v hurt, ill-treat,
molest, persecute, harm,

injure, victimize, maul,
maltreat, do violence,
misuse, desecrate, (good,
value, virtue, benefit, profit,
do a good turn, do no
harm, be good)
abut-v contiguous, contact,
border, adjoin, touch,
come in contact with,
adhere, end to end, close
to, prop, stand, support,
bolster, (interspace, gap,
hole, opening, far
between)
abyss-n space, infinite
space, roomy, spacious,
boundless, vast,
bottomless pit, hell,
(definite space, region,
sphere, area, realm,
domain, tract, territory,
spot, point, niche, nook,
compartment, heaven,
paradise, eden)
academic-adj teaching,
instruction, education,
discipline, lesson,
curriculum, course of
study, school, academy,
scholastic, collegiate,
educational, (misinform,
render unintelligible,
uncertain, conceal)
accelerate-v sharpen,
quicken, excite, urge,
stimulate, foment, speed
up, spurt, rush, dash, bolt,
dart, swiftly, hurry, (slow,
languor, drawl, creeping,
delay, move slowly, creep,
crawl, lag, linger, dawdle,
apply the brake, reduce
the speed)

accept-v assent, admit, agree, concur, avow, own, acknowledge, ratify, approve, consent, comply, concede, confirm, allow, grant, give in, embrace an offer, satisfy, receive, take, (denial, contradiction, refuse, give, donate, bestow, cede, deliver, endow, invest, award, bequest, contribute, hand, pass)

access-n approach, path, route, near, pursue, approximate, impending, method, manner, procedure, track, (recession, withdrawal, deadlock, retirement, departure, recede, remove)

accessible-adj possible, feasible, practical, possible, conceivable, credible, likely, performable, achievable, surmountable, capable, easy (impossible, no chance, absurd, contrary, unlikely, impracticable, inaccessible, impassable, difficult, hard)

accessory-n addition, add, annexation, tack to, append, also, too, complement, addendum, supplement, adjunct, accompany, associated, with, auxiliary, partner, colleague

accident-n occurrence, misfortune, act of God, mishap, mischance, disaster, calamity, contingency, fortune, haphazard, casualty, tragedy, adversity, (well, alert, satisfactory, remedy, utility, happiness)

acclimatize-v habituate, accustom, naturalize, inure, season, tame, domesticate, breed, tend, break in, train, cage, bridle, restrain, harden, familiarize, educate, (unaccustomed, disuse)

accomodate-v fit, suit, conform, adjust, adapt, oblige, furnish, supply, unison, harmony, concord, concert, congruity, keeping, fitness, aptness, relevancy, adaptation, (discord, dissidence, conflict)

accompaniment-n adjunct, accessory, appendage, concomitant, attribute, context, concomitance, affix, augment, garnish, sauce, complement, (remainder, residue, remnant, rest, relic, leavings)

accomplice-n confederate, ally, abettor, accessory, assistant, colleague, recruit, adjunct, help, partner, mate, collaborator, friend, confidant, (opponent, antagonist, adversary, wrangler)

accomplish-v fulfill, do, achieve, effect, execute,

perform, attain, feat,
acquirement, fulfillment,
performance, realization,
achievement, (destruction,
waste, dissolution,
downfall, ruin, fall, crash)
accord-v tally, harmonize,
concur, grant, bestow,
acquiesce, conformity,
uniformity, agreement,
constancy, level, smooth,
dress, (diversified, varied,
irregular, uneven, rough)
accost-v speak, salute,
hail, address, greet,
speech, appeal,
invocation, salutation,
make up
account-n score, record,
recital, narration,
description, answerable,
explicable, liable,
responsible, amenable,
money matters, finance,
bill, budget, tally,
(unaccountable)
accretion-n concretion,
adhesion, increment,
growth, accumulation,
increase, enlargement,
extension, development,
augment, (decrease,
lessening, subtraction,
reduction, shrinking, ebb)
accrue-v bring in, yield,
result, arise, annexation,
increase, supplement,
insertion, affix, additive,
extra, plus, further, also,
(deduction, retrenchment,
amputation, curtailment,
abrasion, deduct)
accumulate-v collect,

gather, hoard, increase,
assemble, amass,
collection, compilation,
levy, gathering, muster,
assembly, (dispersion,
divergence, scattering,
dissipation, spread)
accuracy-n preciseness,
precision, verity,
correctness, just, proper,
true, correct, exact, fact,
truth, gospel, authenticity,
veracity, honest, sober,
(error, fallacy, inexactness,
report, mistake, fault)
accursed-adj fated,
doomed, detestable,
damnable, diabolic,
charge, slur, incrimination,
imputation, recrimination,
blame, censure,
denunciation, inculpation,
plaint, accusation,
(congratulate, compliment,
commendation, praise,
eulogy)
accustom-v inure, season,
familiarize, habituate,
common, general, natural,
ordinary, track, practice,
rut, groove, precedent,
(newness to, leave off,
cast off, break off, violate,
infringe)
ache-v smart, shoot,
twinge, hurt, pain,
discomfort, suffering,
twitch, headache, spasm,
cramp, crick, thrill, sharp,
gnawing, torment,
(pleasure, physical,
sensual, sensuous,
comfort, luxury)

achievement-*n*
performance, fulfillment,
accomplishment, exploit,
feat, trace, vestige,
courage, bravery, valor,
boldness, spirit, defiance,
(cowardice, timid,
baseness, fear, faint heart)

acknowledge-*v* grant,
concede, confess, admit,
own, assent, disclose,
answer, response, reply,
retort, repartee, discover,
conclusive, satisfy,
(inquiry, search, pursuit,
review, scrutiny, analysis)

acquaint-*v* familiarize,
notify, apprise, inform, tell,
communicate, intimation,
represent, round robin,
present, case, estimate,
specification, report,
(conceal, hiding, secret,
screen, disguise,
masquerade)

acquiesce-*v* agree, concur,
accede, comply, close
with, admit, to deign,
acquirement, obtainment,
grant, gift, inheritance,
donation, purchase,
(expenditure, loss, penalty,
dissent, refusal)

acquittal-*n* exculpation,
clearance, clearing,
exoneration, discharge,
absolution, quietus,
reprieve, pardon, absolve,
release, liberate, let off,
(condemnation, accuse,
conviction, restraint)

acrid-*adj* acrimonious, tart,
pungent, bitter, severe,

caustic, biting, keen,
sharpness, roughness,
mustard, pepper, brine,
stinging, unsavory,
virulence, spleen, asperity,
(condiment)

act-*n* ordinance, decree,
deed, exploit, statute, law,
edict, scene, perform, do,
operate, behave, play,
feign, simulate, action,
doing, (inaction,
passiveness, idle,
misbehave, lax)

advocate-*v* recommend,
counsel, suggest,
prescribe, to advise, to
support, advise,
instruction, charge,
enforce, enjoin, (intendant,
husband, moderator,
speaker, proctor)

aeronaut-*n* pilot, flyer,
navigator, aviator, airman,
aviatrix, scout, balloonist,
Icarus, seaman, skipper,
marine, (wayfarer,
voyager, passenger,
tourist, explorer, straggler,
rambler)

aesthetic-*n* artistic, refined,
cultured, cultivated,
appealing, sensibility,
physical, feeling,
sensation, impression,
cultivate, tudor, (opium,
insensible, paralyze, blunt,
callous, dull)

afar-*adv* aloof, abroad,
away, distant, distance,
horizon, reach, spread,
remote, mundane, away,
yonder, farther, apart,

(nearness, proximity, adjacency, breadth, span, close, handy, home)

affable-*adj* approachable, sociable, gracious, friendly, amiable, humility, meek, resignation, modesty, confusion, humble, submit, diminish, (starch, perked, lofty, haughty, mighty, dignified)

affair-*n* event, business, occurrence, matter, concern, question, eventuality, incident, transaction, proceeding, phenomenon, advent, (impending, destined, loom, threaten, await)

affectation-*v* insincerity, pretension, airs, modishness, charlatanism, quackery, artificiality, (modesty, diffidence, timidity, shyness, humility, demureness)

affection-*n* bent, quality, malady, ailment, fondness, tenderness, devotion, nature, spirit, tone, temper, habit, soul, turn, bosom, breast, heart, (experience, response, impression, emotion)

affirmation-*n* ratification, corroboration, allegation, confirmation, assertion, profession, avowal, emphasis, positiveness, dogmatism, (negation, uncertainty, refutation, disclamation)

afraid-*adj* apprehensive,

fearful, timorous, alarmed, cowardly, terrified, uncertainty, demure, suspense, caprice, levity, dilly dally, boggle, (determination, resolve, conclude)

agency-*n* causality, method, impelling force, force, function, office, exercise, maintenance, work, swing, action, official, acting, operant, (inaction, powerlessness)

agent-*n* servant, proxy, doer, actor, operator, perpetrator, executor, representative, go-between, mediate, deputy, consignee, trustee, nominee, (deputy, substitute, vice, proxy, minister)

aggravation-*n* heightening, intensification, vexation, annoyance, acridity, irritation, render worse, acerbate, worsen, (relief, alleviation, mitigation, assuagement)

aggregate-*adj* sum total, sum, all, complete, whole, assemblage, compilation, gathering, muster, meeting, assembly, mob, body, tribe, crew, (divergence, scattering, diffusion, dissipation)

aggression-*n* inroad, encroachment, invasion, attack, assault, charge, offense, incursion, invasion, against, impugn,

assume, harry, invade,
(defense, guard,
resistance, safeguard)
agile-*adj* quick, lithe, active,
nimble, spry, brisk, activity,
liveliness, spirit, dash,
energy, smartness,
alacrity, industry,
movement, bustle, stir,
fuss, (inactivity, inertness,
dullness, languor, sleep,
sound)
agitation-*n* jar, jolt, shake,
trepidation, shock, flutter,
perturbation, disconcertion,
confusion, turmoil,
turbulence, tumult, stir,
ripple, jog, dance, flutter,
(order, rest, stability)
agony-*n* anguish, pain,
suffering, torment, torture,
smart, twitch, spasm,
headache, cramp,
discomfort, throb, piercing,
rack, (pleasure, sensual,
comfort, luxury, enjoy, at
ease, cozy, snug)
agreement-*n*
understanding, accord,
keeping, unison,
reconcilement, union,
harmony, consonance,
(disagreement, dissent,
inequality, disharmony,
unconformity, discord)
agriculture-*n* agrarian,
rural, farming, husbandry,
cultivation, tillage,
gardening, florist, field,
meadow, flower,
plantation, (taming,
breeding, aviary, fishery,
trainer)

aid-*v* assistance, help,
succor, promotion,
cooperation, furtherance,
advocacy, defense,
patronage, countenance,
alleviation, support, lift,
advance, relief, rescue,
(hindrance, opposition,
neglect)
ailment-*n* affection, illness,
disorder, disease, malady,
sickness, infirmity,
complaint, attack, seizure,
stroke, canker, virus,
plague, pestilence, (health,
soundness, vigor, perfect,
robust, bloom, recover)
alarm-*n* fear, dread, scare,
fright, panic, warning,
signal, summons, excite,
agitate, arouse, startle,
affright, terrify, appall,
caution, prediction, omen,
beacon, give notice,
beware, sentinel,
watchman
allay-*v* ease, assuage,
lessen, mitigate, slacken,
pacification,
accommodation,
arrangement, adjustment,
terms, compromise,
armistice, suspension of
hostilities, (warfare,
fighting, crusade)
allegiance-*n* duty, homage,
obedience, loyalty,
observance, compliance,
submission, passiveness,
devotion, obey, control,
follow, service,
(insubordination, violation,
non compliance)

analogy-*n* resembling, like, associated, related, correspondent, parallel, similar, semblance, affinity, agreement, look like, (diversity, disparity, difference, novelty)

analysis-*n* decomposition, inquiry, consideration, study, disintegration, break-up, investigation, dissection, resolution, dissolve, (combination, mixture, union, incorporation)

analyst-*n* recorder, historian, chronicler, compiler, notary, clerk, registrar, secretary, scribe, biographer, time keeper, almanac, calendar, journal

anarchy-*n* rebellion, chaos, terrorism, lawlessness, disorder, turmoil, confusion, disarray, jumble, huddle, muddle, hash, (order, regularity, uniformity, symmetry)

ancestry-*n* line, lineage, family tree, family, race, descent, parent, father, dad, pedigree, tribe, clan, descent, parental, forefathers, maternity, mother

anchor-*n* stay, grapnel, safeguard, protection, hold, kedge, killick, link, connective, hyphen, bracket, bridge, (separation, parting, segregation, divorce, break)

anchorage-*n* harbor, safety, roadstead, mooring, refuge, lodgement, establishment, settlement, place, station, (displace, dislodge, exile, remove, unload)

ancient-*adj* aged, hoary, antique, archaic, old, venerable, antiquated, maturity, decline, decay, primitive, classic, (newness, novelty, youth, modernism)

anecdote-*n* story, tale, sketch, account, narrative, description, statement, report, summary, brief, relate, recite, recount, sum up, tell, give, graphic, epic

angel-*n* divine messenger, ministering spirits, invisible helpers, good man, worthy, model, paragon, hero, demigod, Innocent, saint, (bad man, evil doer, sinner, wicked)

anger-*n* enrage, inflame, arouse, irritate, annoy, exasperate, provoke, offend, infuriate, resentment, displeasure, wrath, indignation, (favorite, pet, idol, fondness, love, dear)

angle-*n* guise, aspect, phase, crook, fork, obliquity, cusp, bend, notch, ankle, measurement, elevation, distance, triangle, square, diamond

animate-*v* actuate, excite, cheer, enliven, encourage,

inspire, motion, action,
intention, inducement,
draw, inspire, (dissuade,
reluctance, detour, hold,
repel)
annex-v add, attach, join,
affix, junction, union, unite,
lump, fix, bind, fasten,
stitch, buckle, button, knit,
lock, (disjoined,
disconnect, disengage,
divorce, cut, adrift)
annihilate-v exterminate,
eradicate, destroy, end,
wreck, demolish,
extinction, blow, doom,
ravage, sacrifice, abolish,
perish, (evolve, bring forth,
birth, produce, perform)
announce-v report,
declare, predict, foretell,
tell, inform, proclaim,
assert, notice,
communicate, acquaint,
(conceal, hide, mystify,
masquerade, cunning)
annoy-v trouble, bother,
vex, harass, molest,
disturb, irritate, tantalize,
worry, badness, hurtful,
inflict, harm, injure,
oppress, persecute,
(produce, profit, benefit,
goodness, merit)
annul-v nullification,
diffuseness, cancellation,
counter order, invalidation,
retraction, repeal,
abolishment, rescission,
abrogation, (commission,
delegate, consign, assign)
anoint-v rub, lubricate,
salve, oil, divinity, wisdom,

goodness, justice, truth,
unity, eternity,
preservation, (scourge,
halter, stake, truncheon,
stocks)
anonymous-adj
unacknowledged,
unknown, unnamed,
misnomer, alias,
pseudonym, nickname,
(nomination, designation,
title, head, namesake)
answer-n reply, response,
acknowledgment, rebuttal,
retort, return, respond,
say, rebut, acknowledge,
echo, replication,
(question, inquiry, request,
search)
antagonism-n animosity,
antipathy, hostility,
opposition, enmity,
counteraction, polarity,
clashing, collision,
resistance, (concurrence,
cooperation, agreement)
antecede-v preexist,
precede, go before,
precedence, first, head,
lead, introduce, prefix,
prelude, preface, former,
before, (sequence, after,
succeed, follow, suffix)
anteroom-n hall, lobby,
antechamber, receptacle,
enclosure, receiver,
apartment, vessel, portico,
porch, veranda, lobby, hall,
vestibule, chamber, bower
anticipate-v expect, await,
forestall, be early, surmise,
predict, preparation,
provide, disposition,

forecast, cultivate,
(disqualify, unfitted,
shiftless, unprepared)
antidote-*n* emetic, remedy,
counter poison, help,
antiseptic, corrective,
sedative, recipe,
prescription, (poison, virus,
venom, scourge)
antipathy-*n* repugnance,
clashing, opposition,
abhorrence, detestation,
dislike, incompatibility,
reluctance, backward,
disgust, (desire, wish,
want, need, longing)
apathetic-*adj* insensible,
indifferent, cold, unfeeling,
impassive, insensibility, no
desire, disregard, no
interest, (sensible, morale,
softness, warm, tender)
ape-*n* simian, monkey,
mimic, mock, simulate,
imitate, copying,
simulation, semblance,
mirror, reflect, repeat,
echo, match, follow,
counterfeit
apostasy-*n* renunciation,
abjuration, recantation,
defection, retraction,
disavowal, revocation,
abandonment, recreancy,
relapse
appall-*v* nauseate, revolt,
disgust, terrify, putrefy,
painful, trouble, curse,
hurt, displease, annoy,
perplex, tease, irk, vex,
(refresh, comfortable,
cordial, genial)
apparatus-*n* machinery,

outfit, equipment,
contrivance, instrument,
engineer, mechanism,
organ, appliance, gear,
tackle, implement, utensil
apparent-*adj* perceptible,
obvious, seeming, clear,
patent, manifest, visible,
appearing, conspicuous,
distinct, evidence,
(invisible, dim, mysterious,
confused)
appearance-*n* sight, show,
phenomenon, prospect,
representation, display,
stage setting, exposure,
(vanishing, fading,
evanescence, departure,
occultation, withdrawal)
appease-*v* satisfy, allay,
pacify, placate, quiet,
soothe, mollify, pleasure,
moderate, soften,
tranquilize, swag, lull,
compose, (violent, sharp,
quicken, excite, incite)
append-*v* subjoin, add,
affix, attach, annex,
supplement, subjoin,
reinforce, augment,
accrue, introduce, insert,
more, include, (subtraction,
amputate, abscind, pare)
appetite-*n* passion,
craving, want, hunger,
longing, desire, wish,
need, exigency, inclination,
greed, covetous, ravenous,
(anorexia, apathy, listless)
applause-*n* acclamation,
praise, plaudit, acclaim,
clapping, approbation,
commendation, cheer,

good word, blessing, approval, (dislike, reprehend, chide, admonish)

applicable-*adj* convenient, pertinent, suitable, appropriate, relevant, adequate, service, available, ready, tangible, advantageous, (useless inefficacy, worthless)

appoint-*v* nominate, ordain, assign, establish, prescribe, commission, delegate, consign, authorize, accredit, engage, hire, (annulment, nullification, conceal, cancel)

apportionment-*n* allotment, assignment, consignment, partition, allocation, division, distribution, disperse, spread, intersperse, (crowd, muster, levy, gather, flood)

appraise-*v* rate, judge, estimate, assess, value, survey, reckon, measure, standard, rule, compass, gage, gauge, yard, meter, coordinates, ordinate, latitude

apprehend-*v* arrest, seize, imprison, dread, distrust, perceive, see, understand, known, ascertain, recognize, realize, (ignorant, unexplored, bewilderment)

approach-*v* drawing near, advance, access, advent, admission, convergence,

pursuit, drift, gain upon, converge, (avoidance, recession, go away)

approbation-*n* sanction, approval, advocacy, favor, renown, kudos, popularity, commendation, eulogy, homage (detraction, disrepute, disapprobation)

appropriate-*adj* becoming, fit, suitable, timely, proper, adapted, agreeable, expedient, advisable, convenient, worthwhile, applicable, (undesirable, unfit, clumsy, awkward)

apt-*adj* clever, quick, dexterous, skillful, influence, important, rampant, dominant, regnant, predominant, support, (powerless, uninfluential, irrelevant, inertness)

arable-*adj* productive, fertile, tillable, farming, georgic, agronomy, horticulture, florist, field, meadow, garden, ornamental

arbitrary-*adj* overbearing, imperious, harsh, tyrannical, dictatorial, peremptory, domineering, despotic, austere, (lenient, mild, gentle, tolerant, forbearing)

argument-*n* data, case, discussion, debate, controversy, wangling, contention, dispute, examine, pros and cons, (deceptive, sophistical, irrelevant, evasive)

aristocrat-*n* patrician, lord, noble, nobleman, empire, monarchy, royalty, (democracy, demagogy, republic, magistrate, socialism, anarchy, relaxation, toleration, freedom)

arrangement-*n* provision, preparation, array, assortment, allotment, distribution, analysis, organize, sort, distribute, (disorder, disarrangement, disturb, confuse)

arrive-*v* advent, coming, debarkation, landing, reception, welcome, goal, destination, harbor, haven, port, (egress, departure, embarkation, exit, leaving)

arrogant-*adj* airs, swagger, haughtiness, pretension, ostentation, insolence, take, demand, usurp, appropriate, seize, assume, dignity, pride, self-respect

arsenal-*n* armory, depot, magazine, storehouse, arms, weapons, armament, partisan, battery, gunnery, missile, shrapnel

artful-*adj* adroit, tricky, crafty designing, sly, shrewd, dexterous, falsity, deception, untruth, lying, misrepresentation, perjury, forgery, (frankness, truthfulness, sincerity)

artificial-*adj* false, sham, unnatural, affected, counterfeit, imitation, deception, untruth, delusion, collusion, treachery, trick, cheat, (truthfulness, veracity, frankness, honesty)

artistic-*adj* talented, beautiful, graceful, accomplished, cultural, exquisite, aesthetic, skillful, clever, ability, ingenuity, capacity, (unskillful, stupidity, indiscretion)

asceticism-*n* austerity, penance, puritanism, abstinence, cynicism, mortification, maceration, flagellation, fasting, ascetic, cynical

ascribe-*v* assign, impute, attribute, refer, theory, reference, pedigree, rationale, (accident, fortune, hazard, chance, random, luck, casualty)

ask-*v* implore, beseech, inquire, interrogate, beg, entreat, request, question, search, research, pursuit, review, scrutiny, sifting, (answer, respond, reply, rebut, retort)

askew-*adj* oblique, crooked, awry, distorted, inclination, slope, slant, leaning, beveled, tilt, bias, twist, swag, oblique, descend, decline

ass-*n* dolt, booby, donkey, fool, idiot, wiseacre, simpleton, ninny, oaf, lout, loon, addle, innocent, babbler, (sage, wise man, mastermind, thinker, authority)

assassin-n cutthroat, killer, murderer, slayer, homicide, manslaughter, slay, butcher, victimize, massacre, strangle, stifle, (alive, breathe, respire)

assemblage-n collection, concourse, conflux, gathering, mobilization, meet, concentration compilation, (disjunction, dispersion, divergence)

assert-v allege, claim, avow, maintain, state, affirm, belief, credence, credit, assurance, faith, trust, confidence, dependence, (misbelief, discredit, infidelity, dissent, retraction)

astringent-adj styptic, sour, tart, austere, binding, contraction, reduction, lessening, shrinking, collapse, decrease, (large, expand, widen, enlarge, grow)

astute-adj acute, bright, shrewd, quick, intelligent, capacity, comprehension, intellect, sagacity, judgment, cunning, brains, (imbecility, dull, incompetence, idiocy)

athletic-adj acrobatic, strong, robust, powerful, gymnastic, strength, energy, vigor, force, main, spring, elasticity, tone, (weakness, debility,

relaxation, languor)

atonement-n indemnification, expiation, redemption, conciliation, propitiation, recompense, compromise, (impenitence, obduracy, callousness)

attack-v encroachment, onset, onslaught, encounter, assault, charge, aggression, thrust, kick, punch, assail, invade, (defense, protection, guard, shield)

attention-n alertness, heed, observance, intentness, scrutiny, study, mindfulness, thought, consideration, reflection, (inattention, neglect, oversight, disregard)

audacity-n overconfidence, gall, impudence, temerity, insolence, rashness, imprudence, indiscretion, presumption, (caution, discretion, calculation, deliberation)

auspicious-adj fortunate, favorable, propitious, promising, expedient, occasion, opportunity, suitable, proper, (unsuitable, improper, lose, waste)

authority-n authorization, power, warrant, right, dominion, dictation, command, influence, facts, evidence, collateral, (laxity, obedience, servant, submission)

auxiliary-adj assistant,

collaborator, adjuvant,
helping, aiding, ancillary,
support, lift, favor, relief,
rescue, ministry, aid,
(prevention, stoppage,
enemy, opponent)
avail-v benefit, profit, serve,
succeed, suffice,
usefulness, adequacy,
conduce, gainful,
advantageous, valuable,
(inadequacy, unskillful,
lost, seek)
averse-adj reluctant, loath,
opposed, counter,
unwillingness, renitency,
reluctance, indifference,
backward, slowness,
(willing, mind, heart,
incline, eager)
await-v contemplate,
impend, anticipate,
expectation, approach,
future, coming, heritage,
posterity, close, next,
eventual, (past, gone,
former, ancient, antiquity)
award-v adjudication,
compensation, bestowal,
conferment, decision,
giving, donation,
presentation, accordance,
delivery, endowment,
(receiving, acquisition,
acceptance, admission)
awkward-adj unskillful,
ungainly, clumsy,
ungraceful, incompetency,
inability, inexperience,
fumble, boggle, blunder,
flounder, stumble, (skill,
expert, craft, competence)
axiom-n aphorism, truism,

postulate, rule, proposition,
saying, adage, saw,
proverb, sentence, motto,
word, morale, reflection,
(absurdity, imbecility,
nonsense, paradox,
muddle)
axle-n arbor, pivot, axis,
spindle, rotation,
revolution, gyration, whirl,
surge, screw, gimbals,
gyrate, twirl

B

babble-v chatter, prattle,
rave, gibber, murmur,
gurgle, gossip, empty
sound, nonsense, jargon,
gibberish, jabber, bombast,
(meaning, expression,
bearing, substantial)
backsliding-v apostasy,
retrogression, lapse,
countermovement,
regression, retreat,
withdrawal, retirement,
recession, reflection,
(progression, advance,
ongoing, headway)
backward-adv delayed,
dull, stagnant, tardy, loath,
disinclined, reluctant,
remiss, retrograde,
unwillingness, reluctance,
(willingness, punctual,
inclination, leaning)
bad-adj sinful, imperfect,
rancid, unsuitable, wicked,
tainted, hurtful, virulence,
injurious, deleterious,
noxious, aggrieve,
oppress, (good,

excellence, merit, virtue,
worth)
baffle-v outwit, confound,
check, balk, frustrate, foil,
nonplus, restrict, restraint,
blockade, hindrance,
obstacle, drawback,
(assistance, help, support,
lift, advance)
bag-n container, pouch,
sack, protrude, sag,
capture, entrap, catch,
receptacle, enclosure,
receiver, compartment,
sac, pocket, sheath
bait-n worry, badger, lure,
trap, decoy, harass,
deception, falseness,
untruth, fraud, deceit,
misrepresentation,
delusion, juggling,
(veracity, truthfulness,
sincerity)
balance-n evenness,
scales, equilibrium,
steadiness, parallel,
match, compare, contrast,
identification, collate,
confront, (crooked,
uneven, unbalanced)
balk-v shy, stop, back,
thwart, disappoint, foil,
frustrate, hindrance,
deception, falseness,
untruth, fraud, deceit, trick,
cheat, (true, frank, open,
candor, sincerity)
ball-n hop, dance, party,
shot, sphere, globe,
projectile, roundness,
cylinder, drum, rotund,
balm-n ointment, balsam
sedative, moderation,

gentleness, calmness,
relaxation, mitigation,
lullaby, (violence,
vehemence, might,
turbulence)
banish-v expatriate, exile,
dismiss, expel, eject,
exclude, punish, emission,
evacuation, drainage,
reject, discard, cut, (admit,
introduce, inject, insertion)
bare-adj simple, mere,
nude, naked, undraped,
empty, destitute,
unfurnished, disclose,
uncover, reveal, expose,
(cover, screen, shake, full,
furnish)
bark-n skin, rind, shell,
cortex, howl, yelp, yap,
bay, cry, growl, yip, roar,
bellow, grunt, snort,
squeak, purr, mew, croak
barren-adj arid, sterile,
unfertile, unprofitable,
fruitless, worthless,
impotence, waste, desert,
unproductive, inoperative,
(fertility, multiplication,
productive, generate)
barter-v trade, exchange,
bargaining, swap, traffic,
marketing, interchange,
reciprocation, shuffle,
retaliate, (substitution,
supplanting, alternative)
base-n groundwork, footing,
foundation, foothold,
substratum, basic, lowest,
fundamental, platform,
dishonesty, disgrace,
shabbiness, (integrity,
rectitude, honesty, faith)

bound-adj spring, vault, jump, confine, circumscribe, limit, restrain, swiftness, spurt, rush, dash, race, lively, gallop, (slowness, creeping, loiterer, retire)

bounty-n subsidy, grant, generosity, liberality, munificence, benevolence, giving, donation, consignment, charity, (receiving, acquire, assignee)

braid-v plait, interweave, Interlace, intertwine, joining, union, unite, bind, attach, fix, splice, truss, tether, (disjoin, disconnect, disengage, separate)

branch-n wing, arm, member, ramification, offshoot, limb, bough, twig, fork, divide, bifurcate, diverge, radiate

brand-n stamp, stain, sort, kind, grade, stigma, firebrand, burning, cauterization, ignite, (cooling, refresh, congeal, starve)

bravado-n boasting, bluster, vaunting, braggadocio, flourish, bombast, brag, resonance, exult, crow

breadth-n broadness, width, expanse, amplitude, spaciousness, tread, span, reach, bore, caliber, thickness

break-v fracture, shatter, sever, rend, violate, tame, transgress, infringe, subdue, interruption, interval, gap, (adjoin, touch, contact, adhere, coincide)

breathe-v inhale, respire, live, exist, divulge, utter, whisper, disclose, puff, blow, dust, blast, breeze, gale, blowing, fanning

brevity-n briefness, shortness, succinctness, terseness, conciseness, little, curtail, abridge, curt, compact, stubby, (long, length, span, elongate)

bribe-n graft, price, allurement, seduction, hush-money, recompense, fee, corrupt, suborn, tempt

brigand-n thief, bandit, thug, robber, highwayman, freebooter, filcher, buccaneer, swindler, forger, fence

bright-adj vivid, intense, deep, intelligent, apt, clever, lustrous, radiant, luminous, flashing, glistening, glowing, brilliant

brisk-adj alert, lively, swift, quick, nimble, velocity, fly, gallop, vanish, brief, quick, sudden, short, spasmodic, cursory, (long, eternity, persistence)

bristling-adj sullen, angry, perverse, thorny, spiny, spiked, sharpness, barbed, horned, nib, tooth, (dull, bluntness, obtuse, bluff)

brittleness-n frailness, fragility, delicateness, splintery, crack, snap, split, splinter, crumble,

(toughness, strength, tenacious, resisting)

broadcast-v diffuse, scatter, disseminate, utter, spread, disperse, sow, dispense, disband, dispel, (assemblage, collection, levy, gathering)

broken-v shattered, divided, disconnected, docile, infirm, gentle, domesticated, weakness, languor, fragility, (strength, power, energy, vigor)

bubble-n sparkle, gurgle, effervescent, foam, boil, nothingness, zero, never, unsubstantial, burp, (substantial, article, something, substance)

buckle-n twist, bend, warp, fastening, fastener, clasp, link, junction, union, unite, bond, bridge, braid, hook, girdle, (disjoin, disconnect, divorce, cut)

buffoon-n pantomimist, fool, jester, clown, mummer, comedian, humorist, wag, wit, dandy, joker, charlatan, mime

bulk-n amount, volume, measure, largeness, mass, expanse, greater part, whole, integrity, collectiveness, lump, (division, segment, fragment, piece)

bulletin-n statement, report, journal, news, information, word, advice, dispatch, publicity, notice, (secret, mystery, riddle,

conundrum)

bully-n brawler, tyrant, roisterer, swaggerer, threaten, bluster, domineer, browbeat, combatant, litigant, competitor, rival, (submissive, surrender, resignation)

bulwark-n rampart, barrier, fortification, safeguard, defense, protection, guard, shield, self defense, ditch, dike, (attack, assault, charge, thrust)

bungler-n muddler, lout, blunderer, fumbler, clown, duffer, novice, clod, lubber, muff, swab, yokel, greenhorn, (proficient, master, veteran, soldier, experienced)

buoyant-adj light, floating, resilient, springy, sanguine, foamy, rise, hover, spire, soar, tower, swim, surge, (descent, fall, drop, downfall, tumble)

bureaucracy-n officialism, red-tape, authority, influence, power, command, empire, sway, (laxity, loose, freedom, tolerate)

burglar-n bandit, robber, housebreaker, thief, filcher, swindler, forger, coiner, fence, smuggler, wrecker

burlesque-n buffoonery, farce, take-off, parody, comedy, drollery, ridiculous, ludicrous, preposterous, monstrosity,

(formality, prudery,
demureness, modesty)
burn-v sear, parch, char,
destroy, blaze, flame, hot,
swelter, boil, torrid,
tropical, sultry, stifling,
stuffy, suffocating,
oppressive, (cold, cool,
chill, frigid, inclement)
burrow-n tunnel, mine, dig,
excavate, penetrate,
rooted, inhabit,
domesticate, moored,
anchored, established,
lodged, (displacement,
banishment, removal,
dislocate)
bushy-adj shaggy, hairy,
clumpy, dense, jungle,
prairie, grass, hedge, rush,
week, foliage, growth,
woody
business-n employment,
occupation, undertaking,
pursuit, avocations,
financial activities, affair,
concern, case, interest,
(inaction, inactivity, leisure)
busy-adj occupied, active,
engrossed, employed,
engaged, industrious,
diligent, officious, flurry,
rustle, stir, perturbation,
(idle, dawdle, mope,
inactivity, relaxation)
buttress-n abutment, prop,
truss, brace, support, aid,
block, anvil, shore, jamb,
beam, rafter, (suspend,
hand, fast to, pensile,
hanging)
buy-v procure, purchase,
acquire, invest, shop,

market, buyer, vendee,
patron, customer, client,
pay, market, (sell, sale,
dispose of, mortgage,
auction)
bygone-adj old, former,
departed, antiquated,
obsolete, gone by, past,
yore, away, latter, look
back, ancestry, lapse
byword-n proverb, saying,
object of scorn, nickname,
pet expression, by-name

C

cab-n carriage, hansom,
taxicab, hackney, hack,
vehicle, conveyance, van,
wagon, cart, coach,
caravan, car
cabinet-n closet, room,
repository, case, ministry,
council, committee,
chamber, board, bench
cackle-v chuckle, giggle,
cluck, clack, gabble, chit-
chat, small talk, babble,
gossip, converse, tattle,
verbal intercourse,
(soliloquize, say, think
aloud)
cage-n confine, restrain
incarcerate, imprison,
enclosure, receptacle,
reservatory, compartment,
hole, nook, stall
cajole-v coax, wheedle,
deceive, delude, flatter,
praise, soothe, humor,
exaggerate, charm,
(scandal, defamation,
slander, derogate)

cart-*n* wagon, pushcart, dray, tumbrel, vehicle, transport, displace, displant, unload, empty, transfer, vacate, (lodgement, stow, installation, localize)

carve-*v* quarter, slice, dissect, mold, hew, cut, disjunction, separation, parting, divorce, detach, divide, split, (join, unite, close, together)

castrate-*v* neuter, spay, geld, emasculate, purify, cleanliness, lavation, clear, purgative, (impurity, contamination)

casual-*adj* random, accidental, occasional, incidental, contingent, external, conditional, fortuitous

casualty-*n* misfortune, disaster, calamity, mishap, accident, event, adventure, crisis, emergency, contingency, consequence, (loom, await, impend)

cause-*v* birth, beginning, origin, prime, principle, producer, generator, creator, determinant, motive, root, basis, foundation

caustic-*adj* pungent, biting, burning, acrimonious, corroding, mordant, repulsive, discourteous, blunt, gruff, harsh, austere, (courtesy, politeness, compliment)

caution-*n* discretion, heed, circumspection, wariness, forethought, vigilance, watchfulness, admonition

cave-*n* grotto, den, cavern, lair, hole, abode, dwelling, domicile, lodging, nest, arbor, cell, retreat, roost

cavil-*v* quibble, haggle, carp, mangle, dissent, dislike, object, to, disvalue, outcry, (sanction, advocacy, esteem, repute)

cavity-*n* opening, hole, dent, depression, hollow, excavation, dip, scoop, excavate, tunnel, burrow, (projection, bulge, swell, nob)

cease-*v* discontinue, halt, end, stop, terminate, refrain, closure, desist, pause, rest, interrupt, suspend, cut, (start, continue, initiate, sustain, uphold)

cede-*v* surrender, give up, concede, yield, relinquish, submission, resignation, homage, succumb, submit, (combatant, belligerent, competitor)

celebration-*n* observance, commemoration, jubilation, ovation, triumph, inauguration, honor, installation, coronation

celestial-*adj* holy, unearthly, divine, beatific, Elysian, heavenly, solar, empyreal, starry, otherworldly

celibacy-*n* misogyny, purity,

singleness, bachelorhood,
virginity, maidenhood,
spinster, unmarried,
(marriage, wedlock, union,
mate)
censure-*n* faultfinding,
hypercritical, carping,
condemnatory, disesteem,
dislike, disapprove, object
to, frown, (approval,
sanction, esteem, praise)
ceremonial-*adj* ritualistic,
formal, pompous, solemn,
display, show, parade,
ostentatious, showy,
grand, flashing
certainty-*n* sureness,
certitude, assuredness,
safety, inevitable, fact,
infallibility, dogmatic,
(unbelief, uncertainty)
cessation-*n*
discontinuance,
interruption, respite,
intermission, interval,
recess, impediment, halt,
lull, suspension, truce
chafe-*v* vex, fret, gall,
annoy, rub, warm, pain,
suffering, twitch, soreness,
crick, sharp, piercing,
gnawing, (pleasure,
sensual, comfort, luxury)
chaff-*v* refuse, husk,
persiflage, raillery, ridicule,
deride, travesty, mock,
sarcastic, ironical, banter,
rally
chagrin-*n* vexation,
mortification, painfulness,
anxiety, annoyance,
irritation, worry, ordeal,
trouble, fret, (happiness,

enjoyment, comfort, ease)
chance-*n* luck, fortune,
unforeseen occurrence,
fate, lot, destiny, fortuity,
risk, gamble, uncertainty,
jeopardy, happen, come,
arrive, befall, turn up,
(attribution, intention)
channel-*n* duct, waterway,
conduit, canyon, chasm,
aqueduct, canal, moat,
ditch, water gate
chant-*n* melody, song,
psalm, canticle, hymn,
vespers, mass, prayer,
service, vigils
chapter-*n* part, section,
division, passage, branch,
portion, segment, parcel,
piece, detachment, verse,
clause, (totality,
collectiveness,
completeness, bulk)
char-*v* parch, sear, burn,
carbonize, scorch, boil,
heat, fusion, inflame, roast,
toast, cauterize, incinerate,
(refrigerate, cool, fan,
refresh)
charitable-*adj* unselfish,
generous, liberal, kind,
altruistic, donor,
eleemosynary, gratis
charlatan-*n* fraud, cheat,
impostor, impersonator,
quack, deceiver, hypocrite,
pretender, humbug
charm-*n* fascination,
attractiveness, amulet,
talisman, incantation, lure,
draw, seduce, conjure,
hypnotize
chasm-*n* pit, abyss, gap,

fissure, cleft, hole,
opening, orifice, passage,
channel, gully, mine,
gallery, (closure, blockade,
shut, obstruct)

chaste-*adj* unaffected,
classic, virtuous, undefiled,
simple, virginal, symmetry,
finish, uniform, balanced,
equal, regular, (distortion,
warped, irregular)

cheat-*v* swindle, defraud,
trick, beguile, dupe,
delude, deceive,
deception, falseness,
fraud, delusion, treachery,
(truthful, veracity,
frankness, honesty)

checkered-*adj* varied, plaid,
irregular, alternating,
uneven, barred, checked

cheer-*n* yell, shout, festivity,
hospitality, enliven, inspirit,
approval, sanction,
esteem, praise, applaud,
joyous

cheerless-*adj* dismal,
somber, gloomy,
depressing, sad, dreary,
despondent

cherish-*v* prize, treasure,
nurture, revere, love,
fondness, liking, affection,
feeling, tenderness, (hate,
alienation, coolness)

chew-*v* grind, eat, crunch,
masticate, gulp, gluttony,
feed, devour, swallow,
take, dispatch, munch,
gnaw, (discharge,
secretion, ejection)

chief-*n* first, principal,
foremost, supreme, main,

head, leader, commander,
important, paramount,
significant, (insignificant,
trivial, nothing, trash)

childish-*adj* simple-minded,
infantile, silly, weak,
credulous, puerile,
youthful, young, shallow,
foolish, (wisdom, intellect,
cunning, mature)

chivalrous-*adj* knightly,
brave, courteous, gallant,
war, tenure, courage,
honor, generosity

choke-*v* strangle, suffocate,
congest, clog, stifle,
obstruction, blockage,
closure, bolt, seal, clinch,
(opening, yawning)

chop-*v* cut, hack ,split, hew,
dissection, separation,
division, fracture, rupture,
crack, (attach, fix, affix,
join, union, unite)

chronic-*adj* unceasing,
survive, lasting, inveterate,
constant, eternity,
perpetuity, persistent,
standing, survival,
(transient, passing,
fleeting, flying)

chronicle-*n* registry, annals,
archives, account, epoch,
almanac, calendar, journal,
diary, pendulum,
(anticipation, disregard,
neglect)

cipher-*n* cryptogram, code,
monogram, cryptograph,
naught, zero, numeration,
pagination, recension,
summation, (catalog,
inventory, schedule, index)

circle-n globe, ring, orb, disk, circlet, encircle, circumnavigate, gird, circumscribe, surround, compass, inclose

circulate-v spread, report, pass, change hands, propagate, revolve, rotation, revolution, gyration, whir, whirl

circumference-n periphery, perimeter, circuit, girth, outline, perimeter, ambit, circuit, lines, contour, profile, zone, belt, (verge, brink, brow, side)

circumscription-n bound, limit, confinement, case, restriction, enclosure, restraint, envelope, (perimeter, zone, belt, girth, band)

circumstance-n situation, condition, environment, surroundings, position, time, place, occurrence, event, quandary, fix, predicament, dilemma

circumvent-v thwart, elude, frustrate, outwit, baffle, prevent, preclusion, interruption, hindrance, (assist, help, promotion, patronage)

cite-v arraign, summon, allege, quote, adduce, illustrate, bring forward, charge, imputation, accuse, taunt, (vindication, acquittal, apology, gloss, excuse)

civil-adj urbane, well-bred, mannerly, respectful, secular, courteous, behavior, breeding, gentility, (discourteous, ungainly manners, rude, insult)

civilize-v polish, refine, cultivate, humanize, breeding, good, polite, conform, admissible, (comical, ridiculous, absurdity, ludicrous)

claim-v requirement, plea, assert, contend, demand, require, deserve, title, pretense, prerogative, imposition, requisition

claimant-n accuser, heir, prosecutor, pretender, petitioner, solicitor, applicant, suitor, beggar, hunter

clamor-n outcry, uproar, racket, tumult, din, contention, agitation, cry, shout, roar, scream, cheer, hoot, holler

clamp-n fastener, clasp, brace, band, joining, union, connection, unite, attach, affix, (disconnection, disunion, division)

clan-n faction, breed, brotherhood, set, sort, family, association, paternity, parent, father, sire, lineage, pedigree

clash-v conflict, collide, dispute, contend, impact, collision, concussion, shock, disagreement, discord, dissidence, (concert, conformity, uniformity)

colonize-v establish, settle, found, people, place, situate, locate, localize, make a place for, plantation, camp, (displaced, misplaced, exile, removal)

combination-n aggregation, union, mixture, composite, coadunation, synthesis, inosculation, (disjunction, decomposition)

command-v regulation, order, ordinance, act, bidding, direction, injunction, commandment, ruling, instructions, dispatch, message, (lowness, debasement, depression)

commence-v begin, start, enter upon, outset, inception, genesis, birth, originate, conceive, source, dawn, embarkation, initiate, (end, close, terminate, conclude)

commend-v recommend, praise, acclaim, approve, approbation, applause, clap, esteem, sanction, admiration, appreciate, (dislike, insinuation, ostracism)

comment-n observation, remark, criticism, annotation, interpretation, argument, controversy, debate, reasoning, (mystify, evasion, intuition, instinct)

commission-n warrant, charge, instruction, authorization, mandate, brevet, permit, delegation, consignment, nomination, charter, installation, investiture, accession, (annulment, prohibition)

commit-v perpetrate, consign, intrust, perform, action, doing, performance, exercise, citation, execute, achieve, (inaction, abstinence, passive)

common-adj conventional, usual, prevalent, current, customary, regular, vulgar, ill-bred, general, universal, (special, designate, realize, determine)

commonplace-adj tedious, prosy, monotonous, ordinary, usual, unimportant, worthless, paltry, (important, prominence, significant, concern)

commotion-n disturbance, tumult, turmoil, disorder, agitation, stir, tremor, shake, ripple, jog, jolt, jar, (oscillation, vibration, liberation)

communion-n intercourse, converse, partnership, association, talk, participation, possession, partaking, (possessor, holder, occupant)

compact-n deal, contract, understanding, bargain, engagement, agreement, stipulation, covenant, terse, condensed, thick,

constricted, compressed,
dense, (contention,
disagreement)
companion-*n* partner,
chum, colleague,
associate, accompany,
coexist, attend,
synchronize, (alone,
isolate, disjoin, one, sole,
solitary)
company-*n* association,
partnership, group, crowd,
cast, syndicate, firm,
companionship,
assemblage, (dispersion,
disjunction, divergence)
compartment-*n* niche,
enclosure, division, part,
portion, item, segment,
fragment, (collectiveness,
completeness, bulk, mass)
compassion-*n* condolence,
sympathy, tenderness,
mercy, pity,
commiseration, fellow-
feeling, yearning,
forbearance, (inclemency,
severity, malevolence)
compatible-*adj*
harmonious, congruous,
suitable, consistent,
agreeable, concert,
conformity, uniformity,
(discord, dissidence,
variance, unfitness)
compel-*v* constrain, force,
coerce, impel, drive,
compulsion, make, press,
coactive, oblige,
necessitate
compendium-*n* epitome,
bulletin, review, brief,
analysis, recapitulation,

summary, excerpt, note,
abstract, digest,
(dissertation, theme,
discourse)
compensation-*n*
repayment, payment,
requital, pay,
remuneration, reward,
honorarium, solatium,
mediocrity, generality,
compromise
competence-*n* proficiency,
ability, capability,
sufficiency, means, rich,
luxuriant, affluent, wealthy,
abundant, (insufficient,
meager, shortcoming,
small, scarce)
competent-*adj* capable, fit,
qualified, efficient
competitor-*n* contestant,
rival, entrant, aspirant,
claimant, antagonist,
adversary, opposition,
disputant, enemy, (helper,
adjunct, friend, ally,
confidant)
compile-*v* arrange, amass,
collect, make, write,
assemblage, group,
cluster, clump,
accumulation, heap, pile,
(unassembled, dispersed,
sparse)
completion-*n* attainment,
achievement, execution,
fulfillment, performance,
accomplishment,
conclusion
complex-*adj* complicated,
intricate, involved,
confused, confusion,
disarray, uproar, riot,

rumpus, jumble, huddle,
(orderly, regular, neat, tidy)
complexity-n
entanglement, intricacy,
complication, perplexity,
compositeness
compliance-n assent,
agree, acquiesce, submit,
obey, conformity, normal,
typical, formal, (abnormal,
unusual, eccentric)
complicity-n connivance,
conspiracy, collusion,
confederacy, cooperate,
concur, combine,
understand, unite,
(opposition, antagonism,
counteract, against)
component-n integral part,
constituent, ingredient,
member, subdivision,
radical, intrinsic, inherent,
immanent, subsistent,
essential, inwrought,
innate, inbred,
(extraneousness, whole)
compose-v make up, form,
construct, fashion,
constitute, assuage, calm,
improvise, create,
reception, (exclusion,
omission, reject)
composed-adj serene,
calm, unruffled, tranquil,
collected, unexcitable
composition-n
compounding, constitution,
formation, construction,
blend, mixture, texture,
nature
comprehend-v conceive,
grasp, understand,
comprise, aware,

cognizant, conscious,
acquainted, (shallow,
unknown, superficial, half-
learned)
comprehensive-adj
widespread, synoptic,
inclusive, extensive,
wholesale, full
compress-v condense,
reduce, abridge, thicken,
squeeze, compact,
contract, reduction,
lessening, shrinking,
(extension, spread,
obesity)
comprise-v embrace,
embody, contain,
comprehend, include,
admission, inclusion,
enclose, receive
compromise-n settlement,
arrangement, adjustment,
agreement, composition,
commute, compound,
arrange, imperil, hazard,
jeopardize
compute-v reckon, count,
estimate, evaluate, record,
note, memorandum,
archive, scroll, register,
(obliterate, cancel, scratch,
erase, strike out)
concavity-n hollow, dip,
depression, cavity, antrum,
trough, furrow, depression,
dip, hollow, (rejection,
swelling, bulge, protrusion)
concealment-n
masquerade, secretion,
latency, cover, disguise,
mask, camouflage, screen,
veil, shroud, shelter,
secrecy, privacy, secret

concede-*v* assent, yield,
acknowledge, surrender,
cede, confess, grant,
admittance, ratification,
acquiesce, (dissent,
discordance,
disagreement, discontent)

conceit-*n* egoism, epigram,
quip, whim, fancy, pride,
vanity, complacency,
glorification, airs, self-
satisfied, (modesty,
humility, blushing, reserve,
constraint)

conceive-*v* visualize, fancy,
devise, realize, grasp,
comprehend, form,
produce, become pregnant

concentrate-*v* gather,
collect, converge, focus
center, fix, assemble, core,
nucleus, heart, centralize

concession-*n* permission,
acknowledgement,
admission, reduction,
allowance, grant, gift

conciliate-*v* propitiate,
reconcile, satisfy, disarm,
placate, mollify, reason,
call, inducement,
consideration, (dissuade,
remonstrate, warn,
against, repel)

conciseness-*n*
succinctness, brevity,
terseness, abridgment,
laconicism, condensation,
compression

conclude-*v* arrange, finish,
settle, terminate, infer,
end, deduce, resolve

conclusive - *adj*
unanswerable, convincing,
indisputable, final,
concluding, deduce

concoct-*v* make, hatch,
invent, contrive, prepare,
falsehood, untruth, lying,
perjury, misrepresentation,
forgery, (veracity, sincerity,
candor, truthful)

concord-*n* accord,
symphony, agreement,
harmony, consonance,
unison, correspondence,
amity, congruence,
unanimity, alliance,
conciliation

concrete-*adj* solid, definite,
substantial, hard, exact,
specific, adherence,
together, aggregation,
consolidation, tenacious,
(non-adhesion, loose,
relaxation)

condescend-*v* descend,
deign, vouchsafe, stoop,
humility, meek,
submission, resignation,
(dignified, stately, proud)

condiment-*n* seasoning,
sauce, flavoring, relish,
salt, mustard, pepper,
spice, relish

condition-*n* stipulation,
modification, proviso,
situation, plight, fitness,
assumption, postulate

condolence-*n* pity,
sympathy, commiseration,
compassion, consolation,
comfort

conduct-*v* deportment,
guise, behavior, carriage,
comportment, demeanor,
operate, work, manage,

govern, regulate, supervise

confederate-n associate, ally, accomplice, companion, transient, passing, evanescent, fleeting, flying

confer-v deliberate, consult, discuss, converse, bestow, advise, consul, suggestion, prompt, recommend

confere-n consultation, interview, meeting, parley

confess-v acknowledge, admit, divulge, reveal, disclose, assent, accept, accede, concur, (dissent, demur, disagree, protest)

confident-adj certainty, trust, self-reliance, spirit, assurance, expectant, sure, hopeful, optimistic, self-sufficient, candid, open, unsuspecting, gullible

confine-v restrain, imprison, incarcerate, cage, bound, enclosure, limit, inclose, surround, imprisoned, buried

confirm-v endorse, uphold, corroborate, substantiate, warrant, vouch, certificate, facts, record, docket, (disprove, other side, oppose)

confiscate-v sequestrate, seize, appropriate, taking, capture, appropriation, catch, nab, (return, restore, redeem)

conflict-n battle, combat, encounter, discord, dissension, antagonism,

opposition, counteract, antagonize, (cooperate, concur, combine)

conformity-n agreement, accord, harmony, resemblance, congruity, compliance, observance, acquiescence, concession, submission, consent

confound-v confuse, jumble, overthrow, perplex, bewilder, wonder, marvel, astonish, admire, (expect, foreseen, common)

confront-v brave, defy, front, resist, fore, face, outpost, pioneer, advance, (rear, guard, stern, behind, after)

confuse-v muddle, disturb, disconcert, fluster, bewilder, mistake, deranged, mislay, disorder, unsettle, (arrange, preparation)

confusion-n embarrassment, discomfiture, tumult, turmoil, jumble, (dispose, place, pack, file)

confutation-n disproval, disproof, refutation, refutal, invalidation, retort, answer, (demonstrate, prove, establish)

congeal-v thicken, set, condense, coagulate, stiffen, harden, density, solidness, mass, cake, (thin, fine, tenuous, rarefy)

congenial-adj sympathetic, harmonious, adapted, compatible, agreement,

accord, adapt, fitness,
harmonize, (disagree,
hostile, repugnant)
congratulation-*n* best
wishes, felicitation,
compliment, gratulation,
condolence
congregation-*n*
aggregation, gathering,
fold, flock, brethren,
assemblage, collection,
muster, (dispersed,
broadcast, sprinkle)
congress-*n* parliament,
convention, legislature,
assembly, council,
committee, court,
chamber, board, staff
conjecture-*n* speculation,
inference, surmise,
supposition, assumption,
postulation, condition
conjugate-*v* coupled,
mated, united, bijugate,
paronymous, verbal, literal,
derivation, root,
(corruption, slang, cant)
connect-*v* attach, unite,
link, associate, correlate,
relation, reference,
correlation, similarity,
(disconnection, remote,
irrelevant)
conquer-*v* vanquish,
subdue, defeat, overcome,
prevail, success, advance,
conquest, victory, (fail,
repulse, rebuff, defeat,
overthrow, slip)
consanguinity-*n* kindred,
relationship, parentage,
paternity, connection,
propinquity, alliance,

affiliation, affinity
conscientious-*adj*
scrupulous, painstaking,
exact, faithful, trusty,
upright, duty, obligation,
liability, (relaxation, failure,
evasion)
conscious-*adj*
understanding, aware,
keen, sensible, cognizant,
senses, observation,
intuition, judgment,
(imbecility, brutality,
without reason)
conscription-*n*
impressment, compulsory
enlistment, draft, compel,
force, make, drive, coerce
consecrate-*v* hallow,
devote, dedicate, apply,
utilization, work, yield,
manipulate, (disuse,
abstain, spare, neglect)
consent-*v* compliance,
assent, acquiescence,
concurrence, agreement,
concession, permission,
permit, accession,
acknowledgment, (dissent,
refusal)
consequence-*n*
proceeding, outcome,
result, decision,
termination, settlement,
prominence, self-
importance
consequential-*adj*
sequential, deducible,
derivable, inferable,
secondary, supercilious,
resultant
consider-*v* regard, notice,
heed, believe, adjudge,

deliberate, reflect, ponder,
(vacancy, thoughtless,
absent)

considerable-*adj*
extraordinary, intense,
notable, weighty, big,
massive, substantial

consideration-*n* regard,
observation, notice,
kindliness, consequence,
inducement, deference,
esteem, perquisite

consign-*v* delegate, assign,
commit, authorize, send,
deliver, dispatch, ship,
allotment, assignment,
charge, task,
apportionment

consistent-*adj* compatible,
harmonious,conformable,
homogeneous, accordant,
agreement, accommodate,
conventional, (abnormity,
infringement, irregular)

consolation-*n* comfort,
solace, assuagement,
sympathy, encouragement,
relief, softening, alleviation,
restorative, (aggravated,
exasperation, embitter)

consolidate-*v* incorporate,
federate, merge, solidify,
compact, coherence,
adhere, holdfast, tenacity,
(looseness, relaxation,
freedom, disjunction)

consonance-*n* accordance,
tunefulness, concord,
harmony, accord

conspicuous-*adj*
prominent, famous,
renowned, eminent,
notable, obvious, glaring,

salient, (invisible,
concealment, obscure)

conspirator-*n* plotter,
accomplice, confederate,
traitor, combine, scheme,
concur, intrigue, plot

constant-*adj* incessant,
unflagging, continual,
steadfast, stanch, loyal,
agree, uniform, level,
smooth, (diversify, varied,
uneven)

constitute-*v* establish, set
up, found, appoint, form,
frame, compose,
(exclusion, rejection,
omission, separate)

constitution-*n* structure,
construction, state,
condition, code, law,
charter, temperament,
disposition, nature

constraint-*n* necessity,
coercion, repression,
unnaturalness, bind,
contract, squeeze,
compress

construction-*n* formation,
structure, build,
explanation, translation,
erection, creation

consultation-*n* interview,
deliberation, conference,
council

consume-*v* annihilate, burn,
demolish, devour, use up,
exhaust, drain, expend,
destruction, ruin, downfall,
(fabricate, produce,
performance,
achievement)

consummate-*v*
unmitigated, sheer,

perfect, finished, profound,
intense, complete, fill,
replenish, (deficiency,
wanting, defective)
contact-*n* meeting, union,
conjunction, adhesion,
contiguity, proximity,
apposition, abutment,
touch, adhere, attach,
append, adjoin, (interval,
distance)
contagion-*n* pestilence,
epidemic, transmission,
virus, communication,
poisonousness, toxicity
contagious-*adj*
transmittable,
communicable, catching,
contain-*v* comprise,
embody, include,
incorporate, hold, portion,
segment, fragment, parcel
container-*n* vessel, utensil,
vase, jar, bag, bottle
contaminate-*v* pollute,
taint, corrupt, foul, defile,
uncleanliness, impurity,
decay, filth, dregs, (clean,
launder, wipe, mop,
disinfect)
contemplate-*v* consider,
design, ponder, purpose,
reflect, muse, view, sight,
glimpse, behold, discover,
(blindness, undiscerning)
contempt-*n* scorn, disdain,
detestation, abhorrence,
despise, disrepute,
insignificant, immaterial,
trivial, (important,
prominence, concern,
superior)
contemptuous-*adj*

derision, mockery, sneer,
spurn, abhor,
underestimate (respect,
reverence)
contend-*v* hold, maintain,
allege, strive, struggle,
debate, dispute, reasoning,
argument, proposition,
(chicane, mystification)
content-*n* real meaning,
significance, intent,
implication, substance,
essence, gist, volume,
extent
contention-*n* altercation,
struggle, strife, feud,
contest, litigation,
disagreement, debate,
dispute, belligerency
contents-*n* constituents,
ingredients, cargo, filling,
matter
contingency-*n* prospect,
likelihood, situation, case,
predicament, incidental,
casual, provisional,
conditional, accidental
continual-*adj* incessant,
repeated, constant,
unceasing, perpetuity
continuance-*n* pursuance,
maintenance, extension,
permanence, duration,
perpetuation, stay
contortion-*n* deformation,
twist, distortion,
crookedness, warp,
irregular, unsymmetrical,
misshapen, ill-
proportioned, stumpy,
(symmetrical, shapely,
regular, uniform)
contour-*n* form, outline,

shape, figure,
circumference, parameter,
zone, belt
contraband-*n* forbidden,
illegal, smuggled, illicit,
deception, deceit, juggle,
cheat, hoax, decoy, waylay
contract-*n* arrangement,
bargain, compact, promise,
guarantee, promissory,
pledged, (release,
absolute, unconditional)
contradict-*v* deny, dissent,
refute, disprove, gainsay,
(identical, equivalent, the
same)
contrariety-*n* antagonism,
opposition, repugnance,
clashing, disagreement,
antipathy, discrepancy,
inconsistency, contrast
contrary-*adj* opposed,
adverse, opposite,
antagonistic, hostile,
perverse
contrast-*v* dissimilarity,
unlikeness, disparity,
antithesis, foil
contribute-*v* conduce, tend,
advance, subscribe,
donate, giving,
consignment, charity,
generosity, (acquisition,
acceptance, admission)
contrivance-*n* gear, device,
apparatus, scheme, trick,
stratagem
control-*v* dominion, power,
sway, direction, regulation,
might, force, energy,
pressure, strength, ability,
(disability, helplessness)
controversy-*n* dispute,

argument, debate, quarrel,
altercation, contention,
reasoning, discussion,
comment, (evasion,
quibble, pervert, mystify)
conundrum-*n* puzzle,
riddle, enigma, secret,
maze, profound, labyrinth,
paradox, (information,
intelligence, advice, report)
convalesce-*v* recover,
rally, improve, revive,
restoration, renovation,
resume, cure, heal,
remedy, (relapse,
retrogradation, return)
convenient-*adj* serviceable,
suitable, opportune,
advantageous, adaptable,
expedient, eligible, seemly,
becoming, (unfit,
undesirable)
convention-*n* caucus,
meeting, council,
assembly, usage, custom,
practice
conventional-*adj* habitual,
customary, formal, usual,
common, general, familiar,
regular, vernacular,
(infraction, disuse, violate,
infringe)
convergence-*n* confluence,
concurrence,
concentration, concourse,
focalization, meeting,
assemblage
conversion-*n*
transmutation, change,
transformation,
metamorphosis, growth,
regeneration, assimilation
convey-*v* transport, carry,

bear, grant, cede, will,
transfer, deportation,
carriage, delegate, consign
convict-_v_ find guilty, doom,
prisoner, captive, criminal,
rascal, scoundrel, villain,
ruffian, jail-bird, (good
man, hero, angel, saint)
conviction-_v_ view, opinion,
sentence, penalty, belief,
credence, faith, assume,
esteem, (unbelieving,
doubtful, misgiving)
convince-_v_ satisfy, assure,
convert, persuade, belief,
faith, confidence, reliance,
certainty, (doubtful, fallible,
suspicious)
convoke-_v_ collect, muster,
gather, convene, summon,
assemblage, crowd,
throng, mob, hoard,
(disperse, scatter, diffuse)
convoy-_v_ escort, attend,
conduct, guard, watch,
support, accompany,
custody, safety, security,
surety, (insecurity,
jeopardy, risk, hazard)
convulse-_v_ stir, shake,
disturb, rend, wring, pain,
suffering, aching, spasm,
piercing, sharp, (pleasure,
sensual, comfort, luxury)
cool-_adj_ wary, unfriendly,
self-possessed, chilly,
lukewarm, easygoing,
placid, compose, calm,
freeze, chill, harden
cooperation-_n_ combination,
joint operation, union,
participation, concert,
collaboration

coordinate-_n_ organize,
adjust, harmonize,
arrange, preparation,
assortment, allotment,
catalog, tabulate,
(dislocate, disarrange,
break up)
copious-_adj_ plentiful, full,
abundant, profuse, ample,
sufficiency, adequacy,
enough, fullness,
(incompetence, deficiency,
poverty)
copy-_n_ counterpart, effigy,
facsimile, likeness,
similitude, semblance,
imitation, model,
representation, study
cord-_n_ string, twine, rope,
bond, tie, fastening,
shackle, rein, rivet,
padlock, anchor
cordial-_adj_ hearty, friendly,
genial, warm, sincere,
pleasure, sensual, comfort,
luxury, enjoy, (torment,
anguish, agony)
core-_n_ nucleus, kernel,
heart, gist, pith, substance,
center, middle, axis,
concentric
corner-_n_ niche, nook,
monopolize, control, spot,
point, premises, place,
pigeon hole, compartment
corpse-_n_ carcass, dead
body, skeleton, remains,
cadaver, carrion, bones,
relic, mummy, fossil
corpulence-_n_ fleshiness,
portliness, obesity, fatness,
bulk, greatness, expanse,
large, big, ample, (small,

pygmy, minute,
undersized)
correct-v reprove, punish,
chastise, remedy, mend,
discipline, rectify, repair,
set right, strict, accurate,
true, perfect, unerring
correlation-n reciprocity,
interdependence,
mutuality, correspondence,
comparison, relative,
cognate, (irrelative,
irrespective, arbitrary)
correspondence-n letters,
writings, epistle, news,
dispatch, bulletin,
accordance, agreement
corrigible-adj tractable,
amenable, submissive,
docile, improvement,
better, increase, ripen,
mature, (worse,
deteriorate, degenerate)
corrode-v rust, decay,
wear, waste, deteriorate,
(improve, elaborate,
promote, cultivate,
advance)
corrupt-adj base,
dishonest, tainted, rotten,
spoiled, profligate,
dissolute, immoral, infect,
taint, pervert, debase
cosmic-adj otherworldly,
heavenly, terrestrial,
universal
cost-n expense, charge,
outlay, disbursement,
expenditure, expensive,
dear, high-priced,
(discount, reduction,
allowance, rebate)
council-n committee, court,

chapter, chamber, board,
directorate, syndicate,
cabinet, staff, parliament,
(precept, direction, charge)
count-v estimate, consider,
figure, reckon, compute,
enumerate, numbering,
calculation, recite
countenance-n expression,
aspect, visage, features,
patronage, favor, front,
foreground, advance,
(behind, rear, stern, rum)
counterfeit-v fictitious,
bogus, spurious, fake,
imitation, false, copy,
duplication, mirror,
reproduce, (original,
unimitated)
counterpart-n duplicate,
complement, facsimile,
replica, match, mate,
similarity, likeness, affinity
counterpoise-n balance,
counterweight, equipoise,
counterbalance, ballast,
indemnity, equivalent,
bribe
countersign-v watchword,
authentication, seal,
password, identification,
secondary evidence,
corroboration, (unattested,
unauthenticated)
countless-adj innumerable,
incalculable, numberless,
illimitable, infinite,
immense, immeasurable
country-n nation, state,
power, home, territory,
district, rural regions, field,
meadow, garden,
ornamental

couple-n join, pair, yoke, link, tie, mate, firm, fast, taut, taught, secure, set, intervolved, (sunder, divide, disjoin, dissect, cut up, carve)

courage-n bravery, valor, fearlessness, heart, resoluteness, daring, spirit, boldness, dash, gallantry, heroism, mettle, nerve, grit, fortitude, resolution

courier-n messenger, runner, traveler, envoy, emissary, reporter, informer, correspondent

course-n procedure, path, behavior, succession, channel, drift, trend, progress, flight, routine, (await, loom, predestine, doom)

court-n palace, castle, staff, retinue, train, bar, session, bench, make love, woo, cajole, invite, solicit, praise, (forbearance, refraining, avoidance, evasion, elusion)

courtesy-n politeness, refinement, cultivation, gentility, urbanity, culture, elegance, civility, polish, (discourtesy, repulsive, disrespect, impudent)

courtship-n suit, courting, wooing, flirtation, endearment, caress, fondling, embrace, salute, kiss, amorous, (glum, morose, frumpish, surly)

cove-n inlet, bay, harbor, lagoon, gulf, concavity, depression, dip, hollow, indentation, cavity, dent, pit, basin, (convexity, prominence, projection, swelling)

covenant-n agreement, pact, compact, bargain, agree, stipulate, undertake, observe, comply, perform, (fail, neglect, omit, elude, evade, ignore, infringe)

covering-n screen, shield, shelter, protection, carapace, concealment, seclusion, hide, mystification, (uncover, inform, enlighten, open)

covet-v want, crave, envy, long for, desire, wish, greedy, hunger, hanker, solicitude, anxiety, yearning, aspiration, (cold, frigid, lukewarm, careless, listless)

cowardice-n graveness, pusillanimity, timidity, timorousness, baseness, effeminacy, abject fear, faintheartedness

cower-v shrink, crouch, quail, fawn, grovel, fear, timidity, diffidence, apprehensive, solicitude, anxiety, misgiving, (trust, confidence, reliance, faith)

coy-adj demure, retiring, shrinking, shy, tremble, shake, shudder, nervous, restless, despondent, (hope, trust, aggressive, outspoken, forward)

crabbed-adj tempered,

surly, cross, perverse,
peevish, illegible, intricate,
squeezed
crack-v burst, break split,
seam, rut, cleft, rip, fissure,
sunder, divide, separate,
disjoin, isolate, abscind,
(attach, fix, join, unite,
connect, hold, bind)
craft-n handicraft, trade,
artfulness, trickery, deceit,
vessel, boat, expertness,
art, skill, dexterity,
adroitness, competence,
(quackery, folly, stupidity,
indiscretion)
cram-v crowd, jam, stuff,
choke, guzzle, gorge,
assemble, muster, group,
cluster, pack, bunch,
(disperse, disjunction,
scatter, sow, spread)
cramp-n hamper, restrain,
handicap, paralyze,
cripple, incapacitate,
contract, reduce, diminish,
(expand, extend, augment,
develop, swell)
crass-adj stupid, raw, elude,
gross, ignorant,
incomprehension,
simplicity, shallow,
superficial, green,
(instructed, learned,
educated, enlightened)
crave-v yearn for, long for,
beseech, ask, beg, pray,
desire, petition, ravening,
hungry, famished, desirous
crawl-v grovel, fawn, cower,
drag, lag, lumber, creep,
saunter, plod, trudge,
moderate, slow, (speed,

scuttle, gallop, rush,
velocity)
crazy-adj mad, lunatic, sick,
crack-brained, shaky,
fanaticism, oddity,
eccentricity, twist, insane,
crazed, frantic, raving,
(sanity, soundness,
rationality, lucidity)
create-v make, originate,
form, bring into being,
occasion, devise,
conceive, invent, breed,
propagate, envisage
creation-n invention,
conception, causation,
origination, formation,
constitution, cosmos,
universe
creator-n originator, maker,
author, producer, god,
supreme being
creature-n lower animal,
beast, individual, mortal,
dependent, slave, being,
thing, something, matter,
substantial, (nonentity,
shadow, phantom, nothing,
naught)
credence-n reliance, trust,
assurance, acceptance,
acknowledgment, credit,
faith, dependence,
(uncertain, doubtful,
incredulous)
credibility-n belief,
believable, trustworthiness,
honesty, faith, trust,
confidence, reliance,
repute, honor, merit,
esteem, prestige
credulity-n gullibility,
infatuation, self delusion,

self deception, naivete,
silly, stupid, infatuated,
simple, (incredulous,
skeptical, suspicious,
distrustful)

creed-n dogma, faith,
. doctrine, belief, firm,
implicit, persuasion,
articles, canons,
catechism, (doubt, distrust,
disputable, unworthy)

crest-n culmination, tip,
height, top, plume, seal,
device, ridge, summit,
vertex, apex, zenith,
pinnacle, (base, bottom,
nadir, foot, fundamental)

crew-n mob, company,
gang, throng, sailors,
squad, crowd, horde, body,
tribe, party, clan,
brotherhood, (adrift, stray,
dishelvelled, streaming,
scatter)

cringe-v flinch, shrink,
wince, fawn, grovel,
submit, yield, non-
resistance, obedience,
surrender, succumb,
parasite, bow, stoop,
servile, supple, (bully,
dictate)

cripple-n disable, hurt,
incapacitate, enfeeble,
helpless, prostration,
paralysis, palsy, apoplexy,
exhaustion, (potent,
capable, virtue,
qualification)

crisis-n emergency, trial,
extremity, exigency, crux,
full of incident, eventful,
stirring, bustling, (loom,

await, eventually,
forthcoming)

criterion-n standard, norm,
measure, test, rule,
conformation, support,
ratification, corroboration,
authentication, (oppose,
unauthenticated, non-
conformity)

critical-adj disparaging,
faultfinding, judicious,
analytical, crucial, turning
point, reprove, flay,
censure, examine,
analyze, judge

crooked-adj deceptive,
fraudulent, sneaking,
warped, awry, twisted,
askew, distorted,
(symmetrical, shapely,
finished, beautiful)

cross-n intersection,
traversing, decussation,
hybridization, passage,
entwine, weave, twist,
wreathe, dovetail

crouch-v bend, stoop,
fawn, cower, cringe, low,
neap, debased, underlie,
slouch, wallow, grovel,
depress, (tower, pillar,
dome, height, elevate)

crown-n diadem, coronet,
crest, top, reward, garland,
prize, accredit, empower,
commission, represent,
(dismiss, cancel, repeal)

crucial-adj decisive, final,
determining, supreme,
demonstrate, prove,
establish, show, verify,
(refute, disprove, expose,
rebut)

curt-*adj* blunt, brusque, rude, abrupt, brief, short, succinct, concise, brevity, abbreviate, compress, compact, (lengthy, endlong, interminable)

curtail-*v* lessen, reduce, abridge, abbreviate, cut, retrench, mutilate, amputate, abscind, thin, prune, (add, annex, reinforce, supplement)

curtain-*n* veil, screen, hanging, blind, drapery, conceal, hide, masquerade, hiding place, reserve, (mention, acquaint, informant, outpouring)

custody-*n* imprisonment, care, bondage, charge, protection, keeping, confinement, durance, duress, arrest, (liberate, free, redemption, acquittal)

custom-*n* rule, fashion, precedent, practice, patronage, trade, usage, regular, usual, habitual, normal

cut-*v* divide, split, sever, shape, reap, gather, separate, part, detach, divorce, rupture, (attach, fix, firm, fast, join, unite)

cynical-*adj* sardonic, surly, satirical, contemptuous, misanthropic, disdainful

D

dabble-*v* trifle, potter, moisten, paddle, splash, dilute, immerse, wash, sprinkle, drench

dagger-*n* stiletto, knife, poniard, sword, weapon, armament, saber, resentment, displeasure, animosity, wrath

dainty-*adj* exquisite, pretty, delicate, particular, meticulous, delicious, appetizing, tasty, attractive, lovely, (annoying, nuisance, infestation, molestation)

dally-*v* philander, flirt, dawdle, prolong, idle, protract, delay, suspend, waive, retard, postpone, procrastinate, (prompt, immediate, haste, sudden)

damage-*n* injure, impair, harm, mutilate, hurt, deteriorate, wane, degenerate, decay, injury, loss, (fructify, ripen, mature, promote)

damp-*adj* humid, moist, foggy, watery, moisture, wet, dank, infiltrate, muggy, drench, dewy, (dry, arid, drought)

dance-*v* prance, glide, move, flutter, perform, party, ball, cotillion, hop, jump, oscillate, agitate, pulsate, effervescence

danger-*n* jeopardy, hazard, peril, risk, insecurity, precariousness, venture, instability, exposure, (safe, secure, impregnability, invulnerability)

dangle-*v* wave, hang,

swing, be suspended,
droop, sling, pendulum,
depend, pensive, loose,
flowing, (support, aid, prop,
stand, anvil, stay)

dare-v challenge, venture,
brave, face, defiance,
threat, defy, bluster,
(agree, accord,
sympathize)

darkness-n blackness,
murk, swarthiness,
obscurity, duskiness,
gloominess, dimness,
dinginess, lightless,
opacity, tenebrous

dart-n throw, hurl, direct,
spurt, shoot, scud, propel,
project, fling, cast, pitch,
chuck, toss, (pull, haul,
draw, lug, rake, drag, tow,
trail, train)

dash-v break, crush,
shatter, depress,
discourage, frustrate,
imbue, blend, speed, rush,
sprint, mark, stroke, line,
trace, hint, tinge, grain

daunt-v frighten, alarm,
cow, discourage, fear,
timid, anxiety, solicitude,
care, apprehension,
(courage, bravery, valor,
spirit)

daze-v bewilder, dazzle,
stupefy, blind, spark, flash,
blaze, scintillation, shine,
glow, glitter, twinkle,
brighten, (dark, obscurity,
gloom, dusk, extinction)

dazzle-v impress,
confound, bedazzle, awe,
refraction, distortion,

illusion, false light

dead-adj lifeless, deceased,
defunct, departed, late,
inanimate, extinct, fatal,
mortal, destructive,
murderous

deaden-v incapacitate,
muffle, paralyze, numb,
subdue, invalid,
prostration, exhaustion,
impotent, (potency, ability,
elasticity, magnetism)

deal-v allot, distribute,
dispense, inflict, give,
deliver, administer,
arrange, allotment, sort,
classify, (derangement,
disorder, disorganize)

dearness-n expensiveness,
high price, costliness,
overcharge, extravagance,
sumptuous, valuable,
(cheapness, dislike, hate,
loathe)

debar-v hinder, forbid,
check, obstruct, exclude,
deny, prohibit, bar, stile,
barrier, restraint, prevent,
impediment, obstacle, (aid,
assistance, promote,
reinforce)

debase-v deprave, degrade,
depreciate, lower,
dishonor, disgrace,
deterioration, degradation,
corruption, adulteration

debate-v discussion,
argument, controversy,
contention, conversation,
oral communication,
reasoning, comment,
(answer, response, reply,
replication)

debt-*n* liability, debit, obligation, claim, due, deferred payment, deficit, insolvency, (credit, trustworthiness, reliability, reputation)

decay-*v* putrefy, crumble, rot, wither, fall to pieces, decompose, pare, reduce, attenuate, scrape, render smaller, (expand, spread, extend, overgrown)

decease-*v* demise, dying, departure, passing, death, dissolution, release, rest, extinction, bereavement, (respiration, vitality, animation, subsist)

deceit-*n* falsehood, sham, fraud, treachery, trickery, double dealing, perversion, hollowness, quackery, prevarication, (truthful, veracious, scrupulous)

decent-*adj* ordinary, clean, virtuous, passable, modest, pure, indifferent, middling, mediocre, average, tolerable, (unparalleled, superhuman)

deception-*n* insidiousness, duplicity, deceit, wiliness, sophistry, cunning, dissimulation, falsehood, imposition, misrepresentation, bluff, chicanery, treachery, (veracity, frankness, truth, honesty, sincerity)

decide-*v* resolve, settle, determine, choose, decree, arbitrate, fix upon, judge, result, conclusion, valuation, (misjudge, bias, warped, partiality)

decipher-*v* translate, decode, discover, explain, make out, interpret, definition, explanation, solution, answer, (misrepresent, misinterpret, distort)

decision-*n* resolve, decree, verdict, firmness, will, purpose, judgment, result, conclusion, deduction

declaration-*n* proclamation, avowal, announcement, bulletin, assertion, notice, profess, acknowledge, state

decline-*v* waste, age, die, decay, refuse, repel, shun, spurn, slope, declivity, descent

decomposition-*n* dissolution, break-up, disjunction, disintegration, cariosity, putrefaction, putridity (cleanliness, combination)

decoration-*n* embellishment, trimming, adornment, ribbon, laurel, medal, ornament, wreath, festoon, (simplicity, plain, homely, unaffected, chaste)

decoy-*n* lure, inveigle, entice, entrap, ensnare, deception, falseness, untruth, fraud, deceit, guile

decrease-*v* diminution, lessening, mitigation, reduction, abatement,

shrinkage, contraction,
shorten, abbreviate,
(increase, augmentation,
addition, accumulation)
decree-*n* ordinance, edict,
mandate, verdict, decision,
regulation, command,
order
decrement-*n* diminution,
decrease, deduction,
attenuation, abatement,
waste, loss, (addition,
adjunct)
decry-*v* disparage, slander,
belittle, underestimate,
censure, degrade,
depreciation, undervaluing,
modesty, (overestimating,
exaggeration, vanity)
dedicate-*v* devote, offer,
consecrate, inscribe, mark,
name, figure, repute,
enthrone, celebrate,
glorify, (disrepute,
discredit, disgrace, stain)
deduction-*n* curtailment,
subtraction, removal,
excision, abstraction,
consequence, implication,
derivation, corollary,
discount, allowance,
(addition, attach, join,
interpose, append)
deed-*n* feat, exploit, action,
performance, document,
evidence, confirmation,
warrant, credential,
admission, (vindication,
counter-protest, oppose,
rebut, countervail)
deep-*adj* bottomless,
profound, unfathomable,
abstruse, astute,

designing, cunning,
concavity, submerged,
(shallow, superficial)
deface-*v* mutilate, distort,
injure, disfigure, mar,
blemish, deteriorate,
shapeless, formless,
deform, (conformation,
formation, build, trim,
fashion)
defame-*v* slander, abuse,
disparage, revile, taint,
smirch, sully, disrepute,
discredit, shame, disgrace,
(regard, respect, dignity,
splendor)
· **defeat**-*v* vanquish, subdue,
conquer, refute, rebut,
silence, overcome, failure,
abortion, inefficacy,
ineffectual, (success,
advancement, good
fortune, prosperity)
defect-*n* flaw, fault, lack,
deficiency, imperfection,
weakness, shortcoming,
error, failing, blemish,
deficient, unsound
defense-*n* security, guard,
protection, preservation,
resistance, vindication,
support, advocacy, plea,
espousal, fortification,
entrenchment, palisade,
(attack, aggression,
encroachment, offense,
onslaught, assail)
defenseless-*adj*
unshielded, powerless,
unarmed, helpless,
exposed, (strength,
adamant, resistless,
invincible)

defensible-*adj* impregnable, invulnerable, supportable, maintainable, excusable, justifiable

defer-*v* retard, postpone, delay, procrastinate, adjourn, yield, comply, give in, capitulate

defiance-*n* challenge, threat, provocation, opposition, disobedience, insurgency, rebellion, insubordination, revolt, (obedience, submission)

deficient-*adj* lacking, short, wanting, insufficient, inadequate, shortcoming, inferior, minority, small, subordinate, (superior, supreme, great, advantageous)

define-*v* construe, expound, explain, bound, limit, circumscribe, description, meaning, distinct

definite-*adj* clear, plain, positive, specific, particular, limited, precise, concrete, certain, surety, (doubtful, uncertain, vague, fallibility)

deflect-*v* curve, bend, turn, swerve, diverge, deviation, stray, introvert, divert, digress, departure, (set, undeviating, straight, directly)

deformity-*n* misproportion, disfigurement, ugliness, crookedness, malformation, distortion, (symmetrical, shapely, beautiful, parallel, uniform)

defraud-*v* swindle, hoax, trick, dupe, cheat, deceive, untruth, fraud, guile, misrepresentation, chicane, (truthful, frankness, sincerity, honesty)

defray - *v* settle, meet, liquidate, discharge, pay, acknowledgment, release, receipt, repayment, satisfaction, reimbursement, (non-payment, default, repudiation)

defy-*v* face, confront, brave, oppose, challenge, threaten, dare, defiance, disobey

degrade-*v* shame, disgrace, humiliate, dishonor, fall, abasement, deteriorate, despicable, unbecoming, scandalous, (dignity, stateliness, splendor, noble)

degree-*n* gradation, grade, step, extent, measure, point, amount, mark, rate, standard, height, range, scope, intensity, strength,(quantity, instantaneity)

deify-*v* idolize, venerate, canonize, immortalize, exalt, repute, distinction, dedication, consecration, enthronement, celebration, (dishonor, shameful, stain, disgrace)

deity-*n* omnipotence, god, omniscience, providence, supreme being, creator, almighty, hold, preserve, atone, redeem

dejection-*n* despondency, melancholy, depression, pessimism, despair, sorrow, sadness, grief, dolefulness, distress, weariness, (cheerfulness, happy, geniality, gaiety)

delay-*v* retard, obstruct, linger, defer, impede, postpone, procrastinate, put off, adjourn, late, tardy, belated, (immediately, briefly, shortly, quickly)

delectable-*adj* pleasant, delightful, tasty, delicious, pleasurable, savory, relish, delicacy, appetizing, zestful, (acrid, repulsive, nasty, sickening, nauseous)

delegate-*v* substitute, envoy, agent, proxy, assign, consign, entrust, authorize, empower, commission, assignment, deputation, (annulment, nullification, cancel)

delete-*v* cancel, expunge, erase, obliterate, efface, (record, note, register, endorse, memo)

deliberate-*v* meditate, reflect, reason, ponder, well-considered, gradual, voluntary, leisurely

deliberation-*n* coolness, caution, prudence, deliberateness, slowness, discretion, prudence, calculation, foresight, (impetuous, levity,

imprudence, presumption, audacity)

delicacy-*n* daintiness, luxury, elegance, tidbit, discrimination, tact, culture, sensitiveness, frailty, infirmity, savoury, palatable, ambrosia

delicious-*adj* delectable, dainty, pleasing, luscious, palatable, tasty, relish, good, ambrosia, zest, appetizing, sweet, nectarous, (offensive, repulsive, nasty, nauseous)

delight-*n* please, gratify, charm, enchant, enjoy, pleasure, fruition, satisfaction, happiness, rapture, ecstasy, (annoyance, irritation, worry, plague)

delineate-*v* block, depict, sketch, portray, set forth, illustrate, represent, imitate, sculpture, engrave, design, draft, trace, (distort, exaggerate, daub, scratch)

delinquent-*adj* derelict, remiss, neglectful, rough, rowdy, ruffian, bully, incendiary, thief, murderer, criminal, (model, paragon, hero, innocent, benefactor)

delirious-*adj* crazed, raving, mad, insane, light-headed, lunacy, eccentricity, maniacal, reasonless, demented, (sanity, soundness, rationality, sobriety, lucidity)

deliverance-*n* liberation, release, rescue, reprieve, extrication, emancipation, redemption, salvation, (restraint, retention)

delude-*v* dupe, bluff, trick, fool, hoodwink, deceive, false impression, deception, hallucination, fault, blunder, (fact, reality, accuracy, delicacy, rigor)

deluge-*v* downpour, flood, inundation, rainstorm, supersaturate, excessive, superabundant, overflowing, (insufficient, meager, paltry, empty)

delusion-*n* illusion, magic, fallacy, misconception, hallucination, conjuring, infatuation, oddity, (sane, rational, reasonable)

demand-*v* order, impose, ask, exact, question, require, claim, requisition, request, market, ultimatum

demolish-*v* devastate, ruin, overthrow, wreck, crush, explode, invalidate, defeat, (establish, prove, make good, verify)

demonic-*adj* devilish, hellish, possessed, fiendish, vampire, ghoul, fiend, supernatural, weird, unearthly, haunted

demonstration-*n* verification, proof, substantiation, conclusiveness, testimony, exhibition, mass-meeting, (confutation, refute)

demoralize-*v* incapacitate,

unnerve, undermine, corrupt, deprave, pervert, render-powerless, disqualify, (powerful, puissant, potent, capable)

demur-*v* protest, cavil, object, wrangle, scruple, remonstrance, disbelieve, dissent, unwilling, hesitate, (determination, resolve, vigor, resoluteness)

demure-*v* precise, priggish, solemn, sad, sedate, shy, bashful, retiring, modesty, reserve, constraint, blushing, (vain, pretentious, conceit, selfishness)

den-*n* sanctum, cave, lair, study, retreat, cell, abode, dwelling, lodging, domicile, residence, habitation

denial-*n* repudiation, negation, contradiction, disallowance, disbelief, disavowal, protest, recusancy, (affirmance, declaration, oath, assurance)

denomination-*n* persuasion, designation, name, side, specification, kind, sect, class, division, category, province, domain

denote-*v* betoken, signify, represent, express, imply, convey, designate, specify, indication, feature, type, characteristic

denounce-*v* arraign, charge, censure, rebuke, blame, curse, damn, accuse, reprehend, chide,

admonish, disapprove, (approval, approbation, advocacy, esteem)
density-*n* solidness, body, compactness, thickness, impenetrability, impermeability, coherence, ignorance, crassness, ineptitude, opacity, dullness, obtuseness, (intelligence, rarity)
dent-*n* depression, hollow, indentation, cavity, concavity, dip, cavernous, excavate, burrow, tunnel, (convex, project, swelling, bilge, bulge, protrusion)
denunciation-*n* defiance, condemnation, curse, arraignment, imprecation
deny-*v* differ, protest, contradict, reject, doubt, discredit, dissent, discontent, disagreement, non-conformity, (assent, acquiescence, admission, unanimity)
department-*n* jurisdiction, bureau, office, division, part, function, capacity, sphere, orb, field, line, walk, routine
departure-*n* embarkation, start, exit, leaving, egress, parting, withdraw, adieu, farewell, removal, (return, remigration, arrive)
depend-*v* trust, credit, rely, hang, be contingent, uncertain, casual, doubtful, dubious, vague, hesitant, (positive, absolute, definite, decisive, without

question)
depict-*v* delineate, portray, represent, picture, describe, mimic, illustrative, imitate, figurative, (distort, exaggerate, misrepresent, daub)
deplore-*v* bewail, lament, regret, mourn, complain, grievous, sad, pitiable, repine, (content, satisfaction, ease, cheerfulness)
deport-*v* banish, transport, exile, remove, send, transit, displace, drift, bring, fetch, transpose
deposit-*v* installment, pledge, payment, alluvium, place, situate, locate, settlement, establish, (displace, eject, removal, unload)
deposition-*n* sworn evidence, affidavit, allegation, dethronement, expulsion, archive, docket, certificate, (efface, obliterate, erase, cancel)
depository-*n* warehouse, storehouse, vault, store, repository, conservatory, closet, reservoir, cistern
depravity-*n* badness, corruption, perversion, degeneracy, wickedness, impairment, injury, damage, loss, wrong, aggrieve, annoyance, (improvement, amendment, reform, revision)

deprecation-*n*
remonstrance,
disapprobation, protest,
disapproval, mediation,
expostulation, intercession
depreciate-*v* lessen, fall,
drop, slight, undervalue,
underrate, disparage,
slander, affront
depression-*n* sinking,
cavity, hollow, dip,
diminution, humiliation,
abasement, subversion,
melancholy, dispiritedness,
gloom, despondency,
sadness, (cheerfulness,
elevation)
deprive-*v* bereave, strip,
dispossess, despoil, rob,
clutch, capture, distress,
divestment, extortion,
eviction, (restitution,
replevin, redemption,
atonement)
depth-*n* profoundness,
extent, profundity,
intensity, completeness,
abundance, (shallowness,
veneer, superficiality)
deputy-*n* substitute, proxy,
surrogate, delegate, agent,
representative, alternate
derangement-*n*
discomposure, disorder,
confusion, embarrassment,
mess, tangle, inversion,
mania, insanity, madness,
(sanity, arrangement)
dereliction-*n* abandonment,
relinquishment, neglect,
omission, desertion,
failure, fault, evasion,
(duty, respect, homage)

deride-*v* disdain, scorn,
jeer, mock, ridicule,
irruption, snigger, satirize,
parody, travesty
derive-*v* secure, get, gain,
account for, deduce, infer,
etymologize, trace,
estimation, valuation,
appreciation, assessment,
(discover, find, determine,
evolve)
derogatory-*adj* scandalous,
unbefitting, ignoble,
discreditable, disrepute,
degrade, dishonor, expel,
disgrace, (distinct, repute,
dignity, rank, standing)
descend-*v* dismount, slide,
go down, tumble, detail,
special, particular, specific,
proper
descent-*n* drop, plunge, fall,
declination, comedown,
gravitate, decline, sink,
spring, issue, (ascent,
ascension, rising,
originate, upgrowth)
description-*n* statement,
account, record, report,
summary, outline,
depiction, representation
desert-*n* waste, wilderness,
forsake, abandon, leave,
run away, worth, due,
recompense, meed
deserter-*n* fugitive, truant,
runaway, apostate,
changeful, reactionary,
apostatize, (arbitrary,
dogmatic, positive,
uninfluenced)
design-*v* arrangement,
make-up, depiction,

drawing, aim, intent, project, pattern, model

designate-v show, specify, indicate, name, call, particularize, individualize, special, proper, detail, definite, (general, prevail, generic, collective, broad)

desire-v inclination, fancy, wish, whim, propensity, fondness, need, want, exigency, urgency, hunger, necessity, passion, (dislike, indifference, satiety)

desist-v halt, discontinue, stop, quit, cease, abstain, interrupt, pause, rest, suspend, (continue, persistence, sustain)

desolate-adj uninhabited, deserted, waste, forlorn, miserable, forsaken, lonely, seclusion, solitude, isolation, (sociality, visit, welcome, hospitality)

despair-n dejection, misery, despondency, wretchedness, anguish, hopelessness, desperate, relinquish, (hope, trust, confidence, reliance, faith)

desperate-adj wild, frantic, frenzied, raging, reckless, despairing, incurable, impossible, impervious, impassible, (practical, feasible, compatible)

despise-v scorn, condemn, disdain, disregard, hate, disgust, contempt, derisive, withering, pitiful, despicable

despond-v lament, mourn, despair, falter, sink, melancholy, sad, dejected, depressed, heaviness, dismal, demure, gravity, (cheerful, geniality, gaiety, liveliness)

despotism-n imperialism, tyranny, autocracy, oppression, authority, influence, patronage, power, prerogative, jurisdiction, (anarchy, relaxation, remission, abdication)

destination-n port, goal, halting place, point, mark, end, close, termination, conclusion, finale, consummation, (beginning, commencement, opening, outset)

destiny-n fortune, fate, lot, fatalism, prospect, decree, expectation, impending, future, (eventuality, incident, proceeding, advent)

destitute-adj poor, penniless, lacking, bereft, needy, deficiency, inadequate, emptiness, poorness, depletion, (sufficient, adequate, enough, luxury)

destruction-n demolition, ruination, dissolution, devastation, cataclysm, perdition, extermination, annihilation, extirpation, (preservation, production)

desultory-adj disconnected, digressive, rambling, fitful,

aimless, erratic, broken,
spasmodic
detach-v disconnect, sever,
unfasten, loosen,
separation, segregation,
portion, division, squad,
detail, (unite, join, together,
connect)
detail-n item, particular,
feature, party, patrol,
description, account,
statement, report,
summary, specification,
delineation, representation
detain-v withhold, delay,
retard, secure, retention,
retain, detain, keep,
custody, tenacity, grasp,
gripe
detect-v discern, reveal,
expose, unearth, perceive,
discover, find, determine,
evolve, fix upon,
determine, (result,
conclusion, upshot,
deduction)
deter-v discourage, hinder,
restrain, hold back,
dissuade, deprecation,
dampen, deport, against,
remonstrate, disincline,
(induce, entice, allure,
bewitch)
deterioration-n impairment,
detriment, injury, harm,
debasement, damage,
loss, degeneration,
vitiation, dilapidation,
disrepair (improvement,
betterment, amendment)
determination-n firmness,
resolution, resolve,
judgment, decree, result,

conclusion, evaluate,
assess, estimate,
(misjudge, positive,
intolerant, impracticable)
determine-v impel, insure,
influence, ascertain,
conclude, define, decree,
designate, specify
detest-v loathe, abhor,
abominate, despise,
dislike, disgust,
disagreeable, disincline,
repel, sicken, nauseous,
(desire, wish, fancy,
fantasy, want, need,
inclined)
detraction-n derogation,
disparagement, scandal,
defamation, calumny,
contempt, disapprobation,
(approbation, flattery)
devastate-v ravage, sack,
pillage, lay waste, ruin,
destructive, subversive,
ruinous, incendiary,
extinguish, (produce,
create, construct, erect,
fabricate)
develop-v promote, build,
evolve, grow, enlarge,
produce, perform, flower,
generate, impregnate,
prolific, induce,
(destruction, dissolution,
ruin, annihilate, abolish)
development-n
consequence, outgrowth,
growth, expansion,
evolution, effect,
eventuality, resulting from,
emanate, (cause, origin,
source, element, principle)
deviation-n divagation,

digression, aberration, variation, alteration, diversion, declination, swerve, warp, drift, (continuance, direction, straightness)

device-n stratagem, trick, design, contrivance, appliance, emblem, type, figure, representation, characteristic, diagnostic

devious-adj circuitous, erring, rambling, indirect, diversion, digression, refraction, departure, aberration, (course, aligned, direct, straight)

devise-v create, contrive, scheme, originate, will, bequeath, plan, scheme, design, project, suggestion, resolution

devoid-adj destitute, void, lacking, wanting, absent, not present, empty, truant, vacant, elsewhere, inexistent, (present, fill, pervade, permeate, occupy, moored)

devote-v destine, preordain, addict, consecrate, dedicate, apply, utilize, resolve, determination, desperation, vigor, (fickle, levity, weakness, waver, hesitate)

devotee-n zealot, fanatic, fan, enthusiast, believer, religionist, inclination, desire, magnet, attraction, aspirant, solicitant, (reluctance, lackadaisical, half-hearted)

devotion-n loyalty, passion, fidelity, worship, homage, yearning, gallantry, benevolence, attachment, rapture, adoration, (hate, detest, abominate, abhor)

devour-v consume, annihilate, swallow, masticate, rumination, gulp, eat, edible, succulent, potable, bibulous, (eject, emission, egestion, evacuation)

devout-adj sincere, reverent, pious, religious, holy, beatification, regeneration, conversion, veneration, (irreverence, hypocrisy, bigot, impiety, sacrilege, blasphemy)

dexterous-adj clever, adroit, expert, proficient, handy, skillful, dexterity, competence, facility, mastery, cleverness, (bungle, unskillful, thoughtless)

diabolic-adj impious, infernal, devilish, satanic, fiendish, hurtful, injurious, deleterious, malignity, malevolence, (goodness, excellence, beneficial, proficient)

dialect-n tongue, speech, brogue, cant, idiom, vernacular, colloquialism, slang, expression, provincialism

dictate-v suggest, prescribe, direct, order, charge, compose, draw up, advice, council, instruction,

enforce, recommend
dictatorial-*adj* domineering,
overbearing, autocratic,
peremptory, superiority,
insolence, arrogance,
overbearance, (servile,
obsequious, supple,
cringe)
die-*v* fade, expire, perish,
depart, to be killed, mold,
seal, punch, matrix, death,
dissolution, departure, (life,
vitality, respire, vivification,
animation)
dietetic-*adj* alimental,
dietary, nutritious,
treatment, help, remedy,
medicine, antiseptic,
corrective, restorative,
sedative, (bane, curse,
rust, leaven, poison)
difference-*n* unlikeness,
dissimilarity, variety,
diversity, heterogeneity,
dissonance, disparity,
contradiction, contrast,
incongruousness, dispute,
contend, bicker, (identity,
similarity)
differentiate-*v* separate,
discriminate, adapt,
distinguish, set apart,
sever, estimate,
refinement, diagnosis,
(uncertain, unmeasured,
overlook)
difficulty-*n* arduousness,
impracticability, hardness,
impossibility, tough,
scrape, entanglement,
(smooth, facilitate, ease,
unclog)
diffuseness-*n* verbosity,
amplification, wordiness,
verbiage, loquacity,
looseness, exuberance
digest-*v* classify, settle,
arrange, summarize,
assimilate, transform,
endure, think out, reflect,
cogitate, consider,
(vacant, unoccupied,
inconsiderate)
dignity-*n* honor, nobility,
distinction, stateliness,
august, lofty, majestic,
haughtiness, vainglory,
supercilious, (humble,
disgrace, service,
submissive)
digress-*v* diverge, swerve,
ramble, wander, deviate,
stray, straggle, sidle, rove,
dodge, meander, veer,
(straight, aligned,
undeviating, course)
dilapidated-*adj* crumbling,
decayed, ruined, worn out,
deterioration, debasement,
recession, retrogradation,
(improvement, melioration,
betterment, amendment)
dilate-*v* amplify, stretch,
expatiate, enlarge, expand,
increase, develop,
rarefaction, germination,
growth, (contraction,
reduction, diminution,
decrease)
dilemma-*n* perplexity, mess,
difficulty, strait, difficulty,
impractical,
embarrassment,
impossibility, tough, hard,
(manageable, wieldy,
submissive, yielding)

disconsolate-*adj* sorrowful, melancholy, hopeless, forlorn, desolate, dejection, depression, prostration, (liveliness, life, vivacity, jocularity, mirth)

discontent-*n* uneasiness, dissatisfaction, regret, disappointment, soreness, mortification, repining, (content, serenity, gratification, happiness)

discontinuity-*n* disunion, fracture, disconnection, cessation, disruption, (continuity, succession, sequence)

discord -*n* dissidence, clash, dissension, disagreement, difference, variance, division, schism, faction, (concord, harmony, agreement)

discount-*v* concession, abatement, allowance, qualification, poundage, rebate, depreciation

discourage-*v* depress, deter, dishearten, daunt, divert, dissuade, deport, remonstrate, warn, disincline, (stimulate, excite, inspirit, persuade)

discourse-*n* discuss, declaim, talk, lecture, expatiate, explain, exercise, task, curriculum, course, elementary, teach, (bewilder, uncertain, mystify, conceal)

discourtesy-*n* incivility, rudeness, impoliteness, tactlessness, rusticity, unmannerly, disrespect, impudence, barbarism, (courtesy, politeness, gentility, refinement)

discovery-*n* ascertainment, detection, exposure, finding, revelation, contrivance, unearthing, invention, device, design, (concealment, veil, cover, camouflage, screen)

discredit-*v* shame, debase, disbelieve, disgrace, disrepute, dishonor, tarnish, defile, pollute, humiliate, reproach, (distinguish, elevate, dedicate, ascent, exaltation)

discretion-*n* prudence, option, volition, freedom, wariness, caution, wary, judicious, choice, elect, preference, choose, (indifference, indecision, neutrality)

discrimination-*n* distinction, differentiation, diagnosis, estimation, discernment, acuteness, clearness, acumen, insight

discuss-*v* examine, analyze, reason, argue, debate, consider, study, controversy, inquire, question, investigate, (answer, retort, discover, rationale)

disdain-*v* derision, scorn, haughtiness, arrogance, airs, contempt, insolence, indifference, unconcern,

careless, (anxiety,
impetuosity, propensity,
willingness)

disengage-v disentangle,
disconnect, sever, free,
extricate, clear, liberate,
release, emancipation,
dismissal, (confine, duress,
restraint, repress)

disfigure-v deface, impair,
mutilate, mangle, mar,
ugly, deformity,
inelegance, blemish,
squalor, eyesore, gaunt,
(beauty, elegance, grace,
form, gloss)

disgrace-n dishonor,
shame, degrade, discredit,
humiliate, corrupt,
recreant, venal, insidious,
perfidious, arrant, (upright,
honest, equitable,
impartial)

disguise-n camouflage,
mask, concealment, blind,
cloak, pretense, hide,
mystify, secrecy, reserve,
cover, screen, (enlighten,
acquaint, knowledge,
publicity)

disgust-v repugnance,
loathing, aversion,
repletion, dislike, gall,
abomination, sicken,
repel, (desire, passion,
crave, care for, affect)

dishonest-adj fraudulent,
false, crooked,
dishonorable, deceptive,
untruth, guile,
misrepresentation,
distortion, (veracity,
honesty, frankness,

truthful, true)

disinfect-v purify, cleanse,
fumigate, sanitize,
ventilate, immaculate,
clear, clarify, deodorize,
refine, (dirt, filth, soot,
contaminate)

disinherit-v oust, disown,
deprive, cut off, transfer,
alienate, assign, limit

disintegrate-v break up,
crumble, disband,
disperse, decompose,
powdery, pulverulent

disjunction-n disunion,
disconnection, parting,
partition, break,
disengagement

dislike-v disinclination,
displeasure, disfavor,
reluctance, repugnance,
abomination, antipathy,
abhorrence, hatred

dislocate-v disarrange,
displace, disjoin, disunite,
derange, separate,
disjunctive, asunder,
distinct, unconnected

dismal-adj gloomy, somber,
depressing, funereal,
sorrowful, mournful,
annoyance, grievance,
nuisance, vexation,
(gratify, delight, gladden,
captivate)

dismantle-v destroy,
undress, strip, disrobe,
worthless, inadequate,
waste, cripple, lame,
useless, (utility,
usefulness, conducive,
remunerative)

dismiss-v send away,

banish, discharge, let go,
disband, eject, relinquish,
abandon, dispense,
riddance, (retain, keep,
detain, custody, tenacity)
disobedience-n unruliness,
insubordination, mutiny,
intractableness, revolt,
obstinacy, noncompliance
disorder-n disarrangement,
confusion, untidiness,
disarray, derangement,
anomaly, disunion,
anarchy, chaos, clutter
disown-v repudiate, deny,
renounce, disclaim, reject,
retract, dispute, ignore,
rebut, disavow, protest,
(affirmation, declare,
positive, emphatic)
disparage-v belittle, decry,
discredit, underrate,
abuse, scoff at,
underestimate, depreciate,
modesty, minimize,
(oversensitive, exaggerate,
vanity, magnify)
dispatch-v dismiss, slay,
alacrity, expedition,
promptness, urgency
dispense-v allot, portion,
distribute, bestow,
administer, apportion,
disperse, diffuse, shed,
spread, dissemination,
(assemble, collect, gather,
muster, compilation)
dispersion-n distribution,
scattering, propagation,
dissipation, dissemination,
allocation, apportionment
displacement-n transfer,
dislocation, replacement,

disturbance, eject,
expulsion, dismissal
displease-v vex, disturb,
annoy, offend, maltreat,
sicken, repel, disenchant,
disagreeable, distasteful,
(pleasant, agreeable,
amuse, delectable)
disposition-n emotion,
temperament, passion,
predisposition, tendency,
inclination, propensity
disprove-v refute, rebut,
defeat, confute, negative,
expose, invalidation,
conviction, clincher,
(categorical, decisive)
dispute-v clash, wrangle,
bicker, confute, argue,
debate, challenge, quarrel,
disqualify-v incapacitate,
disfranchise, unfit, disable,
helpless, exhaust, invalid,
inefficiency, collapse,
(attribute, quality, qualify)
disquiet-v turbulence,
uneasiness, commotion,
anxiety, restlessness,
changeable, versatility,
mobility, vacillation,
(stability, vitality, solidity)
disregard-v affront, slight,
insult, overlook, underrate,
belittle, inconsiderate,
escape one's attention,
(attention, consideration,
reflection, regard)
disrepute-n dishonor,
discredit, disfavor,
disesteem, derogation,
abasement, degradation,
ignominy, disgrace
dissatisfy-v offend, vex,

provoke, annoy, anger, displease, chafe, anxiety, concern, grief, bitterness, tribulation, (happiness, felicity, comfort, delight)

dissemble-*v* feign, hide, disguise, mask, simulate, deception, untruth, guile, misrepresentation, pretense, sham, (veracity, truthfulness, frankness, sincerity)

dissent-*v* nonagreement, nonconsent, difference, variance, discordance, schism, disaffection, secession

dissertation-*n* treatise, theme, thesis, essay, discourse, investigation, commentary, lecture, sermon

dissimilarity-*n* unlikeness, divergence, variation, difference, novelty, originality, diversity, disparity, (similarity, resemblance, similitude, semblance)

dissolve-*v* end, destroy, abolish, disintegrate, vanish, evaporate, fade, liquefy, decompose, disappear, (visible, perceptible, perceivable, discernible)

dissonance-*n* controversy, incongruity, dissension, discordance, harshness, disagreement, discretion, (agreement, accord, unison, harmony)

dissuasion-*n* expostulation, diversion, remonstrance, deprecation, constraint, check, control

distance-*n* remoteness, span, space, interval, coldness, frigidity, reservation, aloofness, out skirts, (nearness, proximity, propinquity)

distasteful-*adj* unsavory, unpalatable, bitter, disagreeable, uninviting, unsatisfactory, painful, irritating, grievance, (pleasure, attraction, loveliness)

distinct-*adj* apart, explicit, separate, characterize, clear-cut, distinguishable, disconnected, disjoined, divide, sever, (attach, entangle, twine, cohere, incorporate)

distinguished-*adj* famous, celebrated, noted, illustrious, eminent, superior, supreme, majority, (inferior, smaller, subordinative, deficient)

distortion-*n* deformation, contortion, twisting, perversion, irregular, misrepresentation, misunderstanding, exaggeration, (interpret, decipher, understand, explanatory)

distress-*n* sorrow, agony, affliction, anguish, grief, misery, misfortune, pain, concern, unhappiness, infelicity, (enjoyment, gratification, fruition, relish)

dregs-*n* settlings, lees, sediment, residue, trash, refuse, riffraff, common, low, beggarly, uncivilized, (aristocrat, noble, gentlemen, distinctive)

dress-*n* attire, clothe, drape, deck, berate, scold, adorn, embellish, garments, raiment, apparel, vesture, garb

drink-*v* sip, quaff, tipple, carouse, imbibe, absorb, toast, pledge, libation, potation, draft, gulp, swallow, (eject, emission, emit, evacuate)

drive-*v* impel, oblige, force, urge, steer, manage, control, ride, travel, thrust, aim, compel, enforce

driver-*n* coachman, whip, charioteer, teamster, chauffeur, director, manager, master, taskmaster

droop-*v* despond, decline, sink, wither, fade, hang, lean, drop, decay, retrograde, go down, downhill, (improve, meliorate, betterment, mend)

drop-*v* slide, sink, fall, discontinue, collapse, faint, discard, give up, drip, trickle, descent

dross-*n* rubbish, garbage, trash, waste, leavings, sediment, grounds, unimportant, insignificant, trivial, (important,

prominence, consideration, material)

drought-*n* parched, aridness, thirst, lack, dearth, scarcity, insufficient, inadequate, scantiness, famine, (sufficient, enough, adequate, fullness)

drown-*v* suffocate, drench, submerge, overpower, overwhelm, deaden, victimize, choke, stifle

drunkenness-*n* inebriety, intemperance, drinking, inebriation, insobriety, intoxication, libations, bacchanalia

dryness-*n* aridity, aridness, drought, parched, desiccation, dehydration, evaporation

duality-*n* twofold, double, biform, duplicity, polarity, two, deuce, couple, pair, twins

dubious-*adj* questionable, doubtful, suspicious, uncertain, hesitation, perplexity, embarrassment, dilemma, (certainty, gospel, reliable, infallible)

ductile-*adj* pliable, pliant, flexible, malleable, tactile, manageable, compliant, docile, tractable

duel-*n* affair of honor, single combat, fight, competition, rivalry, contest, opposition, satisfaction, (peace, harmony, tranquil, concord)

dullness-*n* stupidity,
slowness, stagnation,
dimness, sluggishness,
apathy, obscurity,
uninteresting, insipid,
unimaginative

dumb-*adj* voiceless,
silence, taciturnity, slow-
witted, stupid, inarticulate,
suppress, mute, (voice,
sound, utter, articulate)

dupe-*n* victim, sucker, easy
mark, fool, puppet,
deceive, trick, fool,
delusion, deception, false

duplication-*n* doubling,
iteration, renewal,
facsimile, copy, imitate,
mirror, reflect, reproduce,
repeat, (original,
unmatched, unique)

durability-*n* permanence,
continuance, persistence,
immutability, stability,
unchangeable, constant,
(erratic, vagrant,
alternating, mobile)

duty-*n* respect, deference,
homage, reverence,
obligation, service,
responsibility, task,
commission, charge, trust

dwarf-*n* midget, pygmy,
Lilliputian, little, urchin, elf,
puppet, shrimp, runt,
minute, (mammoth,
elephant, hippopotamus,
colossus)

dwelling-*n* domicile, abode,
house, residence,
habitation, housing, home,
berth, throne, tenement,
barn, mansion, villa,
hermitage

dwindle-*v* contract, lessen,
shrink, diminish, decline,
decrease, abate,
depreciate, deteriorate,
shorten, (increase,
enlarge, expand, augment,
raise)

dynamic-*adj* magnetic,
power, impelling, driving,
energetic, impulse,
forcible, active, strong

E

each-*adj* apiece, seriatim,
respectively, severally,
individual, special,
particular, separate,
(generally, generic,
universal)

eager-*adj* zealous, ardent,
earnest, fervent, intent,
willing, voluntary, inclined,
favorable, ready, forward,
(unwilling, renitency,
reluctance, indifference)

earliness-*n* promptitude,
punctuality, readiness,
quickness, haste, speed,
swiftness, alacrity,
prematureness, precocity,
anticipation, hastiness,
(lateness, tardiness, delay,
deferring)

earnest-*adj* fervent,
zealous, ardent, grave,
eager, solemn, weighty,
serious, determined

ease-*n* enjoyment,
readiness, contentment,
expertness, cheerfulness,
comfort, resignation,

satisfaction, (discontent, grief, disappointment, mortification)

easy-*adj* unconcerned, smooth, untroubled, unconstrained, gentle, facile, simple, tractable, manageable, compliant

eat-*v* devour, consume, fare, rust, corrode, erode, masticate, consume, nourishment, subsistence, provision, (excrete, discharge, secrete)

ebb-*v* waste, decay, decline, recede, withdraw, return, reflux, recoil, regress, fall, deteriorate, resilience, (progress, advance, proceed)

eccentric-*adj* irregular, peculiar, odd, deviating, erratic, unsettled, demented, possessed, maddened, moonstruck

ecclesiastical-*adj* religious, priestly, clerical, sacerdotal, scriptural, biblical, prophetic, apostolic, canonical

echo-*n* repercussion, repeat, reverberation, reproduce, resound, ring, reflex, hollow, sepulchral, chime, (dead sound, dampen, muffled, thud)

economy-*n* frugality, thriftiness, savings, prevention of waste, parsimony, retrenchment, careful, saving, sparing, (liberality, generosity, munificent, freely,

bountifulness)

edible-*adj* digestible, eating, epulation, masticate, nourishment, sustenance, nurture, subsistence, feed, swallow, gulp, munch, nibble, culinary, nutritive, succulent, potable, bibulous, (discharge, excretion, exude, secrete, emanate, extrude)

edification-*n* performance, achievement, flower, fructify, evolution, development, growth, genesis, bring forth, (destruction, dissolution, consumption, run, breakdown, abolish, annihilation)

educate-*v* instruct, tutor, direction, guidance, preparation, discipline, practice, study, lecture, inoculation, impregnate, enlighten, inform, coach, disseminate, (bewilder, perversion, misinformation, deceive, mislead, unedifying)

effect-*n* consequence, result, outgrowth, development, derivative, (cause, origin, source, foundation, groundwork)

efficient-*adj* skillful, capable, clever, knowledgeable, adroit, masterful, accomplished, ingenuity, endowed, competent, (unskilled, blunder, inability, stupidity, failure, fumble, disqualify)

ego-*n* vanity, conceit, self-esteem, admiration, gaudery, assurance, complacency, praise, glorification, laudation, (modesty, timidity, humility, reserve, demureness, sheepish)

either-*adj* choice, option, alternative, selection, prefer, to set apart, preference, elect, discretion, decision, (neutrality, indifference, waive, abstain, refrain, indecision, neither)

elaborate-*adj* improve, betterment, melioration, amend, elevate, increase, promote, reform, revise, refine, cultivate, enhance, polish, refresh, bolster, revamp, (recede, retrograde, decrease, degrade, deter, impair, deteriorate, degenerate, decline)

elate-*v* cheerfulness, gaiety, geniality, good humor, glee, merriment, hilarity, laughter, rejoice, liveliness, jocularity, mirth, exhilaration, joviality, vivacity, (dejected, depressed, weariness, melancholy, sadness, dismal, despondent, solemnity, sorrowful)

elect-*v* choice, option, discretion, alternative, decision, poll, ballot, vote, selection, pick, choose, cull, separate, prefer,

excerpt, (neutral, indifference, waive, abstain, refrain, reject)

elementary-*adj* simple, homogeneity, sheer, neat, unsophisticated, basic, (combined, complicated, developed, complex)

elevation-*n* height, altitude, pitch, loftiness, stature, prominence, mount, tower, soar, surmount, lofty, rise, mountainous, upper, gigantic, picture, drawing, sketch, (lowness, depression, lowlands, underlie, crouch, slouch, grovel, at a low ebb)

eliminate-*v* deduction, retrenchment, removal, mutilation, amputation, curtailment, withdraw, diminish, abscind, prune, subtract, decrease, (addition, annexation, adjection, increase, supplement, inclusive, reinforce)

elude-*v* refraining, forbearance, avoidance, abstain, eschew, shun, keep away from, shirk, dodge, recede, evade, aloof, (pursuit, chase, hunt, follow, leap, seek, engage, quest, prosecute)

emanate-*v* egress, exit, emersiongence, evacuation, distillation, pouring, discharge, drain, emerge, move, pass, evacuate, escape, outlet, export, expatriation,

remigration, departure,
(ingress, entrance,
introgression, influx,
intrusion, invasion, import,
infiltration)

embark-v departure, port-
of-embarcation, outset,
start, removal, adieu,
farewell, starting point, set
out, quit, vacate,
(admission, insertion,
immigration, insinuation,
penetrate)

embarrass-v difficulty,
dilemma, perplexity,
entanglement,
awkwardness, quagmire,
unwieldy, restriction,
hindrance, impediment,
restraint, (support, uplift,
advance, furtherance,
promotion, favor,
patronage, advocacy)

embellish-v ornament,
decoration, architecture,
lace, fringe, border,
edging, wreath festoon
garland, pattern, improve,
(disfigure, deformity,
delete, blemish, flaw, scar)

embitter-v aggravate,
render worse,
exasperation,
exacerbation,
overestimation,
exaggeration, acerbate,
heightening, (relief,
deliverance, refreshment,
easement, softening,
alleviation, mitigation,
soothing)

emblazon-v bright, vivid,
intense, deep, rich, gay,

gaudy, showy, flashy,
glaring, flaring,
inharmonious,
ostentatious, pomposity,
splendor, (pale, neutral,
monochrome, colorless,
hueless, faint, dull, muddy,
discolored, achromatic)

embolism-n interference,
intervention, dovetailing,
infiltration, parenthesis,
obtrusion, interpenetrate,
obtrusion, (surround,
beset, encompass,
environ, encircle, embrace,
circumvent)

embrace-v contain, hold,
embody, involve, implicate,
inclusion, admission,
comprehension, reception,
intimate, cordial, devoted,
sincere, affection,
(alienation, dislike,
animosity, hostility,
exclusion, rejection, exile,
separation, elimination,
repudiation)

embroil-v derange,
unsettle, disturb, confuse,
muddle, fumble,
perturbation inversion,
complicate, disorder,
involve, convulse,
disconsert, dissension,
division, rupture,
(harmony, agreement,
sympathy, unison, accord,
reunion, conciliation)

embryo-n beginning,
commencement, opening,
inception, initial, onset,
genesis, birth, start,
originate, conceive, initiate,

groundwork, foundation, pivot, hinge, (creation, harvest, result, end, termination, conclusion, finale, consummation, death, finality, finish, close, expiration)

emergency-n critical situation, crisis, pinch, quandary, full of incident, circumstance, adventure, contingency, phenomenon,eventuality, concern (ease, feasibility, flexibility, smooth, lighten, manageable, submissive, disburden)

emigrate-v migrate, traverse, wander, travel, journey, egress, exit, evacuation, emersion, export, emerge, emanate, evacuate, (ingress, entrance, entry, influx, incursion, invasion, import, infiltration, immigration, admission)

eminence-n high, eminent, exalted, lofty, tall, gigantic, Patagonian, towering, elevated, dignity, importance, primacy, elevation, dedication, glorification, enshrinement, consecration, (disrepute, discredit, tarnish, taint, defilement, degradation)

emit-v ejection, emission, effusion, rejection, extrusion, discharge, expulsion, eviction, excrete, secrete, shed, void, effuse, spend, pour

forth, (reception, admission admittance, importation, introduction, absorption, insertion)

emotion-n feeling, affection, suffering, endurance, tolerance, supportance, experience, response, sympathy, sensation, pathos, passion, eagerness, enthusiasm, excitation, (insensitivity, indifference, peacefulness, impassive)

empire-n property, realty, land, acres, ground, command, sway, rule dominion, sovereignty, government, jurisdiction, (laxity, toleration, anarchy, relaxation, deposition, abdicate, depose, dethrone)

employ-v occupation, function, capacity, place, post, vocation, calling, occupy, undertake, transact, task, engagement, profession, commission, subjection, dependence, subordination, bondage, servitude, (freedom, independence, play, free, franchise, liberal, dismissal)

empower-v permission, allow, liberty, indulge, authorize, admission, accordance, might, power, potency, ability, able, qualify, (impotence, disability, incapacity,

invalidity, incompetence,
helplessness, collapse,
exhaust, disqualification)
empty-*adj* void, clear,
vacate, depart, eject, exit,
evict, emission, expulsion,
extrusion, deport, exhaust,
spend, use, consume,
impoverish, drain,
disperse, squander,
(provide, supply, fill,
furnish, replenish, recruit,
provide, admit, ingest,
absorb, gulp)
emulate-*v* excellence,
goodness, merit, virtue,
worth, superiority,
perfection, prime, exude,
imitate, copy, simulation,
follow, model after,
assimilation, (originality,
unparalleled, mistreat,
injurious, detrimental,
mischievous, nocuous)
enact-*v* perform,
movement, evolution,
perpetration, execution,
deed, proceeding,
participate, put-in-motion,
achieve, rule, regulation,
ordinance, statute,
(unlawfulness, inactivity,
idle, refrain, incomplete,
non-performance,
incomplete, neglect)
enamel-*n* polish, varnish,
gilding, embellish, lacquer,
paint, veneer, (blemish,
disfigure, deform, injure,
tarnish)
enchanting-*adj* elegant,
beauty, grace, polish,
radiance, splendor,

gorgeous, dazzling,
refined, idolatrous,
adoration, (repugnant,
shudder, irritating,
revolting, annoying,
provoking, obnoxious,
repulsive, offensive)
enclosure-*n* domain,
territory, district, zone,
compartment, place, spot,
document, envelope, den,
cell, dungeon, (liberate,
free, extricate, open,
spacious, boundless,
uncircumscribed)
encounter-*v* event,
occurrence, incident, affair,
phenomenon,
circumstance, accident,
adventure, crisis,
emergency, experience,
arrive, (depart, exodus,
await, future, impending,
destiny)
encourage-*v* induce,
persuade, lure, bribe,
prompt, inspire, beckon,
stimulate, tempt, seduce,
coax, tantalize, fascinate,
cajole, support, promote,
accommodate, help,
contribute, expedite,
bolster, uphold, (prevent,
obstruct, stop, interrupt,
impede, restrict, restrain,
block, inhibit, discourage,
hamper)
encroach-*v* trespass,
infringe, extravagate,
surpass, overstep, exceed,
invalidate, unlawful,
unauthorized, forfeited,
improper,

disfranchisement,
(sanction, warranty,
immunity, franchise,
vested-interest, deserve,
merit, substantiate)
encumber-v difficulty,
impracticability, tough,
dilemma, perplexity,
entanglement,
awkwardness, delicate,
vexed, impossible,
hindrance, restriction,
obstruction, stumbling-
block, (ease, flexibility,
feasible, smooth,
disencumber)
encyclopedia-n book,
volume, manual,
publication, knowledge,
possess knowledge,
learning, instructed,
educational, enlightened,
informed, bookish,
scholastic, profound,
(uninformed, uncultivated,
ignorant, simplistic,
unexplored)
end-n terminate, close,
finish, final, conclusion,
expire, result, discontinue,
(beginning, start, open,
commence, initial,
inaugurate, genesis)
endeavor-v pursuit,
enterprise, pursuance,
adventure, quest, exert,
labor, resolution, intention,
purpose, determined,
ambition, aim,
(indiscriminate,
promiscuous, incidental,
repose, without purpose)
endorse-v confirmation,

corroboration, support,
ratification, authentication,
admission, indication,
attest, document, refer,
substantiate, verify,
acknowledge, concur,
cooperate, agree, affirm,
consent, recognize, avow,
(dissent, discordance,
protest, contradict,
disagree, conflicting,
disavow, object)
endowment-n cleverness,
talent, ability, ingenuity,
capacity, forte, gift,
intelligence, capability,
expertness, dexterity,
adroitness, proficiency,
competence, excellence,
qualification, bestowal,
donation, investiture,
award, (grant, acceptance,
incompetence, inability,
disqualification, unfit,
inexperienced, awkward)
endure-v durable,
persistent, lasting,
continuing, permanence,
survive, longevity,
prolongation, protraction,
remain, continue, abide,
lingering, eternal,
everlasting, perpetual,
stable, established,
unchanged, subsist, (alter,
change, modify, deviate,
transformation, revolution,
short-lived, perishable,
impermanent)
energy-n power, might,
force, control, ascendancy,
authority, strength,
competency, pressure,

voltaism,
electromagnetism,
influence, enablement,
efficiency, endowment,
susceptibility, friction,
potential, intensity, vigor,
elasticity, (inertness,
dullness, inactivity,
languor, quiescence,
latency, passive, torpid,
sluggish, slow, tame,
lifeless, uninfluential,
incapacity, inefficacy)
enforce-v persuade, prevail,
enlist, engage, animate,
incite, provoke, instigate,
actuate, encourage,
dictate, press, compel,
force, compulsory,
constraint, necessitate,
oblige, stringent, duress,
coercion, (loss of right,
discourage, encroach,
breach, violate, forfeit,
unsanctioned)
engage-v motive, reason,
intention,inducement,
attraction, enticement,
allurement, fascination,
influence, bribe, lure,
campaign, crusade,
expedition, mobilization,
tactics, strategy, battle,
combative, militant,
appoint, commission,
assign, commit, authorize,
(annul, cancel, revoke,
dismiss, abolish, retract,
rescind, reverse, disclaim,
dissolve, null)
engrave-v memory,
remembrance, retention,
reminiscence, recognition,

keepsake, figure, emblem,
motto, put an indication,
label, imprint, Hallmark,
inscribe, (forgotten,
unremembered,
obliteration, mindless,
oblivious)
engulf-v dive, plunge,
submerge, sink,
importation, admission,
ingestion, absorption,
inhalation, suction,
interjection, import,
engorge, inhale, ingest,
(ejection, emission,
epulation, spew, disgorge,
dislodge, expectorate,
eviscerate, deport)
enigmatic-adj uncertain,
doubt, dubiety, hesitation,
perplexity, dilemma,
bewilderment, timid,
vacillation, vagueness,
obscurity, precarious,
casual, random,
hypothetical, paradoxical,
occasional, provisional,
(assurance, reliability,
infallible, unerring, positive,
dogmatic, explicit,
expressive, clear, lucid,
precise)
enjoy-v pleasure, sensual,
gratification, titillation,
comfort, luxury, relish,
revel, bask, cordial,
palatable, fruition,
satisfaction, delight,
refresh, happiness,
rapture, overjoyed,
captivated, ecstasies,
entranced, (suffer, pain,
ache, displeasure,

discomfort, weariness,
irritation, worry, infliction,
vexation, sorrow,
unhappiness)

enlarge-v increase,
augment, extend, develop,
grow, spread, gain,
intensify, enhance,
magnify, exaggerate, add,
expand, swell, inflate,
germinate, larger, amplify,
bulbous, (decrease,
subtract, reduce,
decrease, shrink, diminish,
contract, shrivel)

enlighten-v inform,
acquaint, knowledge,
communicate, announce,
instruct, outpour, report,
expound, explain, detect,
illuminate, reflect,
refraction, shine, glow,
glitter, twinkle, gleam,
glimmer, sparkle, radiate,
(darken, gloom, obscure,
shade, dim, eclipse,
extinguish, dingy, conceal,
disguise, ignore, suppress)

enough-adj sufficient,
adequate, full, abundance,
copious, profuse, galore,
outpouring, abound,
exuberate, inexhaustible,
ample, commensurate,
(insufficient, inadequate,
want, lack, require,
deplete, empty)

enrapture-v pleasurable,
delectability, amusing,
inviting, charm, fascinate,
enchanting, amiability,
seduction, amenity,
loveliness, goodness,

flatter, refresh, enliven,
attractive, alluring,
delightful, felicitous,
(annoying, grievance,
burden, bother, hurt,
displease, disturbing,
enraging, disgusting,
enrage)

entangle-v attach, affix,
bind, clinch, twine, encase,
gird, tether, fasten, secure,
twist, pinion, string, leash,
couple, intervolved,
embroil, unsettle, disturb,
complicate, ravel, dishevel,
tangle, wrangle, breach,
(discontinuity, separation,
dismemberment, sunder,
divide, abscind, rupture,
split, disentangle, unleash)

enterprise-n undertaking,
engagement, venture,
speculate, negotiate,
commerce, interchange,
quest, pursue, follow,
pursuit, course, (abstain,
refrain, escape, retreat,
reject, disengage, elude,
elusive, evasive)

entertain-v observance,
attention, application,
diligent, recognize,
mindful, regardful,
examine, scrutinize,
consider, social gathering,
joviality, hospitality,
welcome, festive,
fraternize, visit, consort,
reception, party,
(seclusion, exclusion,
privacy, reclusion,
isolation, desertion,
solitary)

enthusiasm-*n* emotion, sensation, cordiality, eagerness, zeal, excitation, lively, experience, warm, quick, feverish, flamboyant, fanatical, hysterical, impetuous, impressed, moved, touched, affected, penetrating, (distract, inactive, indifferent, preoccupation, disregard, disconcerted, inattentive)

entrance-*n* inlet, orifice, mouth, porch, portal, portico, door, gate, threshold, vestibule, origin, source, begin, commence, enter, debut, inaugurate, ingress, entry, influx, immigration, (egress, exit, evacuation, emerge. discharge, conclude)

entrap-*v* snare, trap, ambush, misinform, deceptive, cunning, deceitful, elusive, insidious, risk, danger, peril, insecurity, jeopardy, precariousness, instability, vulnerability, endanger, (safety, security, protect, invulnerable, defensible, tenable, secure)

entrust-*v* commission, delegate, assign, procure, errand, appoint, nominate, return, install, employ, empower, represent, bestow, give, present, consign, dispense, endow, award, gift, donation, grant, benefaction, (acquire, receive, accept, assign, beneficiary, admit, cancel, repeal, dismiss, abolish)

enunciate-*v* pronounce, accentuate, aspirate, deliver, vocal, phonetic, articulate, distinct, remark, emphatic, assert, affirm, report, express, state, communicate, present, (retract, repudiate, rebut, silence, mute, suppress, muffle, raucous, husky, dry)

envoy-*n* messenger, emissary, ambassador, marshal, crier, trumpeter, courier, representative, functionary, diplomat, delegate, commissioner

equal-*adj* sameness, symmetry, balance, evenness, monotony, level, equivalent, match, capability, capacity, quality, attribute, endowment, virtue, gift, qualification, susceptibility, (helplessness, inability, incompetence, inept, unevenness, inequality, partial)

eradicate-*v* extract, remove, eliminate, extricate, exterminate, eject, eviscerate(insert, implant, inject, import, introduce, infuse)

erect-*v* form, fabricate, produce, create, construct, manufacture, build, organize, establish,

achieve, complete,
perform, forge, carve,
chisel, constitute, institute,
accomplish, evolve,
(destroy, destruct,
dissolve, break, disrupt,
ruin, smash, annihilate,
demolish)

erratic-*adj* inconstant,
versatile, changeable,
unstable, vacillate,
fluctuate, vicissitude, alter,
shifting, unstable, vary,
fickle, restless, spasmodic,
divert, deviate, wandering,
(stable, unchangeable,
constant, immobile, sound,
stiff, solid, established,
permanent, firm, settled)

eruption-*n* violent,
vehement, impetuous,
boisterous, effervescent,
turbulent, severe,
ferocious, raging,
exacerbate, malign,
forceful, spastic, explode,
volcanic, rampage, riotous,
(moderate, temperate,
relaxed, gentle, sober,
quiet, calm, tranquil,
pacify, sedative, balmy,
smooth)

escape-*v* release,
disengage, liberate,
discharge, emancipate,
dismiss, deliverance,
absolve, extricate, acquit,
free, dismantle, untie,
violate, transgress,
derelict, neglect, evade,
(responsible, accountable,
conscientious, restrain,
hinder, coerce, repress,

custody, arrest,
incarcerate, unrestricted)

essential-*adj* inherent,
important, intrinsic,
quintessence, incarnate,
backbone, principle, main,
major, chief, consummate,
prominent, necessary,
required, indispensable,
urgent, exact,
(insignificant, meaningless,
immaterial, minuscule,
diminutive, minor,
infinitesimal, paltry)

establish-*v* found, settle,
permanent, vested,
produce, create, construct,
form, fabricate,
manufacture, produce,
institute, evolve, develop,
generate, genesis,
contrive, build, accomplish,
(ruin, smash, crash,
destroy, abolish, suppress,
overthrow, demolish,
ravage, devastate, wreck,
consume)

esteem-*v* credit, assurance,
faith, trust, confidence,
presumption, dependence
on, reliance, conviction,
implicit, unshaken, dogma,
credence, credulous,
confident, assured,
sanctioned, advocacy,
approved, (dislike,
denunciation,
condemnation,
scandalous, discredit,
suspicious, doubtful,
skeptical)

et cetera-*adj* add, annex,
increase, increment,

supplement, affix, append,
furthermore, along with,
insert, and-so-forth,
access, include, upward,
(none, naught, deduction,
removal, abstraction,
curtailment, decrease.
abscind, decimate)

eternity-n perpetuity, ever,
immortality, everlasting,
perpetuation, forever,
endless, eternal,
ceaseless, evergreen,
imperishable, always,
lasting, continual, lingering,
permanent, (temporary,
perishable, briefly,
transient, sudden, quick,
short)

ether-n buoyancy, lightness,
volatility, levity, gossamer,
float, airy, weightless,
sublimated, inflation,
sponginess, absence of
solid, thin, tenuous, hollow,
(density, solid, compact,
thick, weight, gravity,
heaviness, pressure)

etiquette-n rule, standing
order, precedent, routine,
mode, vogue, conformity,
practice, custom, habit,
manners, breeding,
demeanor, gentility,
decorum, propriety,
carriage, (vulgar, bad
taste, awkward, tactless,
ill-bred, coarseness, rough,
slovenly, ungenteel,
gaudy, horrid, obtrusive)

evade-v conceal, secrecy,
hide, stealth, mask,
disguise, ensconce, muffle,
whisper, suppress, veil,
evasive, deceive, forge,
distort, avoid, escape,
retreat, reject, shun,
(pursue, chase,
scrupulous, frank, open,
candid, straightforward,
outspoken, undisguised)

event-n occurrence,
incident, affair, transaction,
proceeding, phenomenon,
circumstance, adventure,
consequence, happening,
encounter, undergo,
contest, competition,
engagement, tussle,
conflict, (uneventful, idle,
without incident)

evergreen-adj continuous,
progressive, successive,
unbroken, uninterrupted,
perennial, constant, entire,
linear, lasting, persistent,
perpetual, (temporary,
transient, fleeting, short-
lived, impermanent,
spasmodic, unsuccessful)

evil-adj harm, hurt, mischief,
nuisance, ill, tragedy,
badness, bane, outrage,
wrong, injure, grievance,
oppress, persecute, abuse,
overburden, victimize,
molest, (goodness,
excellence, merit, virtue,
value, worth, beneficial,
right, commendable)

evoke-v request, motion,
apply, canvass, address,
appeal, solicit, invite,
petition, beseech, plead,
implore, invoke, urge,
beset, ask, beg, crave,

pray, (protest, effect,
consequence, ignore)
evolution-n pullulate, bring
forth, create, beget, get,
generate, hatch, develop,
produce, form, make, ,
progress, journey, flow,
move, mobilize, (rest, still,
immobile, hold, halt,
remain, stop, stagnate)
exacerbate-v exalt,
strengthen, intensify,
enhance, magnify,
aggravate, exaggerate,
increase, growth, advance,
ascend, sprout,
exasperation, impetuosity,
effervescence, turbulence,
confusion, hysterical,
(moderate, relax,
remission, mitigation,
tranquil, pacify, soften,
decrease, moderate)
exact-adj similar,
semblance, parallelism,
likeness, match, accurate,
precise, gospel, authentic,
true, accurate, actual,
definite, right, correct,
punctual, constant,
unerring, (erroneous,
untrue, false, wrong,
unsubstantial, inaccurate,
different, incorrect)
exalt-v raise, intensify,
enhance, magnify,
exaggerate, increase,
enlarge, develop, spread,
lift, sublimate, erect,
elevate, heighten,
(depress, lower, reduce,
over-throw, decrease,
diminish, lessen, weaken,

depreciate)
examine-v scan, scrutinize,
inspect, review, glance,
consider, account,
indicate, observe, inquire,
request, investigate, seek,
search, explore, ransack,
rummage, (answer,
respond, retort,
acknowledge, escape,
unobservant, thoughtless,
careless, inattentive)
example-n prototype,
original, model, pattern,
precedent, standard, type,
copy, conform, instance,
sample, illustration,
specimen, rule,
agreement, observance,
exemplification, (original
duplicate, imitation,
irregularity, eccentricity,
abnormal, oddity, curiosity,
hybrid, unconventional,
infraction)
exception-n abnormal,
irregular, peculiar, unusual,
unexpected,
unconventional,
remarkable, queer,
exceptional, informal,
unaccustomed, exclusive,
(typical, normal, formal,
orthodox, sound, rigid,
positive, ordinary,
common, conventional)
excite-v energy, intensify,
vigor, strength, pressure,
poignancy, severity,
agitation, effervescence,
stir, stimulate, kindle,
exert, inflame, (inert, dull,
inactivity, languor, passive,

slow, lifeless, dormant)
exclusive-adj special,
particular, specify,
characteristic,
individualize, custom,
unusual, rare, singular,
curious, odd,
extraordinary, strange,
remarkable, noteworthy,
eccentric, peculiar,
abnormal, (conventional,
ordinary, conformity,
symmetry, conventional,
regular, usual)
excuse-v forgive, pardon,
condonation, remission,
absolution, amnesty,
reprieve, exoneration,
release, indemnity, forget,
acquit, vindicate, apology,
justify, warrant, advocate,
defend, contend, (accuse,
charge, impute, reproach,
denounce, inexcusable,
vicious)
exercise-n task, curriculum,
study, lesson, lecture,
sermon, apologue,
parable, action,
performance, perpetration,
movement, operation,
work, labor, execution,
procedure, deed, act,
proceeding, enact,
(passiveness, nothing,
inactivity, unintelligent,
misinformation)
exert-v hold, grasp, grip,
reach, command, use,
employ, exercise,
application, consume,
resort, wield, handle,
manipulate, avail,

(abstinence, relinquish,
discard, dismiss, waive,
neglect)
exhaust-v disarm,
incapacitate, disqualify,
unfit, invalidate, deaden,
cramp, muzzle, paralyze,
fatigue, weariness,
collapse, prostration,
(refresh, restoration,
revival, repair, refection,
recover, electricity, power,
energy, magnetism)
exile-n remove, eject,
unload, displaced,
homeless, seclusion,
privacy, reclusion, recess,
solitude, isolation,
loneliness, estrangement,
exclude, repel, expatriate,
outlaw, ostracize,
(companion, community,
welcome, reception,
gather, visiting, social,
conviviality, fellowship)
exit-n depart, embarkation,
removal, exodus,
valediction, adieu, farewell,
flight, egress, evacuation,
emerge, emanate, export,
(ingress, entrance, influx,
import, invasion,
admission, insertion)
exonerate-v disencumber,
disengage, disentangle,
extricate, unravel, untie,
unload, emancipate,
manage, accomplish,
absolve, dispense,
release, (prohibit, exclude,
embargo, forbid,
restrictive, difficult, hard,
tough, dilemma)

expand-v increase,
enlarge, extend, dilate,
develop, augment, gain,
ascend, exalt, intensify,
enhance, magnify, add,
develop, spread,
increment, (contraction,
consume, lessen, shrink,
collapse, emaciate,
atrophy, lose, reduce,
decrease, limit)

expedient-adj desirable,
suit, fitness, agreeable,
propriety, opportunism,
befit, conform, acceptable,
convenient, worthwhile,
applicable, useful,
(impropriety, unfit,
undesirable, objectionable,
unsatisfactory, improper)

expel-v ejaculate, eject,
discharge, push, fling,
throw, toss, projectile,
propel, project, send,
shoot, launch, deport, emit,
reject, banish, extradite,
exit, drain, evacuate,
(reception, admission,
admit, entrance, ingest,
absorb, receive, inhale)

F

fable-n fallacy,
misconception, error,
laxity, mistake, blunder,
misprint, delusion,
hallucination, deception,
mislead, deceive,
erroneous, untrue,
fallacious, unreal,
unauthenticated, (real,
actual, veritable, true,
exact, accurate, definite,
precise, defined)

fabulous-adj great,
abundant, intense, strong,
immense, enormous, vast,
extreme, excessive,
extravagant, exorbitant,
outrageous, preposterous,
unconscionable,
monstrous, stupendous,
astonishing, incredible,
marvelous, (small, little,
diminutive, minute, paltry,
faint, slender, light, slight,
scanty, meager, sparing,
few, moderate)

face-n exterior, surface,
outside, skin, superficial,
frontal, confront,
encounter, clash, contend,
confront, brave, dare,
summon, meet, stand-up,
valiant, resolute, stout,
determined, (cowardly,
shy, timed, soft, spiritless,
skittish, fearful, cower,
skulk, flinch, interior, inner,
within)

factor-n number, symbol,
figure, cipher, formula,
function, sum, multiplicand,
multiple, dividend, prime,
director, manager,
moderator, taskmaster,
delegate, consignee,
envoy, merchant, trader,
complimentary, positive,
negative, formula

fade-v vacant, empty,
blank, hollow, vanish,
evaporate, dissolve,
disappear, without,
dreamy, shadowy,

ethereal, immaterial,
nominal, nothing, luminary,
(substantial, exist, full,
tangible, essential,
material, reappear)
fail-v feeble, impotent,
relaxed, powerless, weak,
soft, fragile, flimsy,
unsubstantial, rickety,
cranky, drooping, lame,
withered, shattered,
decrepit, languid, spent,
decayed, worn, (strong
mighty, vigorous, forcible,
hard, adamantine, stout,
robust)
faint-adj small, atom,
particle, molecule, granule,
minimum, diminutive,
minute, paltry, slight,
scanty, meager, sparing,
weak, feeble, debilitate,
frail, fragile, languid,
decayed, rotten, wasted,
(strong, mighty, stamina,
muscle, virile, vigor, great,
immense, enormous,
abundant, considerable)
fair-adj colorless,
monochrome, pale, blanch,
hueless, pallid, dull,
muddy, sallow, dingy,
ghastly, lusterless,
moderate, ordinary,
average, indifferent,
(unparalleled, ripen,
mature, shiny, dark, tone)
faith-n belief, credence,
credit, assurance, trust,
confidence, certainty,
conviction, hopeful,
optimism, aspire,
expectation, confidence,

reliance, (hopelessness,
despair, despondency,
pessimism, forlorn, doubt,
misbelief, infidelity,
dissent)
fallacy-n false, illogical,
unsound, invalid,
deceptive, evasive,
irrelevant, vague,
unwarranted,
inconsequential,
inconsistent, fallacious,
(logical, correct,
reasonable, rational,
controversial, debatable,
relevant)
false-adj error, fallacy,
misconception, mistake,
fault, blunder, delusive,
deceptive, heresy, untrue,
incorrect, lie, guile, perjury,
forgery, invention,
fabrication, distortion,
evade, sham, (truthful,
scrupulous, sincere, frank,
honest, sober, exact, real,
authentic, precise, actual,
certain)
falter-v slow, slack, tardy,
leisurely, deliberate,
gradual, languid,
moderate, slouch, shuffle,
totter, stagger, mince,
lumber, linger, loiter,
saunter, plod, trudge,
dawdle, (gallop, canter,
trot, hasten, run, race,
whisk, fast, hurry, fly,
eloquent)
familiar-adj aware,
cognizant, acquaint,
inform, versed, instructed,
learned, lettered,

educated, enlighten,
bookish, accomplished,
profound, recognized,
occurrence, habitual,
usual, ordinary, (unusual,
unconformable, ignorant,
uninformed, shallow,
empty, illiterate)
family-_n_ kin, relation,
fraternity, paternal,
maternal, ancestral, linear,
patriarchal, party, alliance,
linked, banded, united
fancy-_n_ prefer, persuade,
option, select, pick, whim,
humor, drollery,
pleasantry, brilliant, desire,
wish, solicitous, overjoyed,
entranced, enchanted,
ravished, fascinated,
captivated, (afflicted,
worried, displeased,
aching, griped, grieve,
lament)
fantasy-_n_ desire, wish,
fancy, want, need,
inclination, propensity,
liking, fain, anxious,
curious, craving, thirst,
(indifference, neutrality,
coldness, unconcern,
apathy, disdain)
far-_adv_ distance, space,
remote, elongation,
remove, span, away,
inaccessible, out-of-reach,
unapproachable, asunder,
unconnected, (close, tight,
taut, firm, inseparable,
near, proximity, vicinity,
confines, alongside)
farce-_n_ absurd, imbecility,
nonsense, paradox,

inconsistency, blunder,
muddle, preposterous,
senseless, inconsistent,
ridiculous, foolish, witty,
quick, nimble-witted,
jocular, waggish,
whimsical, playful,
pleasant, sparkling, (dull,
dry, commonplace,
pointless, flat, stale)
farewell-_n_ depart, goodbye,
outward, exit, embark,
decampment, forfeiture,
loss, bereavement,
deprivation, lose, bereft,
(recover, regain, retrieve,
inherit, arrival, advent,
land, welcome)
fascinate-_v_ influence,
prompting, dictate,
impulse, instigate,
encouragement, incentive,
incendiary, provoke,
arouse, stimulate, induce,
move, persuade, prevail,
wonder, astonish, amaze,
awe, (expect, common,
ordinary, dissuasion,
disincline, averse,
discourage)
fast-_adj_ firm, close, tight,
taut, secure, set,
intervolved, inseparable,
indissoluble, fickle, erratic,
afloat, alternating, speed,
hasten, scamper, run,
swift, nimble, agile,
expeditious, galloping,
quick, (gradual, slow,
leisurely, tardy, gentle,
easy, deliberate, relax,
stagger, plod, trudge,vary,
vacillate)

field-*n* spacious, roomy,
expansive, capacious,
ample, wide, vast,
uncircumscribed,
boundless, arena, zone,
meridian, territorial,
parochial, provincial,
patch, plot, region, realm,
domain, tract, court,
(niche, nook,
compartment, precinct)

fiery-*adj* violent, vehement,
warm, acute, sharp, rough,
rude, ungentle, bluff,
boisterous, wild, brusque,
abrupt, impetuous,
rampant, turbulent,
disorderly blustery, raging,
uproarious, frenzied,
(moderate, lenient, gentle,
mild, cool, sober,
temperate, reasonable,
measured, calm, quiet,
tranquil, still, slow)

fight-*v* contention, strife,
contest, struggle,
belligerency, controversy,
war, litigation, sparring,
competition, rivalry,
opposition, combative,
contending, embattled,
militant, (tranquil, pacific,
peaceable, untroubled,
harmony, quiet, neutrality,
conciliatory, composing,
amnesty, arrangement)

file-*v* arrange, distribute,
sort, prepare, dispose,
organize, analyze, classify,
digest, divide, catalog,
tabulate, index,
systematize, methodize,

regulate, register,
consecutive, continuous,
progressive, successive,
linear, (broken, interrupted,
unconnected, gap, litter,
scatter, disarrange,
disorganize)

fill-*v* complete, entire,
replenish, totally,
brimming, plenary, occupy,
inhabit, moored, domiciled,
populous, attend, dwell,
reside, lodge, nestle, roost,
permeate, (absent, away,
gone, missing, lost,
omitted, nonexistent,
empty, void, vacant,
devoid)

final-*adj* end, close,
terminate, dissonance,
conclude, finale, period,
term, consummation,
finish, expire, last,
complete, accomplished,
culmination, result,
exhaust, (beginning,
commencement, opening,
outset, inception
introduction, inauguration,
embarkation, initial, first,
incipient, leading)

find-*v* discover, detect, hunt,
determine, evolve,
decision, deduction, gain,
acquire, obtain, purchase,
remunerative, lucrative,
(lose, mislay, forfeit,
deprived)

fine-*adj* thin, narrow,
slender, close, taper, slim,
scant, spare, delicate,
incapacious, contracted,

lean, emaciated, meager,
gaunt, lanky, weedy,
flimsy, slight, (thick, broad,
dense, widen, ample,
extend, spread)

finesse-n clever, talent,
ability, ingenuity, capacity,
endowed, skillful,
dexterous, adroit, expert,
apt, handy, quick, deft,
ready, gain, smart, ready,
proficient, masterful,
thorough, accomplished,
able, ingenious, (bungling,
awkward, clumsy,
unskillful, slovenly, gawky,
inept, incompetent, stupid,
unfit)

fire-n heat, warmth, hot,
torrid, smoking, burning,
alight, afire, ablaze,
unquenched, smoldering,
flow, sweat, sultry, hellish,
inferno, (heavenly,
celestial, cold, cool, frigid,
fresh, keen, bleak,
shivering, bitter, chill,
inclement, biting, icy,
glacial, frosty, freezing)

first-adj initial, beginning,
commence, opening,
outset, inception,
introduction, inaugurate,
manifest, apparent,
entrance, inlet, dawn,
genesis, birth, origin, start,
front, (end, last,
consummation, finish,
terminate, conclude,
expire, definitive)

fish-n chase, hunt, sport,
pursuit, prosecution, quest,
scramble, inquire,

investigate, unearth, ferret
out, seek, search, track,
trail, feel out, (answer,
respond, reply,
acknowledge, discover,
explain, refrain, spare,
abstain, unsought, avoid,
neutral, evasive)

fit-v conform, consistent,
adapt, adjust, graduate,
assimilate, match, suit,
harmony, unison,
appropriate, deft, apply,
meet, dovetail, (unfit,
unsuited, inconsistent,
mismatch, intrusive,
uneven)

fix-v join, unite, attach,
affix, fasten, bind, secure,
clinch, twist, tie, string,
strap, sew, lace, stitch,
tack, knit, button, buckle,
hitch, lash, truss, bandage,
braid, (sunder, divide,
disjoin, sever, abscind, cut,
saw, snip, nip, cleave,
split, chip, crack, carve)

flagrant-adj immoral,
impropriety, scandal,
looseness, demoralization,
corruption, atrocity,
infirmity, weakness, frailty,
(virtuous, merit, worth,
excellence, credit, self-
control, self, denial,
fulfillment)

flat-adj inert, dull, torpor,
languor, quiescence,
inaction, sloth, obstinacy,
passive, sluggish, slack,
tame, slow, blunt, lifeless,
uninfluential, latent,
dormant, low, neap,

debase, nether, crouched,
subjacent, squat, prostrate,
(high, elevated, eminent,
exalted, lofty, tall, gigantic,
towering, soaring)
flatter-v cunning, crafty,
artful, skillful, subtle, feline,
profound, designing,
contriving, intriguing,
strategic, diplomatic,
artificial, sly, insidious,
stealthy, charming,
fascinating, enchanting,
humor, amuse, gratify,
(hurtful, bitter, displease,
annoy, trouble, disturb,
cross, perplex, molest,
tease, tire, irk, bother,
pester, harass, harry,
badger, beset, persecute,
heckle)
flaw-n discontinue, pause,
interrupt, intervene, break,
interpose, disconnect,
separation, gap, opening,
hole, chasm, crack, slit,
fissure, rift, breach, gash,
cut, leak, dike, fault,
erroneous, untrue,
unsound, illogical,
inaccurate, incorrect,
(exact, accurate, definite,
precise, well defined, just,
right, correct, strict, close,
liberal, rigid)
fleece-v tegument, skin,
pellicle, fell, fur, leather,
hide, pelt, cover, theft,
steal, thievery, robbery,
depredation, plunder,
pillage, black-mail,
burglary, buccaneer, strip,
abduct, confiscate,

sequester
fling-v propel, project,
throw, cast, pitch, chuck,
toss, jerk, heave, hurl, flirt,
fillip, dart, lance, tilt, sling,
send, discharge, shoot,
bolt, (draw, pull, haul, lug,
drag, tug, tow, trail,
wrench, jerk, tactile)
float-v navigate, sail,
nautical, naval, coasting,
afloat, transport, tender,
whaler, slaver, coaster,
yacht, launch, buoyant,
ascend, rise, (descent,
drop, fall, gravitate, sink,
droop, settle, decline,
dismount)
flock-n crowd, horde, body,
tribe, crew, gang, band,
party, company, troop,
army, regiment, assemble,
dense, muster, together,
collect, convene,
congregate, accumulate,
(disperse, adrift, stray,
disheveled, dissemination,
dissipation, scatter,
disband, disembody,
dispel)
floor-n ground, base,
foundation, substructure,
pavement, deck, footing,
basis, bottom, nadir, foot,
fundamental, horizontal,
level, even, plan, flat,
smooth, succeed, flushed,
victorious, unbeaten,
(unsuccessful, highest,
top, crest, apex, zenith,
upper most)
flounder-v inconstancy,
versatile, unstable,

vacillate, changing, ever changing, fluctuating, restless, agitating, variable, erratic, fickle, irresolute, capricious, spasmodic, (fixed, steadfast, firm, steady, balanced, valid, immovable, riveted, tethered, anchored, moored, established)

flourish-v prosperity, welfare, well-being, affluence, success, wealth, thriving, fortunate, lucky, flushed, felicitous, effective, flower, (abortive, addle, fruitless, bootless, inefficient, inefficacious, lame, insufficient, unavailing, useless, swamp)

flow-v elapse, lapse, run, proceed, advance, pass, roll, slide, glide, progress, loose, dependent, stream, flux, run, course, move, shifting, restless, nomadic, (still, fixed, stationary, sedentary, quiet, calm, anchor, still, restful)

flower-n produce, create, construct, form, fabricate, manufacture, build, erect, edify, organize, establish, achieve, evolve, develop, grow, genesis, bear, generate, impregnate, (destroy, destruct, waste, dissolve, consume, ruin, crash, smash, extinction, subversive, suicidal, squash, squelch)

fluctuate-v change, inconstancy, versatility, mobility, instability, vacillate, alter, restlessness, fidget, disquiet, agitate, variable, waver, shift, shuffle, flitter, totter, tremble, oscillate, alternate, (tethered, fixed, steadfast, firm, balanced, permanent, constant, unchanged, undeviating, durable, perennial)

flush-v flat, plane, flounder, jet, spurt, squirt, spout, splash, rush, gush, deluge, inundation, stream, flux. flow, brook, torrent, (gust, blast, breeze, squall, gale, storm, tempest)

fly-v flit, elapse, lapse, flow, run, proceed, advance, slide, glide, pass, transient, fleeting, shifting, spasmodic, wild, abrupt, impetuous, turbulent, disorderly, (moderate, gentle, lenient, still, slow, smooth, tame, peaceful, standing, perpetual)

fold-v halve, divide, split, cleave, bisect, enclose, envelope, (circumvent, skirt, twine)

follow-v succeed, next, ensue, conform, observe, obey, comply, supervene, consecutive, continue, sequel, behind, attend, pursue, beset, tread, example, (precede, forerun, lead, advance, prior, former, foregoing,

before, advance, start,
preliminary)
fool-n deceive, false, fraud,
guile, delusion, circumvent,
overreach, maneuver,
cunning, deceptive,
counterfeit, pseudo,
pretend, feign, tricky,
adulterate, rotten, disguise,
simulate, disrespect,
aweless, irreverent,
disparaging, insulting,
rude, derisive, sarcastic,
(respect, regard,
consideration courtesy,
reverence, honor, esteem
estimation, veneration,
admiration, approbation)
foot-n bottom, nadir, sole,
toe, hoof, fundamental,
founded, based, ground,
broad, support,
foundation, base, basis,
bearing, hold, landing, aid,
prop, stand, shore, truss,
beam, rafter, (suspend,
hang, pendulum, swing,
dangle, swag, flap, loose,
flowing)
forbear-v refrain, abstain,
inaction, neutrality,
avoidance, evasion,
elusion, seclusion, flight,
escape, recoil, reject,
unsought, shun, spare,
shirk, dodge, parry,
fugitive, (pursuit, pursue,
enterprise, adventure,
scramble, chase, hunt,
prosecute)
forbid-v prohibit, disallow,
bar, forefend, withhold,
limit, circumscribe, restrict,

taboo, interdict, exclude,
dissent, negative,
unconsenting, unavowed,
discontented, (assent,
admission, agreement,
affirm, recognition,
acknowledge, permit,
indulgent, allow)
force-v power, potency,
might, energy, ascend,
control, authority, ability,
ableness, competency,
efficiency, enablement,
influence, capability,
almighty, adequate,
efficacious, valid, able,
(powerless, impotent,
unable, incapable,
incompetent, harmless,
weaponless, null, void,
nugatory, ineffectual,
failing, inadequate)
forecast-v foresight,
deliberation, prevision,
longsightedness,
anticipation, providence,
surmise, foregone
conclusion, prudence,
foreknowledge,
precognition, prediction,
announcement,
premonition, warning,
prognosis, prophecy,
horoscope, preparation,
rehearsal, provision,
arrange, array,
(unnurtured, uneducated,
premature, undigested,
improvidence)
forefathers-n paternal,
parental, maternal, family,
ancestral, linear,
patriarchal, descendant,

heir, generation, (succeed,
ensue, alternate, after,
latter, follow)
foreign-*adj* irrelative,
irrespective, unrelated,
arbitrary, independence,
adrift, isolated, insular,
extraneous, strange, alien,
outlandish, exotic, intrude,
emigrant, outsider,
inadmissible, (implicate,
integral, member, merge,
constitute, relative,
cognate, referable, akin,
family, allied, affiliated,
fraternal)
foremost-*adj* superior,
supreme, greater,
advantage,
preponderance,
advantageous, prevalence,
nobility, preeminence,
culmination,
transcendence, excess,
major, higher, exceeding,
distinguished, vaulting,
important, (inferior,
minority, smaller, minor,
less, deficient,
subordinate, secondary,
least, under, lower,
diminish)
forestall-*v* subsequently,
afterwards, later,
thereafter, thereupon,
since, beforehand,
anticipate, prior, previous,
precede, posthumous,
premature, before long,
unexpected, postpone,
(adjournment, succeed,
supervene, posterior,
following, after, later,

postliminium, postdate)
forfeit-*v* fail, evasion,
unobservance, omission,
neglect, informality,
infringement, infraction,
violation, transgression,
break, retraction,
repudiation, nullification,
protest, lapse, deprivation,
loss, (fulfillment,
satisfaction, faithful, profit,
earnings, proceeds,
acquire, advantageous,
gainful, remunerative,
paying, lucrative)
forlorn-*adj* dejected,
depression, prostration,
lowness, oppression,
heaviness, gloom,
weariness, melancholy,
sadness, dismal,
despondent, blank,
discourage, dispirit, frown,
spiritless, grieve, affliction,
(cheerful, happy, smiling,
blithe, bright, airy, jaunty,
sprightly, vivacious,
sparking, winsome, frisky,
playful, jocular)
form-*n* copy, facsimile,
counterpart, effigy,
likeness, similitude,
semblance, cast, imitation,
model, representation,
orderly, regular, correct,
methodical, uniform,
symmetrical, unconfused,
arranged, systematic,
(disorderly, promiscuous,
indiscriminate, chaotic,
complex, intricate,
complicated, perplexed,
knotted, tangled,

dislocated)
formula-_n_ rule, routine,
uniformity, constancy,
standard, model,
precedent, conformity,
principle, steady, legal
process, law, code,
statute, canon, ordinance,
decree, numeral, divisible,
prime, fractional, (irregular,
diversified, indiscriminate,
desultory, difference,
illegal, prohibited, unlawful,
illicit, uncharted,
unauthorized, unofficial)
fortuitous-_adj_ casual,
accidental, adventitious,
causeless, incidental,
contingent, undetermined,
possible, unintentional,
haphazardly, random,
speculation, venture,
chance, undesigned,
unpremeditated,
indiscriminate,
promiscuous, undirected,
without purpose, (intended,
advised, determined,
prepense, undertaking,
design, ambition)
fortune-_n_ chance,
indetermination, accident,
hazard, haphazard,
random, fate, lottery,
casually, happen, destiny,
foredoom, predestined,
fatalism, wealthy, rich,
affluent, opulent, moneyed,
capital, afford, (poor,
indigent, poverty, needy,
necessary, distressed,
bereft, bereaved, reduced)
forward-_adj_ early, prime,

timely, punctual, prompt,
summary, discourteous,
disrespect, impudent, ill-
breed, vulgar, unpolished,
rude, saucy, harsh,
austere, sarcastic, biting,
caustic, snarling,
surly, (courteous, polite,
civil, mannerly, urbane,
well-behaved, polished,
cultivated, refined, gallant,
late, tardy, slow, behind,
behind, backward)
foundation-_n_ stability,
constancy, immobile,
sound, vital, stable,
established, fixture, tower,
pillar, fixed, durable,
tethered, anchored,
moored, (unstable,
fluctuation, movable,
vicissitude, shake, totter,
flitter, flutter, flounder,
mobile, transient)
fracas-_n_ disorder,
derangement, irregular,
anomaly, confusion,
disarray, muddle,
hodgepodge, chaos,
medley, scramble,
embroilment, whirlwind,
unsymmetrical, untidy,
(order, uniformity,
symmetry, series, routine,
method, disposition,
arrangement, discipline)
fracture-_n_ separation,
parting, detachment,
segregation, divorce,
supposition, divide,
sunder, sever, cut, saw,
carve, dissect, mangle,
gash, hash, slice, whittle,

disperse, apportion,
(attach, fix, join, unite,
embody, affix, fasten, bind,
secure, tie, pinion, string,
strap, link, marry)
frail-_adj_ weak, relax,
languor, impotence,
infirmity, fragile,
declination, loss, dull,
spent, weatherbeaten,
decayed, rotten worn,
seedy, wasted,
defenseless, feeble,
debilitate, unnerved,
powerless, flaccid,
nervous, soft, womanly,
unsubstantial, (strong,
mighty, vigorous, forcible,
hard, adamantine, stout,
robust, sturdy, hardy,
powerful, potent, valid,
resistless, impregnable,
sovereign, athletic)
frame-_v_ support, aid, prop,
stand, anvil, shore, skid,
rib, truss, bandage, stirrup,
stilt, scaffold, skeleton,
beam, rafter, backbone,
set, fit, mold, tone, tenor,
turn, trim, guise, fashion,
light, style, character,
structural, organic, model,
formal, (dangle, swag, flap,
trail, flow, suspend, hand,
sling, append, pensive,
depend, swing, loose,
flowing)
free-_adj_ sunder, divide,
sever, abscind, splinter,
chip crack, divorce, part,
detach, separate, cutoff,
adrift, loose, disentangle,
isolate, liberate, apart,

rupture, breach, split,
divulge, section, rift,
incision, fission, (attach,
fix, affix, fasten, pinion,
string, gird, tether, moor,
harness, chain, fetter, join,
twine, twist, incorporate,
close, secure, leash,
couple, nail, bolt)
frequent-_adj_ repeat, again,
often, anew, over again,
once more, ditto, many,
iterate, harping,
recurrence, succession,
monotony, rhythm, imitate,
incessant, perpetual,
continual, constant,
habitual, commonly,
(seldom, rarely, scarcely,
hardly, infrequently, few,
never, inconstant)
fresh-_adj_ new, novelty,
recent, immaturity, youth,
innovation, renovation,
modern, mushroom,
renew, green, evergreen,
raw, virgin, neoteric,
newborn, (old, antiquity,
maturity, decline, decay,
senility, seniority,
archaism, ancient,
venerable, prime,
obsolete)
fret-_v_ suffer, pain, dolor,
ache, twinge, twitch, gripe,
headache, hurt, cut, sore,
discomfort, malaise,
spasm, cramp, nightmare,
throb, agitate,
sharp,piercing, throbbing,
gnawing, anguish,
experience, writhe, (enjoy,
luxurious, sensual,

comfortable, cozy, snug,
agreeable, grateful,
refreshing, cordial, genial,
palatable, fragrant,
melodious, lovely,
beautiful)
fringe-n closure,
obstruction, plug, block,
stop, button, shut, bar,
bolt, stop, seal, plumb,
choke, border, (vent,
vomiter, orifice, mouth,
throat, portal)
frivolous-adj foolish,
imbecility, stolidity, dull,
incompetence, frivolity,
irrationality, trifling,
giddiness, eccentricity,
extravagant, absurdity,
shallow, weak, stupid,
idiotic, vacant, bewildered,
bovine, silly, senseless,
nonsensical, inept, giddy,
idle, (sober, prudent,
cautious, staid, solid,
considerate, wise,
watchful, provident,
intelligent, acute, rational,
sound, clever, shrewd,
discerning, penetrating)
front-n cover, guise, outfit,
envelop, involve, sheathe,
foreground, face, advance,
outpost, countenance,
pioneer, insolence, (rear,
back, posteriority, guard,
nape, stern, rump, breech,
dorsal, after, aft, astern,
behind, divest, bare,
dishabille)
frugal-adj economical,
saving, thriftiness,
retrenchment, prevention,

sparing, careful,
parsimony, abstinence,
moderation, temperance,
forbearance, self-denial,
restraint, (pleasurable,
indulgence, self-
indulgence, effeminacy,
excess, dissipation,
generous, bountiful, liberal,
free, unsparing, carte
blanche)
frustrate-v thwart,
disconcert, balk, foil, baffle,
snub, override, circumvent,
defeat, spoil, mar, cripple,
extinguish, dishearten
dissuade, undermine,
meddle, encumber, choke,
bar, block, barricade,
prevent, oppose, (assist,
help, lift, advance, favor,
advocate, sustain,
reinforce, support, uphold,
bolster, nurture)
fuel-n firing, combustible,
coal, anthracite, coke,
carbon, charcoal, turf,
peat, firewood, bobbing,
match, light, incense,
brand, torch, fuse, (non-
combustible, non-
flammable)
fugitive-n temporarily,
awhile, short, briefly,
transient, evanescence,
impermanence, fly, gallop,
vanish, evaporate,
refugee, emigrant,
vagabond, nomad,
wanderer, adventurer,
rover, straggler, rambler,
(durable, lasting,
permanent, survive, long-

standing, persistent,
perpetual)
full-*adj* much, great, might,
importance, considerable,
fair, huge, big, abundant,
intense, strong, sound,
heavy, plenary, complete,
entirety, perfection,
altogether, effectual,
wholly, totally, (incomplete,
imperfect, fault, short,
meager, lame, sketchy,
small, minimum, little,
diminutive, minute)
fumble-*v* jumble, muddle,
toss, hustle, derange,
misarrange, misplace,
mislay, decompose,
disorder, disorganize,
embroil, unsettle, disturb,
touch, feel, handle, thumb,
paw, grope, grabble,
twiddle, (arrange,
distribute, sort, assort,
allotment, apportionment,
analyze, classify, digest)
fumigate-*v* vaporize,
gasify, evaporate, exhale,
volatile, smoke, transpire,
emit, clean, purify,
defecate, purge, launder,
(rot, fester, putrefy, reek,
stink, mold, dirty, filthy,
grimy, soiled, contaminate,
taint, corrupt, liquefied)
function-*n* numeral,
symbol, divisible, prime,
fractional, decimal,
arithmetic, analysis,
algebra, integral, calculus,
useful, serviceable,
subservient, conducive,
efficient, effective,

applicable, advantageous,
expedient, (uselessness,
inefficacy, futility,
inadequate, inefficient,
unskillful)
fundamental-*adj* essential,
quintessence, incarnation,
intrinsic, inherence,
normal, implanted, natural,
radical, hereditary,
congenital, support, base,
basis, bearing, footing,
hold, (dependency,
suspension, hanging,
swing, dangle, append,
extrinsically, extraneous,
incidental, accidental)
fungus-*n* growth, carbuncle,
wart, polypous, fungous,
blister, boil, poison, leaven,
virus, venom, arsenic,
antimony, mildew, dry-rot,
cancer, canker, rust,
(remedial, restorative,
nutritious, peptic, curable,
cellular, spongy,
infundibular)
furbish-*v* improve,
betterment, melioration,
mend, amend, advance,
elevate, increase, reform,
correct, refine, prepare,
provide, forthcoming,
adornment, embellishment,
japanning, varnish,
cosmetic, (pitted,
discolored, imperfect,
impairment, injury,
damage, loss, detriment,
decline, decay,
dilapidation, atrophy,
collapse)
furnish-*v* provide, purvey,

reinforce, supply, find,
cater, victual, forage,
replenish, elaborate,
mature, ripen, mellow,
season, temper, anneal,
commissariat, reserve,
(shiftless, wasteful, spend,
squander, drain,
consume, expend,
exhaust, disperse)

fury-n violence, inclemency,
vehemence, might,
impetuosity,
boisterousness,
effervescence, turbulence,
bluster, uproar, riot,
severe, exacerbation,
orgasm, force, outrage,
shock, trepidation,
perturbation, ruffle, hurry,
fuss, flurry, fluster, (cool,
passiveness, calmness,
composure, tranquil,
serenity, quiet, staidness,
restraint, submissive)

fuse-v join, junction,
attachment, ligation,
corporate, unite, fix, affix,
fasten, bind, secure,
clinch, twist, knit, braid,
splice, gird, tithe, molten
(separate, disjoin,
discontinue, leave,
asunder, adrift, insular, rift,
unconnected, apart)

G

gag-n render mute,
constrained, imprisoned,
pent up, stiff, control
repress, smother,
suppress, rein, hold,

enchain, shackle, bridle,
muzzle, pinion, handcuff,
secure, (liberate,
disengage, release,
emancipate, discharge,
dismiss, deliver, acquittal)

gage-n measure, weigh,
survey, appraise, assess,
estimate, reckon, gauging,
standard, rule, caliper,
meter, rod, check,
compass, rate

gain-v benefit,
improvement, advantage,
interest, service, behalf,
satisfactory, commend,
useful, good, blessing,
fortune, treasure,
happiness, profit, earnings,
income, proceeds, fruition,
harvest, (lose, forfeit,
lapse, privation,
bereavement, deprivation,
riddance, incur, mislay,
minus)

galaxy-n assemblage,
collection, location,
ligation, compilation, levy,
gathering, muster, flux,
verge, meeting, group,
cluster, myriad, multitude,
numerousness, profusion,
multiple, heavenly bodies,
stars, asteroids, nebulae,
milky, way, galactic circle,
(few, scant, thin, rare,
scatter, scarce, infrequent,
handful, minority)

gall-n torment, torture, rack,
discomfort, malaise,
twinge, twitch, pained,
ache, unsavory,
unpalatable, bitter, acrid,

rough, offensive, repulsive, nauseous, loath, unpleasant, (palatable, nice, dainty, delectable, gusty, appetizing, exquisite, luscious, pleasurable, gratification)

gamble-v chance, accident, fortune, hazard, attribute, imputation, ascription, attribution, rationale, speculation, venture, stake, betting, adventurer, (intentional, knowingly, advisedly, designedly, purposely, studiously, deliberately, attribute)

game-n beast, brute, animal, fleshy, zoological, pursuit, enterprise, undertaking, adventure, quest, business, hobby, chase, hunt, sporting, follow, prosecute, fun, frolic, amusement, entertain, diversion, relaxation, solace, pastime, pleasure, merriment, laughter, regatta, (weary, disgusting, tiresome, irksome, uninteresting, dry, monotonous, dull, arid, humdrum)

gang-n assemblage, gathering, collection, compilation, levy, muster, crown, throng, flood, rush, deluge, horde, body, tribe, crew, band, squad, party, go, moving, mobile, mercurial, restless, shifting, nomadic, unquiet,

erratic, (quiet, tranquility, calm, repose, peace, stagnate, unassembled, disperse, sparse, sporadic, adrift, disheveled, streaming)

garble-v mutilate, amputate, abscind, excise, pare, thin, prune, decimate, abrade, scrape, file, geld, diminish, curtail, shorten, disseminate, exclude, bar, leave, reject, repudiate, blackball, relegate, segregate, banish, separate, omit, week, winnow, (containing, constituting, inclusion, admission, comprehension, reception, addition, annexation, addition, affix, subjoin)

garland-n circle, circlet, ring, areola, hoop, bracelet, armlet, round, annular, orbicular, oval, ovate, elliptic, spherical, wreath, fascia, crown, corona, coronet, chaplet, festoon, embroidery, ornamented, embellish, beautified, adorn, (simple, plain, homely, ordinary, unaffected, chaste, severe, bald, flat, dull, convoluted)

garrison-n occupied, indigenous, native, domestic, domiciled, naturalized, vernacular, domesticated, domiciliary, safe, utility, efficacy, serviceable, adequate, efficient, prolific, shelter,

concealment, fortification,
munition, ditch,
entrenchment, barrier,
fence, (aggressive,
attacking, offensive,
obsidianus, incursion,
invasion, encampment,
bivouac)

gasp-v blow, sneeze,
sternutation, hiccup,
cough, waft, respire, puff,
wheeze, snuff, fan,
ventilate, tempestuous,
droop, broken-winded,
fatigue, weariness,
yawning, lassitude,
exhaustion, (refreshed,
recuperative, respire,
breathe, reinvigorate, flow,
profluent, effluence)

gather-v assemble, collect,
locate, compile, lever,
muster, concourse, verge,
hoard, meet, flock,
cumulative, populous,
gainful, profitable, acquire,
remunerative, lucrative,
(loss, forfeit, privation,
riddance, bereaved,
dispossessed, quit,
deprivation)

gay-adj colorful, hue, tint,
dye, shade, pigment,
chromatic, bright, vivid,
intense, deep, fresh,
unfaded, rich, gorgeous,
gaudy, florid, showy,
flaunting, flashy, glaring,
flaring, discordant,
(mellow, harmonious,
sweet, delicate, tender,
refined, dismal, somber,
melancholy, dark, gloomy,
dreadful)

gazette-n publication,
current, notorious, flagrant,
circulated, propagation,
edition, newspaper,
journal, imprinted, edition,
diary, log, book, record,
note, almanac, ledger,
archive, scroll, chronicle,
portfolio, (obliterate,
erasure, cancel, out of
print, unregistered,
unwritten, efface)

gear-n clothes, things,
array, attire, vesture, garb,
apparel, wardrobe, outfit,
equipment, uniform,
regimentals, livery,
accouterment, toggery,
handle, shaft, shank,
blade, tiller, helm, pulley,
crank, winch, lever,
(divested, nude, exposed,
thread-bare, bareness,
exfoliation, disrobe,
dismantle, dishabille)

gem-adj super-excellence,
superiority, perfection,
prime, flower, cream,
goodness, merit, worth,
beneficial, edifying,
satisfactory, jewelry,
bijouterie, trinket, locket,
necklace, bracelet, anklet,
precious, brilliant, (pitted,
injured, deformed,
defective, flow, stain,
tarnished, disfigured,
hurtful, noxious,
detrimental, mischievous,
malignant)

general-adj universal,
miscellany, catholic, every,

all, generic, common,
ecumenical,
transcendental, prevalent,
prevailing, always,
prescription, usage, rule,
standing order, precedent,
routine, rut, groove,
habitual, conformable,
military authority, marshal,
potentate, sovereign,
tyrant, (servant, subject,
retainer, squire, vassal,
slave, unusual,
uncommon, special,
disusage, unconformity,
unaccustomed)

genial-*adj* warm, mild,
ardent, aglow, productive,
bringing forth, birth,
evolution, development,
growth, genesis, perform,
operate, flow, formative,
sensual, voluptuous,
agreeable, cordial, sweet,
melodious, (painful,
aching, sore, gripe, gnaw,
torture, torment, agonize,
crucify, tingle, writher,
rack, fall, destroy,
dissolution, consumption,
subversive, ruinous,
incendiary, deleterious)

genius-*n* intellect,
understanding, reason,
mental, rational,
subjective, faculties,
senses, consciousness,
observation, percipience,
instinct, conception,
capacity, wit, ability,
skillful, dexterous, adroit,
expert, proficient, masterly,
clever, (foolish, inept,

inexperienced,
incompetent, stupid,
unqualified, vacant,
thoughtless, diverted,
narrow-minded, dull,
thoughtless)

gentle-*adj* moderate,
temperate, sober,
calmness, relaxed,
tranquil, mitigate, pacify,
sedative, lessen, slow,
smooth, unexciting,
hypnotic, soft, bland,
lenient, reasonable,
peaceful, mild, demure,
imperturbable, enduring,
(vehement, demonstrative,
violent, wild, furious, fierce,
fiery, hot-headed, madcap,
over-zealous, enthusiastic,
impetuous, passionate,
fanatical)

genuflection-*n* bowing,
courtesy, curtsy,
obeisance, depress, drop,
sink, fall, debase, abase,
reduce, prostration,
subversion, precipitation,
kneel, surrender, kowtow,
homage, (disrespectful,
aweless, irreverent,
disparaging, insulting,
rude, sarcastic, elevate,
raise, erection, upheaval)

gestation-*n* production,
creation, construction,
formation, fabrication,
manufacture, building,
erection, flowering, fructify,
birth, delivery,
confinement, travail, labor,
midwife, obstetrics,
gender, propagation,

impregnation, (destroy,
waste, disruption,
consumption, ruin, smash,
sacrifice, demolish, dispel,
smash, quell, shatter)
ghastly-*adj* pale, uncolored,
achromatic, hueless, pallid,
faint, dull, muddy, dead,
dingy, ashy, cadaverous,
ashen, misshapen, plain,
homely, ugly, deformed,
disfigurement, distorted,
graceless, uncouth,
rugged, rough, gross, rude,
awkward, (beautiful,
elegant, graceful, adorned,
brilliant, radiance,
splendor, gorgeous,
magnificent, pretty,
handsome, dapper, jaunty,
shiny)
giant-*n* gargantuan,
monster, mammoth, whale,
behemoth, leviathan,
colossus, whopper, great,
ample, large, corpulent,
stout, fat, huge, immense,
enormous, mighty,
stupendous, infinite,
brawny, lumpish, strong,
mighty, robust, powerful,
potent, valid, resistless,
(frail, fragile, shatter,
flimsy, unsubstantial,
rickety, little, dwarf, pygmy,
scant, minute diminutive,
puny, infinitesimal, atomic)
giddy-*adj* inattentive,
absent, abstracted, distrait,
lost, preoccupied,
disconcerted, napping,
dreamy, thoughtless,
scatter-brained, wild,

careless, disregard,
heedless, neglectful, fickle,
unsettled, vacillation, timid,
(self-controlled,
determined, decisive,
resolute, vigor, zeal,
devotion, self-possessed,
definitive, peremptory,
flinching, shrinking, firm,
relentless)
gild-*v* cover, canopy,
bandage, cutaneous,
armor-plated, iron-clad,
sheath, wrap, veneer, face,
coating, paint, anoint,
incrustation,
whitewash, envelop,
deceive, falseness,
untruth, fraud, deceit,
guild, misrepresent, trick,
cheat, juggle, collusion,
(line, stuff, incrust, wad,
pad, truth, open)
gird-*v* bind, firm, fast,
close, tight, taut, secure,
set, nail, bolt, hasp, clasp,
rivet, solder, wedge, miter,
attach, affix, secure,
engage, strengthen, vigor,
force, might, robust,
sturdy, hardy, powerful,
potent, dynamic, (weak,
feeble, debilitate, impotent,
relaxed, unnerved,
unstrung, flaccid, soft,
effeminate, frail, flimsy)
glad-*adj* gratification,
pleasure, enjoyment,
fruition, relish, satisfaction,
happiness, felicity, bliss,
beatitude, joy, gladness,
delight, glee, cheer,
comfort, overjoyed,

enchanted, raptured,
ravished, fascinated,
captivated, pleasing,
(suffer, painful, ache,
smart, grieve, mourn,
yearn, repine, droop,
languish, despair,
displeasure, annoyance,
irritation, infliction, anxiety,
grief, sorrow)

glance-v view, look, espial,
ken, glimpse, peep, gaze,
stare, leer, contemplation,
visual, ocular, behold,
perceive, ophthalmic,
sight, examine cursorily,
skim, watchful, (inattentive,
unobservant, blind, close,
dismiss, discard,
discharge, oversight,
disregard, heedlessness,
overlook)

glare-v garish, blazing,
ablaze, rutilant, meteoric,
phosphorescent, aglow,
shining, luminous, bright,
vivid, splendent, lustrous,
flash, sparkle, scintillate,
coruscate, reflection,
refraction, dispersion,
gleam, twinkle, shimmer,
radiate, (dark, dim, dull,
dingy, fade, grimey, shade,
obscure, eclipse, gloom,
extinguish)

glass-n transparent,
pellucid, lucid, diaphanous,
limpid, clear, serene,
crystalline, vitreous,
hyaline, smooth, polish,
gloss, even, flat, sleek,
brittle, fragile, break, frail,
lacerate, (tenacious, tough,

strong, opaque, film, thick,
cloudy, hazy smoky,
murky, dirty, rough,
rugged)

glide-v motion, movement,
move, going, flow, flux, run
course, stir, evolution,
kinematics, step, rate,
pace, tread, stride, gait,
port, cadence, carriage,
transitional, motive,
shifting, mobile, mercurial,
unquiet, (still, fixed,
stationary, sedentary, stay,
pause, lull, tranquil,
deliberate, slow, gradual)

glimmer-n light, ray, beam
stream, gleam, streak,
moon, glow, flush, halo,
glory, luminous, lucid,
bright, vivid, lustrous,
shimmer, sparkle,
scintillate, radiate, (dark,
obscurity, gloom, eclipse,
shade, sunless, somber,
dim, dingy, gloomy,
overcast)

glorify-v dedication,
consecration,
enthronement,
canonization, celebration,
enshrinement, hero,
worthy, notability, rank,
great, eminence,
importance, elevation,
ascent, super, exaltation,
dignify, aggrandizement,
(discredit, disrepute, bad,
disapprobation, dishonor,
disgrace, shame,
humiliation, tarnish, taint,
defilement, pollute)

gloss-n smooth, lubricity,

velvet, silk, satin, slide,
glass, ice, plane, file, mow,
shave, level, roll,
macadamize, polish,
glabrous, slippery,
lubricious, oily, soft,
(render rough, uneven,
knotted, aspergillus, crisp,
gnarled, unpolished,
rough-hewed, gnarled,
crumble, corrugate)

glut-v satiety, satisfaction,
saturation, repletion,
surfeit, weariness, spoiled,
child, cloy, quench, slake,
pall, gorge, surfeit,
swallow, enough, bolt,
devour, gobble up, gulp,
raven, greedy, adequacy,
omnivorous, over-fed,
(fast, starve, clam, famish,
perish, unfed, hungry)

go-v motion, movement,
transit, going, evolution,
wander, gone, lost,
departed, defunct,
negative, elapse, lapse,
flow, run, duration,
proceed, advance, pass,
expire, progress, (stop,
admit, absorb, swallow,
enter, introduce, receive,
import, insert)

Godspeed-n depart, go,
move, begone, farewell,
adieu, good-bye, withdraw,
vacate, leave, evacuate,
abandon, remove, exit,
embarkation, exodus,
flight, (arrive, reach, attain,
overtake, disembark,
welcome, fetch, destined,
reception)

good-adj savory, well-
tasted, tasty, palatable,
nice, dainty, delectable,
gusty, appetizing, delicate,
delicious, exquisite, rich,
luscious, ambrosial, relish,
zest, virtue, virtuousness,
moral, ethic, merit, worth,
(scandal, laxity, looseness,
demoralizing, depravity,
pollution, profligacy,
atrocity, infirmity, error,
defect, deficiency)

gorge-v ravine, break, gap,
opening, hole, chasm,
cleft, mesh, crevice, creek,
cranny, crack, slit, fissure,
crevasse, abyss, gulf, inlet,
frith, strait, gully, pass,
furrow, satiety, satisfaction,
saturation, repletion, glut,
surfeit, weariness, quench,
slake, fatigue,
(fastidiousness, nicety,
epicure, gourmet, dainty,
join, adjoin, touch, meet,
osculate, coincide, coexist,
adhere)

gorgeous-adj beauty, form,
elegance, grace,
unadorned, symmetry,
comeliness, fairness,
polish, gloss, good looks,
bloom, brilliancy, radiance,
splendor, magnificence,
handsome, pretty, lovely,
refined, shapely, colored,
bright, vivid, (achromatic,
hueless, pale ,ugly, plain,
homely, ordinary,
unsightly, deformed,
eyesore, frightful, ghastly,
graceless, gross)

gospel-*n* certainty,
necessary, certitude,
surety, assurance, moral,
infallibleness, reliability,
scripture, positive,
dogmatism, sure, solid,
absolute, positive,
unerring, authentic, official,
evident, (uncertain,
dubious, hesitation,
suspense, perplexity,
dilemma, bewilderment,
vagueness, confused)

grace-*n* style, elegance,
purity, ease, readiness,
polished, classical correct,
artistic, chaste, pure,
academical, easy, fluent,
flowing, tripping,
unaffected, natural,
unlabored, mellifluous,
(stiffness, barbaric,
euphuism, graceless,
harsh, abrupt, dry,
cramped, formal, forced,
artificial, mannered)

gradation-*n* degree, extent,
measure, amount, ratio,
stint, standard, height,
pitch, reach, amplitude,
range, scope, caliber,
shade, tenor, compass,
station, rank, order,
uniformity, correct,
methodical, systematic,
(confusion, disorder,
jumble, huddle, wrong,
fortuitous, perplexed,
quantitative, some, more,
less, any)

gram-*n* essence, small,
little, tenuity, paucity, few,
insignificance, mediocre,

moderate, atom, particle,
molecule, diminutive,
minute, paltry, faint,
slender, slight, scanty,
meager, sparing, modest,
mere, low, infinitesimal,
stark, bare, (vast,
immense, enormous,
extreme, excessive,
extravagant, exorbitant,
outrageous, preposterous)

grammar-*n* punctuate,
syntax, parts of speech,
language, conjugation,
case, declination,
rudiments, elements,
outlines, alphabet, begin,
commence, rise, arise,
originate, conceive, initiate,
open, (end, final, terminal,
consummate, finish,
conclude, solecism, bad,
false, slipslop,
ungrammatical, incorrect)

grand-*adj* important,
momentous, serious,
earnest, noble, solemn,
impressive, commanding,
imposing, urgent, pressing,
critical, prominent, grave,
superior, instant, essential,
vital, absorbing,
considerable, significant,
telling, (poor, paltry, trifling,
trivial, slight, slender, light,
flimsy, frothy, idle, foolish,
powerless, petty, pitiful)

grant-*v* admit,
acknowledge, avowal,
reveal, divulge, allow,
concede, confess,
disclose, transpire,
permission, empower,

license, authorize, absolve, entrust, sanction, license, privilege, favor, (prohibit, forbid, disallow, hinder, restrict, exclude, withhold, bar, veto, limit, ambush, conceal, stalk, cover, recess)

graphic-adj intelligent, clear, explicit, lucid, perspicuity, legibility, precise, simplify, understand, comprehend, distinct, positive, illustrative, expressive, recognizable, obvious, (riddle, paradox, unaccountable, illegible, vague, loose, ambiguous, obscure, perplexed, negative, nebulous)

grasp-v comprehend, understand, catch, follow, collect, master, lucid, luminous, transparent, plain, distinct, explicit, positive, definite, take hold, retain, detain, detention, custody, tenacity, firm hold, grip, secure, (relinquish, abandon, renounce, derelict, surrender, dispense, resign, eliminate)

gratuitous-adj intuitive, instinctive, impulsive, independent, unconnected, inconsistent, fallible, groundless, unproved, evasive, irrelevant, cheap, low, moderate, reasonable, depreciated, unsalable, gratis, without charge,

(expensive, extravagant, exorbitant, extortionate, premium, priceless, precious, overcharged, rationalistic, argumentative, controversial)

gravity-n force, power, pressure, elasticity, electricity, magnetism, galvanism, capability, voltaism, attraction, dynamic, energy, friction, suction, capacity, weight, heaviness, ponderous, load, burden, (levity, lightness, buoyancy, leaven, subtle, airy, weightless, floating, portable, powerless, impotent, valid, effective, influential, productive)

grease-n lubricate, smoothly, anoint, oil, glycerine, lather, wax, payment, settle, discharge, quit, acquit, liquidate, retribution, remit, installment, (disgorge, repay, refund, reimburse, insolvent, bankrupt, gazetted, protest, dishonor, rub, scratch, scrape, rasp, scrub, grind, friction)

greed-n desire, avidity, covetous, ravenous, craving, voracity, gluttony, hunger, longing, hankering, solicitude, impatient, impetuous, over-anxiety, gorge, gormandize, devour,

gobble-up, gulp, raven,
guzzle, cram, fill, (fast,
starve, perish, Lenten,
unfed, famish, indifferent,
cold, neutrality, unconcern)
gregarious-*adj* social,
companion, comradeship,
conviviality, good
fellowship, festivity,
hospitality, heartiness,
cheer, welcome, greetings,
receptive, fraternize,
(seclusion, exclusion,
privacy, retirement,
reclusion, recess, solitude,
isolation, loneliness,
estrangement, voluntary
exile)
grieve-*v* mourn, anxiety,
concern, grief, sorrow,
distress, affliction, woe,
bitterness, heartache,
heaving, aching, bleeding,
misery, tribulation,
wretchedness, desolation,
despair, prostration,
(happiness, felicity, bliss,
beatitude, enchantment,
transport, rapture,
ravishment, ecstasy,
paradise, Elysium)
grind-*v* reduce, contract,
decrease, lessen, shrink,
collapse, emaciation,
consumption, atrophy,
condensation,
compression, compact,
smaller, squeeze, lessen,
narrow, constrict, crush,
dwarf, (expand, increase,
enlarge, extend, augment,
amplify, spread, increment,
growth, develop)

grip-*n* power, retention,
retain, detention, custody,
tenacity, firm hold, grasp,
forfeit, secure, clutch,
swoop, wrench, take,
catch, hook, nab, (return,
restore, reparation,
release, replevin,
redemption, recovery,
recuperate, surrender,
yield, forego, renounce,
abandon, expropriate)
gross-*adj* great, magnitude,
size, multitude, immensity,
enormity, infinity, fullness,
great quantity, volume,
monstrous, incredible,
whole, total, aggregate,
amount, sum-total,
command, hold, grasp,
reach, clutch, regime,
monarchy, (fractional,
fragmentary, sectional,
divided, partial,
compartment, portion,
section, piece)
grotto-*n* alcove, hermitage,
greenhouse, portico, lobby,
court, porch, veranda,
arbor, depression, dip,
hollow, depressed,
concave, cavernous, cave,
cove, (cupola, dome, arch,
balcony, eaves, pilaster)
ground-*n* land, earth,
ground, dry land,
continent, mainland,
peninsula, delta, coast,
shore, soil, clay, loam,
acres, real estate, cause,
origin, source, principle,
element, reason, rationale,
occasion derivation,

(consequently, necessarily,
eventually, derivative, sea,
ocean, water, waves,
billows)

grow-v increase, enlarge,
extension, accession,
augment, gain, strengthen,
intensify, enhance,
magnify, redouble, dilate,
exaggerate, expansibility,
germination, growth,
swollen, develop, amplify,
widen, (reduce, scrape,
compress, lessen, shrink,
collapse, emaciate,
atrophy)

guard-v protect, preserve,
custody, chaperone,
watch, warden, preserve,
shelter, shroud, flank,
secure, trust, defend,
garrison, driver,
coachman, whip, fireman,
(danger, peril, insecure,
jeopardy, risk,
precariousness, exposure,
vulnerability, instability)

gypsy-n vagabond, nomad,
Bohemian, wanderer,
pilgrim, emigrant, fugitive,
refugee, runner, courier,
comet, pedestrian, tourist,
passenger, excursionist,
explorer, adventurer, rover,
rambler, straggler, gad-
about, (dupe, dull,
credulous)

H

habit-n essence, temper,
spirit,humor, capacity,
constitution, character,

type, quality, garment,
garb, palliative, apparel,
wardrobe, wearing
apparel, clothes, array,
outfit, morning dress,
uniform, (divestment,
nudity, bareness, undress,
uncover, denude, disrobe,
extraneousness, accident,
derived from without)

hack-v cut, sunder, divide,
subdivide, sever, abscind,
saw, snip, nib, nip, cleave,
rend, slit, split, splinter,
carve, cut up, dissect,
disintegrate, disperse,
separate, discrete, ass,
donkey, jackass, mule,
horse, (join, attach, unite,
fasten, bind, fix, affix,
buckle, gird, close)

hackneyed-adj dictum,
saying, adage, proverb,
sentence, perception,
enlightenment, glimpse,
inkling, trite, reflection,
conclusion, golden rule,
motto, axiom, maxim,
aphorism, (blunder,
muddle, absurd, imbecility,
farce, rhapsody, sell, pun,
ignorance, blindness)

haggard-adj fatigue,
weariness, yawning,
drowsiness, lassitude,
tiredness, exhaustion,
faintness, collapse,
prostration, (refreshed,
recover, revival, repair,
refection, renew)

hail-n welcome, arrive,
advent, landing, hither,
good day, reach, advent,

reception, home, goal, port, haven, sleet, ice, snow, flake, crystal, drift, frost, icicle, (heat, caloric, fire, spark, flash, flame, blaze, bonfire, fireworks, depart, decampment, leave, outward, whence, hence, farewell, adieu, good bye)

half-*n* bisect, halving, divide, split, cut in two, cleave, dimidiate, separate, fork, bifurcate, cleft, bipartite, fork, prong, gradual, degree, retard, relax, slacken, moderate, rein, curb, leisurely, at half speed, slow, (hurry, accelerate, quicken, haste, rapid, scuttle, scud, gallop, amble, troll, hasten, duplicate, twice, once more, over again, renewal, double)

halt-*v* cease, discontinue, desist, stay, break, leave, hold, stop, stick, interrupt, suspend, enough, truce, weak, debility, stony, loss, drop, crumble, totter, tremble, shake, limp, fade, languish, decline, flag, (strength, power, energy, vigor, force, physical, spring, elasticity, tone, tension, continue, persist, go, sustain, uphold, keep, perpetuate, maintain, preserve)

hammer-*n* repeat, iterate, reiterate, recurrence, succession, monotony, rhythm, recur, revert, reappear, often, blow, dint, stroke, sledge, mall, maul, mallet, flail, batter, pile-driving, punch, bat, axe, (recoil, react, spring, revulsion, rebound, reflex, reverberate, rebuff, repulse, return)

hand-*n* organ of touch, touch, feel, handle, finger, thumb, feel, palpation, tingle, tangible, dextral, right-handed, ambidextrous, right and left, flank, quarter, (numb, intangible, impalpable, insensibility to touch)

handbook-*n* information, enlightenment, acquaintance, knowledge, publication, guide, manual, map, plan, chart, gazetteer, work, volume, tract, pamphlet, circular, portfolio, (conceal, hide, cloak, secrete, cover, screen, cloak, veil, shroud, masquerade)

handsome-*adj* liberal, free, beautiful, pretty, lovely, graceful, elegant, delicate, dainty, refined, fair, personable, comely, good-looking, dapper, jaunty, natty, quaint, (ugly, deformed, inelegance, disfigurement, squalor, monster)

handy-*adj* near, proximity, propinquity, vicinity, nigh, nearby, elongation, background, spread,

neighboring, adjacent,
adjoining, proximate,
intimate, (distant, remote,
far, extend, stretch, away,
apart, asunder)

hang-v dependent,
suspending, swing, dangle,
swag, draggle, flap, trail,
flow, sling, hook up, hitch,
fasten, append, strangle,
garrote, throttle, choke,
stifle, suffocate, smother,
asphyxiate, (support, bear,
carry, sustain, bolster,
hold, shoulder)

hapless-adj unfortunate,
mishap, unblest, unhappy,
unlucky, decayed, poor,
adverse, disastrous,
calamitous, ruinous, dire,
deplorable, anxiety,
solicitude, trouble,
concern, grief, sorrow,
distress, (prosperous,
thrive, flourish, smooth,
well-being, affluent,
success, blessing, lucky)

hard-adj strong, strength,
power, vigor, force, brute
force, mighty, adamantine,
stout, robust, sturdy,
powerful, potent, puissant,
valid, reinforce, stamina,
nerve, muscle, sinew,
steel, energy, grip, bone,
dynamite, rigid, renitency,
inflexible, stubborn, stiff,
firm, (soft, pliable, flexible,
plasticity, tender, supple,
lithe, limber, limp, frail,
fragile, flimsy,
unsubstantial, rickety,
drooping, withered,

shattered)

hardly-adv scarcely, slight,
scanty, limited, sparing,
few, low, below, moderate,
modest, inappreciable,
infinitesimal, mere, simple,
sheer, stark, bare, little,
diminutive, nothing,
morsel, thimble, trifle,
unimportant, insignificant,
trivial, paltry, indifference,
nonentity, (important,
consequence, prominence,
considerable, significant,
concern, emphasis, great,
vast, immense, enormous,
extreme, goodly,
unsurpassed)

hark-v hear, audible,
acoustic, listen, catch a
sound, attentive, mindful,
observant, alive,
awakened, behold,
breathless, heed,
cognizant, recognize,
(absent, abstract,
disregard, heedless,
indifference)

harm-n evil, ill, hurt,
mischief, nuisance,
disaster, accident,
casualty, mishap,
adversity, tragedy, ruin,
destroy, catastrophe,
calamity, bale, bad,
painful, grievance,
injurious, detrimental,
noxious, mischievous,
nocuous, vile, foul, rotten,
(good, excellent, better,
superior, above par, nice,
fine, genuine, favorable,
fair, benefit, advantage,

improvement, interest,
well, right, satisfactory)
harness-v fasten, attach,
fix, affix, bind, secure,
clinch, twist, tie, pinion,
string, strap, sew, lace,
stitch, tack, knit, button,
buckle, hitch, last, truss,
bandage, braid, splice,
swathe, gird, tether, moor,
picket, chain, fetter, yoke,
collar, halter, muzzle, gag,
bit, brake, curb, snaffle,
bridle, rein, (sunder, divide,
subdivide, sever, dissever,
abscind, saw, snip, nib,
nip, cleave, rend, slit, split,
carve)
hatch-v produce, create,
construct, formation,
fabricate, manufacture,
build, architect, erect,
edification, establish,
workmanship, perform,
achieve, complete, flower,
fructify, bring forth, birth,
deliver, evolve, develop,
grow, enclosure, barrier,
barricade, gate, door,
hatch, (destroy, waste,
dissolve, disrupt, consume,
nullify, annul, demolish,
deteriorate, perish, fall)
hateful-adj bad, hurtful,
evil, maltreat, abuse,
injurious, deleterious,
detrimental, noxious,
pernicious, mischievous,
malignant, vile, mean,
wrong, depraved,
shocking, reprehensible,
disapprove, abominable,
detestable, execrable,

cursed, confounded,
damned, infernal, diabolic,
(admirable, estimable,
praiseworthy, pleasing,
tolerable, best, choice,
select, goodness,
beneficial valuable,
serviceable,
advantageous, edifying,
favorable)
have-v possess, own, hold,
tenure, occupy, depend,
monopoly, heritage,
inheritance, heir, engross,
recreate, acquire, get,
gain, win, earn, obtain,
procure, gather, collect,
assemble, pick, find, reap,
secure, draw, confute,
(lose, bereft, dispossess,
rid, minus, deprive, lapse,
forfeit, mislay, exempt)
hazard-n chance, accident,
hap-hazard, random, luck,
casualty, contingence,
adventure, probability,
possibility, odds,
undetermined, fortuitous,
causeless, incidental,
unintentional, danger, peril,
insecurity, jeopardy, risk,
venture, precariousness,
slipperiness, instability,
defenseless, exposure,
imperil, (safety, security,
surety, impregnability,
invulnerability, safeguard,
palladium, guardian)
heap-n big, huge, large,
ample, abundant, full,
intense, heavy, plenary,
high, zenith, vast,
immense, enormous,

extreme, inordinate,
excessive, extravagant,
exorbitant, outrageous,
preposterous, monstrous,
over-grown, towering,
stupendous, prodigious,
astonishing, incredible,
accumulate, lump, pile,
pyramid, (disperse, adrift,
here and there, smallness,
little, few, insignificant,
mediocrity, moderation,
atom, minute,
inconsiderable, paltry,
scant, limited, meager,
sparing, few)
heart-*n* love, fondness,
liking, inclination, regard,
admiration, affection,
sympathy, fellowship,
tenderness, benevolence,
attachment, passion,
devotion, fervor, adoration,
idolatry, Cupid, lover,
amour, betrothed, fiance,
beloved, adorable, sweet,
enchanting, (hate,
disaffection, repugnance,
dislike, antipathy, detest,
abominate, abhor, loathe,
recoil, shatter, shrink,
hateful, irritate)
hearty-*adj* healthy, well,
sound, hale, fresh, green,
whole, florid, flush,
staunch, brave, robust,
vigorous, weather-proof,
willing, voluntary, propend,
inclined, geniality,
cordiality, goodwill,
readiness, earnestness,
forward, eager,
(grudgingly, unwillingly,

adverse, reluctant,
backward, repugnant,
delicate, loss of health,
invalidate, atrophy, decay,
decline, consumption,
fatal)
heat-*n* hot, warm, mild,
genial, tepid, lukewarm,
unfrozen, thermal, fervent,
sunny, torrid, tropical,
estival, canicular, close,
sultry, stifling, stuffy,
suffocating, oppressive,
reeking, baking, burning,
sweltering, glow, flush,
bask, smoke, stew,
simmer, seethe, boil, burn,
broil, blaze, flame,
smolder, parch, fume,
pant, contend, strife,
contest, struggle,
opposition, rivalry, match,
race, steeplechase,
handicap, regatta,
(peaceful, pacific, calm,
tranquil, halcyon, quiet,
cold, frigid, ice, snow,
glacial frosty, freezing,
brutal, hibernal, bitter,
chilly, shiver, fresh,
inclement)
heave-*v* raise, heighten,
elevate, raise, lift, erect,
stick, perch, tilt, upheave,
exalt, hoist, cast, uplift,
remain, stay, stand, lie,
bring, draw-up, hold, halt,
stop, rest, pause, anchor,
(move, motion, shifting,
mobile, restless, nomadic,
lower, depress, dip,
reduce, fall, sink, trample,
duck)

heaven-*n* god like, kingdom, throne, paradise, eden, celestial, resurrection, supernal, unearthly, beatific, eternal home, bliss, happiness, felicity, beatitude, enchantment, transport, rapture, ecstasy, Elysium, (grieve, mourn, yearn, repine, droop, languish, sink, despair, afflicted, demoniacal, haunted, supernatural, weird, uncanny, evil)

hedge-*n* compensate, equate, indemnification, compromise, counter, retaliate, counter-balance, hinder, impede, prevent, forefend, retard, slacken, preclude, inhibit, shackle, obstruct, stop, block, barricade, (aid, assist, help, support, lift, advance, further, promote, relief, advocate, reinforcement)

heir-*n* benefactor, grantee, trustee, holder, generative, descendant, heredity, descent, lineage

hell-*n* abyss, hollow, pit, shaft, well, crater, bottomless pit, unfortunate, unblest, unhappy, unlucky, poor, speculate, venture, stake, random shot, adversity, evil, failure, disaster, gamble, adventure, risk, hazard, stake, (intention, purpose, project, design, ambition, undertake, aim)

helm-*n* handle, hilt, haft, shaft, heft, shank, blade, trigger, tiller, treadle, key, turn screw, screwdriver, direct, manage, govern, conduct, order, prescribe, head, lead, regulate, guide, steer, pilot, drive, throne, chair, dais, (anarchy, relaxation, misrule, subordinate, dethronement, deposition, abdication)

hence-*adv* thence, therefore, since, on account of, because, owing to, wherefore, attribute, impute, refer, derive, theorize, reason, argue, discuss, debate, dispute, wrangle, canvass, comment, (unreasonable, illogical, false, unsound, invalid, unwarranted, inconclusive, casual, fortuitous, accidental, causeless, incidental, contingent, undetermined)

herald-*n* precursor, antecedent, precedent, predecessor, forerunner, leader, bell-weather, harbinger, dawn, prelude, preamble, preface, prologue, prefix, introduction, heading, frontispiece, groundwork, (sequel, suffix, successor, tail, train, wake, trail, rear, retinue, appendix, postscript)

heritage-*n* heirs, posterity, future, next, near, eventual, ulterior,

prospective, tomorrow,
eventual, ultimately,
possess, own, occupy,
hold, tenure, depend,
retain, inheritance, revert,
engross, (exemption,
absence, devoid,
unobtained, past, gone by,
ancient, former, antiquity,
immemorial, bygone,
forgotten, irrecoverable
obsolete)

hermitage-n abode,
dwelling, lodging, domicile,
residence, address,
habitation, berth, seat, lap,
housing, quarters,
headquarters, tabernacle,
throne, ark, home,
fatherland, country,
homestead, stall, fireside,
hearth, stone, household

hesitate-v uncertain,
suspense, perplexity,
embarrassment, doubt,
dubiety, vague, haze, fog,
obscurity, contingency,
puzzle, bewilder, bother,
indecisive, ambiguous,
questionable, precarious,
disputable, (certain,
necessary, assured,
reliable, gospel, positive,
solid, authoritative,
authentic, official, evident,
infallible)

hinder-v impede, prevent,
preclude, obstruct, stop,
interrupt, retard,
embarrass, restrict,
restrain, inhibit, interfere,
discourage, drawback,
stumbling block, foreclose,

prohibit, forbid, disallow,
interdict, exclude,
unauthorized (grant,
empower, charter,
enfranchise, privilege,
warrant, sanction, entrust,
permit, allow, admit,
concede, recognize, favor,
license, authorize, aid,
helpful, subservient)

hiss-n sound, hoot, gibe,
flout, jeer, scoff, taunt,
sneer, quip, fling, wipe,
slap in the face,
disrespect, disregard,
slight, trifle, discourteous,
dishonor, desecrate, insult,
affront, outrage, (respect,
regard, consideration,
courtesy, attention,
reverence, honor, esteem,
admiration, homage)

hit-v blow, dint, stroke,
knock, tap, rap, slap,
smack, pat, dab, slam,
bang, whack, squash,
dowse, whop, swap,
probability, possibility,
contingency, odds, long
odds, run of luck, hammer,
mall, knock, strike, (duck,
recoil, rebound, revulsion,
repercussion)

hobble-v creep, craw, lag,
.slug, draw, linger, loiter,
saunter, plod, trudge,
stump along, move-slowly,
slouch, stagger, mince,
slacken, moderate, easy,
leisurely, deliberate,
gradual, slow-paced, (trip,
speed, hasten, move
quickly, scuttle, scud,

scamper, race, run, shoot,
tear, whisk, sweep, brush,
accelerate)

hobby-_n_ pursuit, purse,
prosecute, enterprise,
adventure, quest, game,
desire, wish, whim,
devotee, aspirant,
solicitant, avid, (indifferent,
neutral, of no interest,
have no desire, cold, frigid,
lukewarm, avoid, shun,
steer clear, deny)

hollow-_adj_ vanish,
unsubstantial, incomplete,
deficiency, short measure,
shortcoming, insufficient,
imperfect, concave, dip,
indentation, cavity, pit,
follicle, depressed,
excavate, furrow, trough,
basin, valley, (convex,
project, sell, bilge, bulge,
protrude, tumor, hump,
hunch, bulb, node, nodule)

holocaust-_n_ kill, put to
death, slay, shed blood,
murder, assassinate,
butcher, slaughter,
suffocate, sacrifice,
destroy, ravage, (creation,
produce, generate,
establish, give life to,
complete)

homely-_adj_ plain,
disfigured, blemished,
pitted, freckled, discolored,
imperfect, injured, simple,
ordinary, chaste, severe,
(polished, festoon, garland,
adorned, decorated,
embellished, detailed,
fleur-de-lis)

honest-_adj_ veracity, truthful,
frank, sincerely, candor,
fidelity, true, scrupulous,
trustworthy, probity,
integrity, rectitude, upright,
honor, purity, fair, just,
equity, impartiality,
principle, grace,
constancy, faithful,
warrant, apologize,
advocate, plead ignorance,
(accuse, charge, tax,
impute, taunt, reproach,
slur, false, deception,
untruth, guile, lying,
misrepresentation, perjury,
forgery, fabrication)

honor-_n_ glory, distinction,
reputation, notability,
notoriety, dedication,
consecration,
enthronement,
canonization, celebration,
enshrinement, glorification,
immortalize, exalt, glitter,
distinguished, great,
eminence, height,
important, (disrepute,
discredit, repute, dishonor,
disgrace, shame,
humiliation, scandal, vile,
turpitude, tarnish, disgrace,
degrade, vile, stain,
shameful, degrading)

hoodwink-_v_ deception,
false, untruth, fraud,
deceit, guile,
misrepresentation,
delusion, trickery,
circumvention, chicane,
juggle, hocus, feint, ignore,
bewilderment, shallow,
superficial, empty, half-

learned, uninformed,
unaware, (knowing, aware,
cognizant, conscious,
acquainted, instructed,
learned, familiar,
scholastic, profound,
accomplished,
ascertained)

hook-*n* attach, fix, affix,
saddle on, fasten, bind,
secure, clinch, twist, tie,
string, strap, sew, lace,
stitch, tack, pin, nail, join,
fast, close, tight, taut, inseparable, entangle,
parting, (sunder, divide,
disengage, subdivide,
sever, cut, snip, nib, nip,
cleave, rend, slit, split,
carve, hack, lacerate,
mangle, rupture, shatter,
shiver, crunch, chop)

hop-*v* leap, jump, spring,
bound, vault, station,
dance, caper, curvet,
caracole, skip, frisky,
bounce, flounce, agitation,
fun, frolic, merriment,
pleasure, amusement,
sport, laughter, reel,
festivity, play, game,
(wearisome, tediousness,
drag, tiresome,
uninterested, monotonous,
humdrum, slow, plunge,
dip, dive, duck, submerge,
douse, sink, engulf,
wallow)

hope-*v* desire, expectation,
trust, confidence, reliance,
faith, belief, assurance,
reassurance, promise,
optimism, enthusiasm,

encouraging, cheering,
bright, rose-colored,
prosperity, welfare, well-
being, affluence, blessings,
thrive, flourish, (adverse,
disastrous, calamitous,
ruinous, dire, deplorable,
unfortunate, unhappy,
unlucky, hapless, despair,
despondence,
abandonment)

horn-*n* receptacle,
recipient, receiver,
reservoir, compartment,
vessel, vase, utensil,
sharp, keen, pyramidal,
spindle, needle-shaped,
spiked, thorny, bristling,
barbed, copious,
abundant, abounding,
enough, rich, sufficient

horrify-*v* annoyance,
grievance, nuisance,
vexation, mortification,
sicken, bore, bother,
plague, pest, sea of
troubles, misfortune,
irritation, painful, disgust,
revolt, nauseate,
disenchant, repel, offend,
shock, fear, apprehensive,
solicitude, anxiety,
mistrust, suspicion, alarm,
tremble, shake, shiver,
shudder, (hopeful, trust,
encourage, aspire,
optimistic, pleasant,
agreeable, pleasure,
delectable, loveliness,
sunny, bright, sweet,
goodness, satisfy, gratify,
satiate, refresh, attract,
allure)

hostile-adj disagreeing, discordant, discrepant, incompatible, irreconcilable, inconsistent, uncomfortable, incongruous, unharmonious, inapt, unapt, unaccommodating, opposed, antagonistic, counteractive, clashing, conflicting, against, disfavor, (cooperation, complicity, participation, collusion, association, alliance, confederation, coalition, fusion, unanimity, combined)

humility-n meek, lowliness, submission, resignation, modest, blush, suffusion, confusion, sense of shame, disgrace, mortification, servile, condescending, courteous, pious, faith, holiness, religious, devout, devoted, reverent, godly heavenly, pure, spiritual, saintly, sacred, solemn, (wicked, evil, unjust, reprobate, irreverence, desecration, sacrilege, dignity, self-respect, pride, haughtiness, vain, arrogance, stately, proud)

I

idea-n notion, conception, thought, apprehension, impression, perception, image, sentiment, reflection, observation, consideration, abstract idea, point of view, theory, fancy, imagination, topic, thesis, text, business, affair, matter, argument, motion, inkling, (indifference, incurious, impassive, ignorance, remote)

identification-n identity, sameness, coincidence, exactness, similar, copy, recognize, equality, comparable, deduce, derived, gather, collect, draw an inference, make a deduction, whet, ween, estimate, appreciate, (discover, find, determine, evolve, contrary, oppose, differ, invert, reverse, turn the tables, contradict, antagonize, oppose)

idiosyncrasy-n essence, endowment, capacity, capability, moods, declension, features, aspects, peculiarities, diagnostic, principle, nature, specialty, particularity, characteristic, mannerism, specific, singularity, version, state, (general, universal, common, ecumenical, transcendental, prevalent, every all, unspecified, impersonal, implanted, extraneousness)

idle-adj shallow, imbecility, incapacity, vacancy of mind, poverty of intellect, weak, wanting, dull,

powerless, frivolous, petty,
inane, ridiculous,
worthless, (paramount,
essential, vial, all-
absorbing, serious,
earnest, grand, impressive,
commanding, imposing)
idol-n favorite, pet, spoiled,
desire, devotee, aspirant,
solicitant, heretic,
antichrist, pagan, heathen,
bigot, (orthodox, sound,
strict, faithful, evangelical)
ignore-v neglect,
carelessness, trifling,
omission, default,
inactivity, inattention,
nonchalance, insensibility,
imprudence, recklessness,
inconsiderate, heedless,
thoughtless, uninformed,
ignored, (knowledge,
cognizance, acquaintance,
insight, familiarity, intuition,
perception, enlightenment)
illegitimate-adj illegal,
unlawful, smuggling,
poaching, prohibited, illicit,
contraband, despotic,
deceitful, delusive,
insidious, untrue, feigned,
fraudulent, artificial,
unsound, (legal,
legitimacy, rule, regulation,
equity, enact, vested,
constitutional, permitted)
illuminate-v light, ray,
beam, stream, gleam,
streak, sun, aurora,
shining, luminous, lucid,
bright, vivid, reflection,
refraction, lighten,
irradiate, color, hue, tint,

intense, unfaded, gay,
(pale, faded, colorless,
decolorize, bleached,
tarnished, blanch, dull,
muddy, dingy)
illustrate-v exemplify, cite,
quote, exemplary,
example, uniformly, in
point, interpretation,
definition, explicit,
translate, define, construe,
decipher, expound,
unravel, disentangle,
resolve, (misrepresent,
pervert, garble, distort,
travesty, stretch,
aberration, irregularity,
exemption)
imbed-v locate, place,
situate, seat, station,
lodge, quarter, post, install,
establish, stow, house, fix,
pin, root, graft, deposit,
vest, pack, give, furnish,
afford, supply, lend,
support, bottom, found,
base, ground, maintain,
(depend, suspend, loose,
flowing, tail, caudate,
hang, displace, vacate)
imitation-n copy,
duplication, repetition,
mirror, reflect, mimic,
reproduce, repeat, echo,
match, parallel, counterfeit,
parody, travesty,
caricature, burlesque,
imitative, verbatim,
duplicate, transcript,
shadow, parody, similar,
impersonate, (original,
prototype, model, pattern,
precedent, standard)

immaculate-*adj* perfect,
best, pure, good, paragon,
unparalleled, supreme,
superhuman, divine,
approbation, faultless,
spotless, impeccable,
unblemished, ripen,
mature, scathless, intact,
harmless, purity, clean,
purify, (decay, corrupt,
mold, must, rot, putrefy,
fester, rank, reek, stink,
dirty, soil, smoke, tarnish,
spot, dirty, filthy, grimy)

immature-*adj* new, novelty,
recent, youth, innovation,
modernism, recent, fresh,
neoteric, new-born, young,
vernal, renovated, brewing,
hatching, forthcoming, (old,
ancient, antique,
venerable, elder, archaic,
classic, seniority, mature,
decline, senility)

immense-*adj* great, large,
considerable fair, above
par, big, huge, ample,
abundant, enough, full,
intense, strong, sound,
passing, heavy, plenary,
high, goodly, noble,
precious, might, sad,
grave, serious, vast,
enormous, extreme,
extravagant, preposterous,
monstrous, (inappreciable,
evanescent, minute,
inconsiderable, paltry,
small, diminutive, mere,
simple, sheer, scanty,
bare)

immortal-*adj* perpetual,
eternal, everlasting,

perpetuity, continual,
endless, unending,
ceaseless, incessant,
unfading, evergreen,
never-ending, enthrone,
signalize, consecrate,
dedicate, enshrine,
(discredit, disrepute,
dishonor, disgrace,
humiliation, momentary,
sudden, instant, abrupt,
hasty, quick)

immovable-*adj* stable,
unchangeable, constancy,
immobile, soundness,
stiffness, fixture, rock,
pillar, tower, foundation,
permanence, remain firm,
settle, establish,
determined, master over
self, self-control,
perseverance, tenacity,
obstinacy, (vacillating,
unsteady, volatile, frothy,
weak, feeble minded,
inconstancy, versatility,
instability, fluctuation,
vicissitude, alteration,
restless)

impartial-*adj* impartiality,
intelligent, keen acute,
alive, discerning, wise,
sage, sapient, reasonable,
sensible, fair, upright,
straightforward, frank,
candid, conscientious,
scrupulous, (undignified,
partial, disloyal,
untrustworthy, corrupt,
debased, thoughtless,
want of intelligence, week,
feeble minded)

impeach-*v* condemnation,

reflection, disparage,
ostracism, dispraise,
censure, detract,
depreciate, exception,
rebuke, reprehension,
reprobation, admonition,
reproach, reprimand,
castigate, lecture,
disapprove, blame, frown
upon, (approbation,
approval, sanction,
advocacy, esteem, good
opinion, praise, applaud,
commend, compliment,
laudatory)
imperative-*adj* required,
need, necessary,
essential, indispensability,
urgency, prerequisite,
uncompromising, inflexible,
relentless, peremptory,
absolute, unsparing,
ironhanded, oppressive,
ruthless, (moderate,
lenient, moderation,
tolerant, mildness,
forbearing, compassion,
indulge)
imperceptible-*adj* mere,
simple, sheer, stark, bare,
inappreciable, infinitesimal,
diminutive, inconsiderable,
slight, scanty, limited,
meager, sparing,
impalpable, intangible,
invisible, molecular,
rudimentary, embryonic,
(hugeness, enormous,
corpulent, fat, plump,
squab, full, lusty,
strapping, consummate,
excessive, stupendous,
astonishing, inexpressible)

imperious-*adj* command,
reign, dynasty, director,
dictatorship, authority,
influence, patronage,
power, jurisdiction, divine
right, administration,
demagogy, socialism,
feudalism, empire,
monarchy, royalty,
(anarchy, toleration,
remission, lax, loose,
dethrone, depose,
abdicate, remiss, free rein)
impetuous-*adj* boisterous,
violence, inclemency,
vehemence, might,
effervescence, turbulence,
bluster, uproar, riot, row,
rumpus, ferocity, rage,
fury, hastily, precipitately,
helter, skelter, urgency,
acceleration, spurt, forced,
march, rush, (leisure, slow,
deliberate, quiet, calm,
undisturbed, moderation,
gentleness, sobriety, quiet,
calmness, sedative,
lenitive, demulcent, balmy,
tranquilize)
imposition-*n* credulity, gull,
infatuation, self-delusion,
deception, superstition,
simple, green, over-
confident, infringe,
encroach, exact, arrogate,
violate, disfranchise,
invalidate, misbehave,
undue, unlawful, illicit,
unconstitutional,
unwarranted,
unsanctioned, (due to,
privilege, prerogative, right,
prescription, title, claim,

pretension, demand,
incredulous, unbelieving,
inconvincible, distrustful)
impossible-*adj*
impracticable,
unachievable, infeasible,
insurmountable,
incompatible, inaccessible,
impassible, unobtainable,
refuse, rejection, declining,
repulse, rebuff, reject,
deny, decline, protest,
disclaimer, (offer, present,
tender, move, start, invite,
possibility, potentiality,
agree, compatibility,
feasibility, practicability,
perhaps, perchance,
surmountable, accessible,
achievable, within reach)
impoverish-*v* weaken,
debility, relaxation,
languor, impotence,
infirmity, femininity,
fragility, inactivity,
withered, haltered, shaken,
crazy, shaky, palsied,
decrepit, consumption,
expenditure, exhaustion,
dispersion, spend, expend,
use, consume, (provision,
supply, caterer, purveyor,
commissary, feeder,
reinforcement, strong,
might, vigorous, forcible,
hard, adamantine, robust,
sturdy, hardy)
impression-*n* sensation,
excite, aesthetic,
perceptive, conscious,
aware, acute, sharp, keen,
vivid, lively, sharpen,
cultivate, tutor, idea,

notion, conception,
thought, apprehension,
image, sentiment,
reflection, observation,
consideration, theory,
conceit, fancy, fantasy,
imagination, (insensible,
unfeeling, senseless,
callous, hardened, case-
hardened)
impressive-*adj* sensational,
eloquent, vigorous,
nervous, powerful,
command of words, bold,
racy, slashing, pungent,
(feeble, tame, meager,
vapid, dull, dry, languid,
monotonous)
imprint-*v* propagate,
spread, advertise, affix,
type, figure, emblem,
cipher, device, represent,
motto, circumscribe,
enclose, imbedded
improper-*adj* inapt, unapt,
inappropriate, discordant,
hostile, incompatible,
irreconcilable, inconsistent,
unconformable,
exceptional, unjust, unfair,
wrong, encroach,
inequitable, unequal,
partial, unfit, (right, fit,
justice, equity, propriety,
impartiality, reasonable,
legitimate, justifiable)
impudent-*adj* insolence,
haughtiness, arrogance,
airs, overbearance,
domineering, impertinence,
sauciness, flippancy,
petulance, bluster,
swagger, presumption,

usurpation, assurance, audacity, hardihood, front, face, brass, shamelessness, effrontery, assumption of infallibility, (servile, supple, oily, pliant, cringing, fawning, groveling, sniveling, mealy-mouthed, precocious)

impulsive-adj impetus, momentum, push, pulsing, thrust, shove, jog, jolt, brunt, booming, throw, explosion, propulsion, percussion, concussion, collision, clash, encounter, deceptive, illusive, plausible, evasive, hollow, irrelevant, (reason, argue, discuss, debate, dispute, logical, sequence, examine, question, rebound, reflex, reverberation, rebuff, return)

inane-adj nothing, naught, nil, nullity, zero, cipher, no one, nobody, never, no such thing, insubstantiality, nonsense, senseless, inexpressible, undefinable, (intelligent, clearness, explicitness, lucidity, perspicuity, legibility, plain speaking, luminous, transparent)

inaugural-adj precursor, precedent, forerunner, pioneer, prelude, preamble, preface, prologue, preliminary, introductory, (sequel, suffix, successor, trail,

rear, appendix, postscript, codicil, epilogue)

inauspicious-adj untimely, intrusive, unseasonable, out of date, inopportune, timeless, untoward, unlucky, unpropitious, unfortunate, unfavorable, unsuited, inexpedient, hopelessness, despair, desperation, despondency, pessimism, forlorn, (hope, trust, confide, rely on, harbor, indulge, confidence, opportune, timely, well timed, seasonable, providential, lucky, fortunate, happy)

incapable-adj impotence, disability, impiousness, imbecility, inapt, ineptitude, invalidity, inefficiency, incompetence, disqualification, helplessness, prostration, paralysis, palsy, apoplexy, exhaustion, collapse, (capability, capacity, faculty, quality, attribute, endowment, virtue, gift, property, qualification, susceptibility, puissance, might, force)

incase-v cover, superpose, overlay, wrap, face, veneer, pave, bind, cap, coat, paint, incrust, limit, bound, encystment, imprisoned, enshrined, (lining, inner coating, covering, filling, stuffing, padding)

incendiary-adj destructive,

subversive, ruinous, deleterious, suicidal, deadly, with a crushing effect, demolish, dispel, dissipate, consume, squelch, exterminate, devastate, extinguish, burn, inflame, roast, toast, fry, grill, singe, parch, scorch, cauterize, sear, char, incinerate, (cool, fan, refrigerate, refresh, ice, congeal, freeze, glaciate, solidification, produce, establish, constitute, generate)

incessant-*adj* monotonous, harping, iterative, mocking, chiming, repeatedly, often again, over again, once more, ditto, encore, everlasting, continual, endless, ceaseless, (instantaneous, momentary, sudden, instant, abrupt)

incidental-*adj* casual, fortuitous, accidental, adventitious, causeless, contingent, undetermined, indeterminate, possible, unintentional, hap-hazard, random probability, possibility, (attribution, theory, ascribe, impute, explanation, ascription, reference to, rationale, imputation)

inclement-*adj* violence, vehemence, might, impetuosity, boisterousness, effervescence, ebullition, turbulence, bluster, uproar, riot, row, rumpus, severe, ferocity, rage, fury, exacerbation, exasperation, malignity, fit, paroxysm, force, convulsion, (moderating, temperateness, gentleness, sobriety, quiet, relaxation, remission, mitigation, tranquilization, assuagement, contemplation, pacification)

inclusive-*adj* addition, annexation, adjection, supplement, subjunctive, annex, affix, superpose, including, inclusive, component, integral, ingredient, element, constituent, contents, appurtenance, (extraneousness, foreign, alien, intruder, ulterior, excluded, exceptional, deduction, retrenchment)

income-*n* earnings, profit, winnings, proceeds, fruit, crop, harvest, benefit, gaining, acquire, obtain, procure, purchase, inheritance, recovery, retrieval, redemption, salvage, remuneration, wealthy, rich, affluent, opulent, moneyed, (poor, indigent, poverty stricken, impoverished, pauper, ruin, destitution, loss, forfeiture, bereaved, dispossessed, lapse, deprivation)

incurable-*adj* hopeless,
despair, despondency,
forlorn, inconsolable,
cureless, remediless,
incorrigible, irreparable,
irrecoverable, ruined,
undone, immitigable,
(hope, trust, confident,
presumptuous, feed,
foster, nourish, healthy,
sound, hearty, fresh,
unscathed)

indebted-*v* owing, debt,
obligation, liability,
arrears, deficit, default,
insolvency, grateful,
thankfulness,
acknowledgement,
allegiance, dueness,
propriety, fitness, sense of
duty, recognition, binding,
imperative, behooving,
(ungrateful, credit, trust,
tick, score, tally, account,
mortgagee)

indefinite-*adj* uncertain,
incertitude, doubt,
suspense, vague, haze,
fog, obscure, ambiguity,
casual, random, aimless,
changeable, fallible,
questionable, precarious,
disputable, invisible,
imperceptible, indistinct,
concealment, confused,
indistinct, (perceptibility,
conspicuousness,
appearance, exposure,
manifestation, obvious,
recognizable, certain,
necessity, surety,
assurance)

indemnity-*n* compensation,

counteract, balance,
hedge, square, give and
take, compromise, excuse,
exoneration, quitting,
release, acquittal,
conciliation, propitiation,
reprieve, reward,
recompense,
remuneration, (penalty,
retribution, confiscation,
forfeit, revenge,
vengeance, retaliation,
rancor)

indenture-*n* compact,
contract, agreement,
bargain, affidavit, pact,
bond, covenant,
stipulation, settlement,
convention, compromise,
cartel, title, deed, authority,
warrant, credential,
diploma, (unattested,
unauthenticated, check,
destroy, weaken,
contradict, vindicate,
disproof)

indicate-*v* examine, scan,
scrutinize, consider,
inspect, review, rivet,
direct, observe, mean,
signify, express, convey,
imply, bespeak, suggest,
allusive, significant,
symbolism, feature,
diagnostic, recognize,
(without meaning,
senseless, nonsensical,
void, vacant, insignificant,
undefinable)

indigence-*n* insufficiency,
inadequacy,
incompetence, impotence,
deficiency, emptiness,

scarcity, want, need, lack,
poverty, famine, poor,
depletion, vacancy,
(sufficient, enough,
adequate, commensurate,
competent, satisfactory,
valid, tangible, copious,
abundant, abounding,
flush)
individual-n human being,
person, creature, mortal,
body, somebody, earthling,
party, head, personal,
individuality, special,
particular, realize,
designate, determine,
private, characteristic,
originality, (general,
universal, miscellaneous,
generic, broad, collective,
every, all, unspecified)
indomitable-adj strong,
might, vigorous, forcible,
hard, adamantine, stout,
robust, sturdy, hardy,
powerful, potent, puissant,
valid, resistless,
irresistible, invincible,
impregnable,
unconquerable,
determined, resolute,
(vacillating, unsteady,
changeable, cowardly,
facile, pliant, reversible,
weak)
induce-v cause, origin,
source, principle, element,
genesis, procure, draw
down, evoke, entail,
provoke, reason, ground,
call, principle, keystone,
element, consideration,
attraction, magnet,

enticement, allurement,
witchery, cajolery,
seduction, (dissuade,
deport, against,
remonstrate, expostulate,
warn, consequence, result,
upshot, issue, outgrowth)
indulge-v lenient, mild,
gentle, soft, tolerant, easy
going, clement,
compassionate, forbearing,
permission, allow, leave,
sufferance, tolerance,
liberty, law, license,
concession grace, favor,
dispensation, exemption,
connivance, (prohibit,
disallow, veto, embargo,
taboo, restrictive, forbid)
ineffectual-adj useless,
inefficacy, futile, inaptitude,
inadequate, inefficiency,
unskillful, inoperative,
incompetent, superfluous,
dispensable, redundant,
unskillful, inadequate,
incapable, invalid,
helpless, exhaustion,
(capable, effective,
endowed, virtuous,
qualified, powerful, potent)
inert-adj dull, inactivity,
torpor, languor, latency,
sloth, irresolution,
obstinacy, passive,
sluggish, heavy, tame,
slow, blunt, lifeless, dead,
uninfluential, latent,
dormant, smoldering,
insensibility, apathy,
lethargic, neutrality,
vegetation, (sensitive,
impressionable,

enthusiastic, spirited,
excitable)
inexorable-*adj* unavoidable,
necessity, obligation,
compulsive, subjection,
imperious, iron, adverse,
fate, compel, inevitable,
irrevocable, impulsive,
(volition, voluntary, willful,
intended, spontaneity,
original, optional,
discretionary, willing)
inexperience-*n* ignorance,
incomprehensive,
simplicity, unexplored,
uncertainty, incapable,
unknown, bungling,
awkward, clumsy,
maladroit, incompetent,
rusty, without former
knowledge, unskillful,
disqualification, (skill,
dexterity, experience,
accomplish, competence,
talent, capacity)
infatuation-*n* impulsive,
impetuous, passionate,
uncontrolled,
ungovernable,
irrepressible,
inextinguishable, burning,
simmering, volcanic,
vehement, demonstrative,
furious, fierce, over-
zealous, enthusiastic,
impassioned, fanatical,
eager, (submission,
resignation, fortitude, even
tempered, tranquil,
tolerance, patience)
infernal-*adj* bad, hurtful,
virulence, wrong, arrant,
rank, foul, vile,

abominable, detestable,
cursed, confounded,
damned, diabolic,
malevolent, grudge, annoy,
malicious, rancorous,
spiteful, caustic, bitter,
envenomed, acrimonious,
grinding, galling,
(benevolent, benignity,
brotherly love, charity,
sympathy, tenderness,
goodness, excellence,
value, merit, virtue,
superiority)
infidelity-*n* dishonor,
dishonest, disgrace,
fraudulent, faithlessness,
betrayal, degrade,
derogate, stoop, grovel,
sneak, unscrupulous,
contemptible, abject,
untrustworthy, (upright,
honest, virtuous,
honorable, fair, right, just,
equitable, impartial, even
handed, square,
straightforward, honest)
infiltrate-*v* intervene,
interference, introduce,
import, throw, insinuate,
dovetailing, permeation,
passage, transmission,
transudation, ingress,
instill, mix, join, combine,
transfuse, tincture, season,
infect, (eliminate,
purification, simple,
uniform, disentangle,
encompass, beset)
infinitesimal-*adj* small,
little, tenuity, paucity,
fewness, mediocrity,
moderation, vanishing

point, atom, particle,
molecule, diminutive,
minute, inconsiderable,
paltry, unimportant,
slender, meager, few,
inappreciable, evanescent,
mere, (vast, immense,
enormous, extreme,
excessive, preposterous,
monstrous, stupendous,
astonishing, incredible,
marvelous)

influence-n change,
alteration, mutation,
permutation, variation,
modification, modulation,
mood, qualification,
innovation, deviation, turn,
diversion, break,
transformation,
transfiguration, pressure,
preponderance,
dominance, reign,
authority, capability,
interest, power, carry
weight, leverage,
(impotence, inertness,
powerless, irrelevant,
permanence, stability,
persistence, endurance,
persist)

information-n knowledge,
cognizance, acquaintance,
privity, insight, intuition,
familiarity, recognition,
appreciation, light,
enlightenment, learning,
lore, scholarly, conceive,
comprehend, understand,
enlightenment, publicity,
communication, intimation,
notice, representation,
(concealment, hiding,

masquerade, secret,
recondite, ignorance,
uninformed,
unconsciousness,
incomprehension)

infraction-n disobey,
violate, infringe, shirk,
defiance, uncomplying,
unsubmissive, unruly,
insubordinate, resisting,
insurgent, riotous,
unbidden, retraction,
repudiation, protest,
forfeiture, lawlessness,
discard, protest, (observe,
perform, compliance,
obedience, satisfaction,
discharge,
acknowledgement, satisfy,
fulfill, carry out)

infringe-v
transgression, trespass,
encroach, transcendence,
surpass, go beyond,
redundance, strain,
disobey, violate, shirk,
defiance, uncomplying,
(obedient, complying,
loyal, faithful, devoted,
restrainable, resigned,
passive, submissive,
henpecked)

infuse-v mix, alloy,
junction, combination,
impregnation, infiltration,
seasoning, springing,
interlard, instill, imbue,
infiltrate, dash, tinge,
tincture, season sprinkle,
attempter medicate, blend,
(pure, eliminate, sift,
uniform, homogeneous,
single, neat, clear, sheer)

ingrained-*adj* custom,
usage, use, prescription,
practice, prevalence,
observance, conventional,
conformity, rule, standing
order, precedent, routine,
rut, groove, habit,
combine, unite,
incorporate, amalgamate,
embody, absorb,
impregnate,
(decomposition, analysis,
dissection, resolution,
unravel, catalytic, disuse,
unusual)

inhibit-*v* restraint,
hindrance, coercion,
constraint, repression,
discipline, control,
confinement, durance,
duress, imprisonment,
emancipation, limbo,
captivity, blockade,
disallow, interdict,
injunction, embargo, ban,
taboo, proscription,
(permit, allow, sufferance,
tolerance, liberty, law,
admit, authorize, warrant,
sanction, entrust)

injury-*n* impairment,
damage, loss, detriment,
laceration, outrage, havoc,
contamination, canker,
corruption, adulteration,
alloy, decay, dilapidation,
deteriorate, weaken, hurt,
harm, scathe, injurious,
deleterious, malignant,
nocuous, evil, wrong,
(beneficial, valuable,
advantageous, profitable,
edifying, improve,

betterment, mend,
amendment, refine)

inkling-*n* supposition,
assumption, postulation,
condition, hypothesis,
postulate, theory, proposal,
suggestion, conceit, rough
guess, conjecture,
surmise, suspicion, hint,
insinuate, allude, desire,
wish, fantasy, leaning,
(indifferent, neutral,
unconcern, nonchalance,
earnestness, anorexia,
apathy)

innocuous-*adj* good,
harmless, hurt,
unobnoxious, beneficial,
valuable, serviceable,
advantageous, profitable,
edifying, salutary, unerring,
above suspicion,
impeccable, (guilty, blame,
culpable, reprehensible,
enormity, atrocity, outrage,
deadly, malpractice)

inoculate-*v* insert, forcible
ingress, implantation,
introduction, insinuation,
intervention, injection,
importation, infusion,
immersion, submersion,
dip, plunge, interment,
imbed, dovetail, inculcate,
indoctrinate, infuse, instill,
infiltrate, ingraft,
(misinform, misdirect,
misrepresent, render
unintelligible, perversion,
extraction, removal,
elimination, eradication,
extirpation, educe, elicit)

inquisition-*n* inquiry,

request, search, quest,
pursuit, examination,
review, scrutiny,
investigation, indication,
exploration, exploitation,
ventilation, sifting,
calculation, analysis,
dissection, resolution,
study, tyrannical
extortionate, grinding,
withering, oppressive,
ruthless, (lenient, mild,
gentle, soft, tolerant,
indulgent, forbearing,
answer, respond, reply,
rebut, retort, rejoin,
acknowledge, explain)
insidious-*adj* deceitful,
deceived, cunning,
delusive, elusive, covens,
untrue, false, fraudulent,
trick, cheat, wile, blind,
feint, sly, stealthy,
underhanded, hidden,
crooked, shrewd,
(artlessness, simplicity,
innocence, candor,
sincerity, honesty, frank,
open minded, free, plain,
outspoken, downright)
insinuate-*v* cast reflection,
reproach, disapprove,
disparage, condemnatory,
damnify, denunciate,
abusive, objurgatory,
clamorous, vituperative,
defamatory, satirical,
severe, withering,
trenchant, sarcastic,
hypercritical, fastidious,
critical, hint, suggestion,
innuendo, (manifest,
apparent, salient, striking,

demonstrative, prominent,
flagrant, notorious,
approbation, approval,
sanctioned, advocate)
insipid-*adj* tasteless,
savorless, flat, stale, fade,
mild, gutless, ingestible,
mawkish, indifferent, cold,
frigid, lukewarm, cool,
unconcerned, phlegmatic,
easy-going, (avidity,
greediness, covetous,
grasping, craving, voracity,
taste, savor, smack, gusto)
insist-*v* argue, reason,
discuss, debate, dispute,
wrangle, bandy, controvert,
canvass, rational,
argumentative, claim,
warrant, controversial,
dialectic, command, order,
ordinance, act, instruct,
dispatch, demand,
imposition, require, charge,
prescribe, (unreasonable,
illogical, false, unsound,
invalid, unwarranted,
inconsequential)
insolvent-*adj* destitute,
indigence, penury,
pauperism, want, need,
distress, difficulties, needy,
poor, poverty-stricken,
debt, obligation, liability,
arrears, deficit,
impecuniosity, mendicant,
nonpayment, (credit, trust,
tally, account, accredited,
wealth, riches, fortune,
opulence, affluence,
independence)
inspire-*v* encourage, infuse,
give, reassure, embolden,

inspirit, cheer, nerve, put,
enliven, elate, exhilarate,
gladden, animate, raise
the spirits, perk up, give
pleasure, (depress,
discourage, dishearten,
dispirit, damp, dull, deject,
lower, sink, dash, knock-
down)

instance-n example,
specimen, sample,
quotation, exemplification,
illustration, accommodate,
conformity, illustrate,
accordance, cite, quote,
inducement, consideration,
attraction, enticement,
allurement, (disincline,
indispose, shake,
dissuade, remonstrate,
warn, without rhyme or
reason)

instant-n moment, second,
minute, twinkling, flash,
breath, crack, jiffy, burst,
hasty, quick, flash of
lightning, present, actual,
current, important,
consequence, prominence,
consideration, (whenever,
occasion, upon, sooner or
later, perpetual, eternal,
everlasting, immortal,
undying)

instinct-n intellect, mind,
understanding, thinking,
principle, rationality,
faculties, senses,
consciousness,
observation, percipience,
association of ideas,
conception, judgment, wit,
capacity, ability, instinctive,

impulsive, gratuitous,
hazarded, unconnected,
(absence of intellect,
imbecility, argumentative,
controversial, debatable)

institution-n school,
academy, university,
college, seminary, alma
mater, party, faction, side,
denomination, communion,
set, crew, band, society,
association, alliance,
league, legal, legitimate,
link, banded, bonded,
unite, join, associate,
corporation, syndicate,
establishment

instruct-v teach,
edification, education,
tuition, guidance,
qualification, preparation,
discipline, exercise, direct,
guide, impress upon,
convince, expound,
command, message,
direction, requirement,
order, (misinform, mislead,
misrepresent, lie, bewilder,
deceive, mystify)

insult-v rudeness,
discourtesy, ill-breeding,
ungainly manners,
disrespect, impudence,
barbarism, misbehavior,
stern, austerity,
modishness, acrimony,
acerbity, irreverence,
slight, neglect,
supercilious, affront,
(respect, consideration,
regard, courtesy, attention,
deference, reverence,
honor, esteem, veneration,

admiration, approbation)

integrate-v consolidate, whole, totality, integrity, totality, entirety, collectiveness, unity, completeness, integration, aggregate, gross amount, altogether, substantially, (incomplete, deficient, shortcoming, insufficiency, imperfect, defective, unfinished, fractional, fragmentary, sectional, divided)

intensify-v increase, augmentation, enlargement, extension, dilatation, expansion, increment, develop, magnify, enhance, aggravate, exaggerate, exasperate, stimulate, activity, agitation, effervescence, stir, bustle, perturbation, energize, kindle, excite, exert, (inertness, inactive, passive, torpid, sluggish, dull, heavy, uninfluential, decrease, diminish, lessen, shrink, wane)

intercede- v mediate, intercessor, peacemaker, negotiator, diplomat, arbitrate, deprecate, expostulate, protest, negative request, (request, motion, overture, demand, canvass, address, appeal)

interest-n influential, important, weight, prevailing, rampant, dominance, predominant,

curious, inquisitive, stare, gape, lionize, pry, paramount, essential, vital, all-absorbing, radical, cardinal, prime, (indifferent, passive, irrelevancy, uninfluential, powerless)

interlink-v join, junction, union, ligation, allegation, accouplement, marriage, inoculation, assemblage, pivot, hinge, dovetail, encase, graft, entwine, attach, intersect, transversely, cross, braid, knot, twine, twist, (disjoin, disconnect, separate, part, segregate, divorce, division, fracture)

intermediate-adj mean, medium, average, balance, mediocrity, generality, middle, compromise, neutrality, link, connect, hyphen, bracket, bridge, bond, tendon, tendril, intervention, insertion, partition, septum, diaphragm, midriff, (circumference, environment, outskirts, suburbs, precincts)

intermit-adj interrupt, interrupted sequence, discontinue, break, fracture, flaw, fault, suspend, interplay, cease, desist, break off, hold, stop,stick, pause, rest, halt, (continue, persistence, repetition, sustain, unvarying,

unreversed, unrevoked,
unvaried)
interpose-v interject,
intercalated, intersperse,
interweave, intrusive,
(encompass, surround,
circumference, encircle,
embrace, circumvent)
interrupt-v discontinue,
disjunction, break, fault,
pause, disconnect,
unsuccessful, spasmodic,
intermittent, few and far
between, alternation,
patchwork, episode,
cessation, resistance,
suspension, stop, rest, lull,
(continue, persist,
repetition, sustain, uphold,
hold up, perpetuate,
maintain, preserve)
intervene-v mediate,
peacemaker, negotiator,
diplomat, moderate, time,
duration, period, term, last,
endure, remain, persist,
elapse, while, interim,
interval, intermission,
interlude, (circumvent,
around, about, without,
skirt, twine round, lap,
border)
interview-n conference,
interlocution, converse,
conversation,
confabulation, talk,
discourse, verbal
intercourse, oral
communication,
commerce, chatty,
colloquial, parley, gossip,
tattle, visit, call,
assignation, appointment,

(seclusion, privacy,
retirement, reclusion,
estrangement,
sequestered, private, snug,
domestic)
intolerance-n prejudice,
narrow-minded, intolerant,
impracticable, besotted,
infatuated, fanatical,
positive, opinioned,
bigoted, crotchety,
unreasonable,insolent,
impertinence, sauciness,
flippant, petulant, (servile,
obsequious, supple,
mealy-mouthed, settle,
pass, comment,
investigate)
intricate-adj disorder,
derangement, irregularity,
unconformity, confusion,
confusedness, disarray
jumble, huddle, litter,
complexity, complexness,
implication, intricacy,
perplexity, network,
involved, raveled,
entangled, disarrange,
(order, regularity,
uniformity, symmetry,
progression, series,
subordination,
systematically, gradation,
uniform)
intrinsic-adj inbeing,
inherence, inhesion,
subjectiveness, essence,
essentialness, incarnation,
principle, nature,
constitution, character,
type, quality, oral,
documentary, hearsay,
external, extrinsic, internal,

demonstration,
(countervail, rebut, refute,
subvert, destroy, check,
weaken, contravene,
objectiveness,
extraneousness, accident,
incidental, accidental)
introduce-v prefix, place
before, premise, prelude,
preface, preceding, prior,
before, former, foregoing,
aforementioned, prefatory,
introductory, preamble,
prologue, precession,
leading, heading,
precedence, (sequence,
coming after, follower,
attend, beset, succeeding,
sequent)
intrude-v disagree,
discordant, discrepant,
hostile, repugnant,
incompatible,
irreconcilable, inconsistent,
interfere, clash,
intervention, partition,
midriff, interpenetrate,
permeate, introduce,
import, interpose,
(surround, beset,
compass, encompass,
environ, enclose, encircle,
embrace)
inundate-v irrigate, deluge,
syringe, inject, gargle,
drench, douse, dilute, dip,
immerse, merge,
submerge, redundance,
many, super abundance,
saturation, transcendency,
exuberance, profuseness,
accumulation, (dry,
flatulent, effervescent,

atmospheric,
meteorological)
invalid-n powerless,
impotence, disability,
disablement, impiousness,
imbecility, incapacity,
indocility, inefficiency,
incompetence,
disqualification,
helplessness, prostration,
palsy, exhaustion,
inefficacy, failure, (power,
potency, might, force,
energy, ability, capability,
faculty, quality, attribute,
valid)
invariable-adj uniform,
homogeneity, accordance,
agreement, regularity,
constancy, always, without
exception, like clockwork,
symmetry, naturalization,
conventionality, example,
instance, specimen,
typical, normal, illustrative,
(exceptional, abnormal,
unusual, unaccustomed,
rare, varied, diversified,
irregular, uneven, rough,
multifarious, multiformity)
invasion-n attack, assault,
assail, charge, impugn,
aggression, offense,
incursion, inroad, irruption,
outbreak, investment,
obsession, bombardment,
fire, volley, platoon, beset,
besiege, beleaguer,
(defense, protection,
guard, ward, shielding,
preservation, guardianship,
resistance, safeguard)
inversion-n derangement,

disorder, eviction,
discomposure,
disturbance, dislocation,
perturbation, interruption,
corrugation, complicate,
involve, perplex, confound,
tangle, litter, scatter, mix,
(classify, divide, file, string,
together, thread, register,
catalog, tabulate, index,
graduate, digest,
methodize)

invest-v purchasing, buying,
procure, rent, expenditure,
expend, disburse,
circulate, remuneration,
fee, contingent, quota,
(premium, bonus, pension,
annuity, jointure, alimony,
pittance, proceeds)

invoke-v address,
allocution, speech,
apostrophe, interpolation,
appeal,invocation,
salutation, request,
entreat, beseech, plead,
supplicate, implore,
conjure, adjure, obtest,
evoke, impetrate,
imprecate, (deprecation,
expostulation, intercession,
mediation, protest)

involve-v include, contain,
hold, comprehend, take in,
admit, embrace, embody,
implicate, drag into,
compose, constitute, form,
containing, convoluted,
winding, twisted, tortile,
intricate, complicated,
perplexed, (simple
exclusion, omission,
exception, rejection,

repudiation, exile,
separation, segregation,
supposition, elimination,
inadmissible, relegate)

irregular-adj diverse,
unevenness, multiformity,
unconformity, varied,
rough, disorder, anomaly,
disunion, discord,
confusion, disarray,
jumble, complexity,
perplexity, turmoil, ferment,
disturbance, convulsion,
riot, unsymmetrical,
intricate, complicated,
(order, uniformity,
methodical, symmetrical,
uniform, arranged,
economy)

irreparable-adj hopeless,
despair, desperation,
despondency, pessimism,
forlorn, incurable, cureless,
remediless, beyond,
remedy, incorrigible,
unpromising, unpropitious,
threatening, hurtful,
painful, pestilence, hurt,
harm, (beneficial, valuable,
serviceable,
advantageous, profitable,
edifying, salutary, hope,
trust, confidence, reliance,
faith, assurance,
reassurance, security)

irrevocable-adj compulsory,
uncontrollable, inevitable,
unavoidable, inexorable,
involuntary, instinctive,
automatic, blind, stable,
unchangeable, constancy,
established, permanence,
fixed, steadfast, firm, valid,

irremovable, riveted,
rooted, settled,
(changeable, mutable,
variable, vagrant,
alternating)

J

jabber-*v* oquacity,
talkativeness, garrulity,
eloquent, jaw, gabble,
chatter, linguistic,
declamatory, open-
mouthed, fluency,
flippancy, flowing, tongue,
verbosity, stammer,
hesitation, impediment,
stutter, falter, mumble,
(oratory, elocution,
rhetoric, declamation)
jail-*n* bolt, bar, lock,
padlock, rail, prison, gaol,
cage, coop, den, cell,
stronghold, fortress, keep,
dungeon, Bastille,
bridewell, house of
correction, hulks, toll-
booth, penitentiary, guard-
room, (liberate,
disengagement, release,
emancipate, dismiss,
discharge)
jam-*v* squeeze, push,
reduce, extricate, express,
pulp, paste, dough, curd,
pudding, poultice, grume,
sugar, syrup, treacle,
molasses, honey, manna,
confection, nectar, pastry,
pie, (sour, vinegar, styptic)
jar-*v* clash, disagree,
interfere, intrude, discord,
capsule, vesicle, vessel,

pod, bottle, decanter,
ewer, cruise, carafe, crock,
kit, canteen, flagon,
demijohn, jug, pitcher,
mug, kettle, chalice,
tumbler, glass, rummer,
horn, saucepan
jargon-*n* paradox, riddle,
unintelligibility,
incomprehensible,
inconceivable, vagueness,
loose, beyond
comprehension, gibberish,
macaronic, confusion of
tongues, (verbal, literal,
titular, conjugate,
derivative, exact,
concordance, clear, plain
speaking, lucidity,
perspicuity, legibility)
jaundice-*n* yellow,
gamboge, cadmium,
aureate, golden, citron,
fallow, sallow, luteous,
tawny, bias, warped,
twisted, hobby, fad, quirk,
one sided, superficial,
partial, narrow, confined,
(deduce, derive, gather,
collect, judge, umpire,
assessor, discover)
jealousy-*n* envious, covet,
invidious, rival, suspicion,
scruple, qualm, unbeliever,
discredit, dissent, (believe,
credit, indifference,
serene)
jerk-*v* agitate, stir, tremor,
shake, ripple, jolt,
trepidation, quiver, quaver,
dance, disquiet, twitter,
flicker, flutter, traction,
draw, draught, pull, haul,

rake, drag, tug, tow, trail, train, wrench, twitch, tousle, propel, project, throw, fling, cast, pitch, chuck, toss, heave, hurl, flirt, flip, (repulse, repel, abduct, repellent, repulsive, diverge, divaricate, radiate, ramify, diverge)

jetty-n projection, prominent, protuberant, convex, nodular, mammillate, papule, arched, bold, bellied, tuberous, tumorous, cornute, odontoid, in relief, raised, salient, roadstead, anchorage, breakwater, mole, port, haven, harbor, pier, seaport, embankment, quay(precipice, breakers, shoals, shallows, bank, shelf, flat, iron-bound, coast, rock)

jilt-v disappoint, disconcerted, aghast, trick of fortune, deception, falseness, untruth, imposition, fraud, deceit, guile, knavery, misrepresentation, delusion, trick, cheat, deceiver, dissembler, hypocrite, shuffler, wolf in sheep's clothing, (dupe, gull, gudgeon, cull, victim, greenhorn, fool)

jobber-n tactician, genius, master mind, head, spirited, cunning, sharp, cracksman, strategist,

proficient, expert, merchant, trader, dealer, monger, chandler, salesman, changer, shop-keeper, tradesman, retailer, Chapman, hawker, huckster, haggler, peddler, broker, (bungler, blunderer, fumbler, lubber, duffer, awkward,squad, notice, greenhorn)

jockey-n rider, horseman, equestrian, cavalier, rough rider, trainer, breaker, driver, coachman, whip, charioteer, postilion, post boy, carter, waggoner, drayman, cab-man, attendant, squire, usher, page, footboy, train-bearer, waiter, tapster, butler, livery servant, lackey, footman, valet, (master, padrone, lord, paramount, commander, captain, chief, sachems, sheik, runner, courier, pedestrian)

jog-v push, walk, march, step, tread, pace, plod, wend, promenade, trudge, tramp, stalk, stride, straddle, strut, foot it, stump, bundle, bowl along, toddle, paddle, roving, vagrancy, marching and countermarching, nomad, vagabondism, migration

join-v connect, union, attachment, attach, fix, affix, fasten, bind, secure, clinch, twist, pinion, string, strap, sew, lace, stitch, tack, knit, gird, tether,

moor, harness, chain,
fetter, firm, fast, close,
tight, taut, group, cluster,
accumulation, assemble,
compile, associate,
(disperse, dissipate,
distribute, apportionment,
spread, cut, scatter, sow,
disseminate, diffuse,
separate, parting, detach)

jolt-v impulse, impetus,
momentum, push, pulsing,
thrust, shove, jog, brunt,
booming, throw, strike,
knock, tap, rap, slap, flap,
dab, pat, thump, beat,
bang, slam, dash, punch,
thwack, whack, hit,
agitate, shake, convulse,
toss, tumble, (recoil,
revulsion, rebound,
reflection, reflex, reflux,
reverberation, rebuff,
repulse, return)

journal-n almanac,
calendar, register,
chronicle, annals, diary,
chronogram, record, note,
memorandum,
endorsement, inscription,
copy, duplicate, docket,
affidavit, certificate,
gazette, newspaper,
magazine, calendar,
ephemeris, diary, log,
archive, scroll, (efface,
obliterate, erase, scratch,
delete, unregistered,
undocumented, without)

judgment-n instinct,
conception, wits, capacity,
intellect, understanding,
reason, rationality,

cogitative, faculties,
senses, observation,
intuition, discrimination,
distinction, differentiation,
(indiscrimination,
uncertainty, indistinctness,
imbecility, without reason)

judicial-adj judge, tribunal,
municipality, bailiwick,
officer, bailiff, sit in
judgment, magistrate,
authority, prefiguration,
auspices, forecast, omen,
prognostication,
premonition, (weak, feeble
minded, fatuous, idiotic,
imbecile, blatant, babbling,
bewildered)

jump-v sudden change,
transilience, leap, plunge,
jerk, start, explosion,
spasm, convulsion, throe,
revulsion, cataclysm, hop,
spring, bound, vault,
saltation, frisky, skip,
dance, caper, curvet,
flounce, start, agitation,
(submerge, douse, sink,
engulf, send to the bottom,
plunge, dip, souse, duck)

jury-n judge, justice,
chancellor, recorder,
magistrate, jurat, assessor,
arbiter, arbitrator, umpire,
referee, archon, tribune,
scapegoat, stop-gap

K

keen-adj strong, energetic,
forcible, active, intense,
severe, vivid, sharp, acute,
incisive, trenchant, brisk,

rousing, irritating, poignant, virulent, caustic, mordant, harsh, stringent, double-edged, (inertness, dull, inert, inactivity, torpor, languor, inaction, lithe, passive, heavy, flat)

keep-v retain, retention, custody, tenacity, firm hold, grasp, grip,clutches, tongs, forceps, pincers, undisposed, tenacious, preserve, safe keeping, conserve, maintain, support, sustentation, salvation, hygienic, (relinquish, abandonment, renunciation, expropriation, dereliction, surrender, dispensation, resignation, riddance, jettison, discard)

key-n opener, perforate, wide open, ajar, gaping, patent, tubular, aperient, cause, origin, source, element, principle, occasioned, pivot, hinge, turning-point, lever, proximate cause, ground, reason, rationale, (derived, derivative, hereditary, dependent upon, owing to, resulting from, due to, closure, occlusion, blockade, shutting up. obstruction,hindrance, plug, block, cork, bar, shut)

kick-v assault, thrust, lunge, pass, push, cut, fire, volley, assail, strike, impulse, whip,attack, aggressive, strike out, fling, insolent, flippant, pert, forward,

impertinent, (defense, protect, guard, ward, shield, self-defense, preservation, resistance, safeguard, repel, stand one's ground)

kidnap-v take, reception, deglutition, appropriation, prehension, presentation, capture, apprehension, seizure, abduction, subtraction, abstraction, confiscation, eviction, rapacity, extortion, clutch, swoop, wrench, grip, haul, take, catch, scramble, (return, restitution, restoration, reinvestment, recuperation, release, give up, bring back, recoup, reimburse, recuperate, recover, revert)

kill-v destroy, violent death, homicide, manslaughter, murder, assassination, massacre, mortal, fatal, lethal, dead, deathly, suicidal, strangle, smother, kill with kindness, consume, burn, idle, trifle, (life, vivacity, spirit, dash, energy, animation)

kindle-v excite, affect, touch, move, impress, strike interest, animate, inspire, impassion, smite, infect, stir, provoke, raise up, summon up, arouse, fire, enkindle, apply the torch, sent on fire, inflame, stimulate, produce, work, handiwork, fabric, performance, creature, upshot, develop, (tranquil, passive, impassibility, coolness, unexcitable, imperturbable, dispassionate, sedate)

king-_n_ potentate, sovereign, monarch, despot, tyrant, crowned head, emperor, majesty, protector, president, judge, empire, royalty, regal, dominant, paramount, supreme, influential, imperial, stringent, (absence of authority, anarchy, relaxation, loosening, remission, misrule, insubordination, depravation of power, remiss, unwarranted)

kiss-_v_ endearment, caress, embrace, salute, smack, buss, osculation, courtship, wooing, suit, philander, flirt, obeisance, bow, courtesy, curtsy, scrape, loving, love token, (repulsive, noncomplacent, accommodating, gallant, ungentle, rough,rugged, bluff, blunt, gruff, tart, sour, surly)

kleptomania-_n_ steal, theft, thievery, robbery, deception, abstraction, pillage, light-fingered, piratical, predaceous, plunder, rifle, sack, loot, ransack, spoil, spoilt, despoil, strip, monomania, eccentricity, fanaticism, infatuation, craze, oddity, (sane, rational, generous,

restitution, return, restore, reimburse, reforge, recoup, redeem, recuperate, remit, rehabilitate)

knavery-_n_ deception, falseness, untruth, imposition, fraud, guile, misrepresentation, delusion, gullible, conjuring, cunning, craftiness, subtlety, chicanery, juggler, concealment, sharp practice, (natural, pure, native, simple, plain, inartificial, untutored, unsophisticated, unaffected, sincere, frank, open)

knee-_n_ angular, bent, crooked, aduncous, uncinate, aquiline, jagged, serrated, furcate, forked, dovetailed, knock-kneed, obeisance, homage, genuflection, courtesy, curtsy, prostration, kneel to, (deprecation, expostulation, intercession)

know-_v_ knowledge, cognizance, acquaintance, privily, insight, familiarity, appreciation, intuition, consciousness, conceive, comprehend, take, realize, understand, aware, ascertained, (ignorance, shallow, superficial, green, rude, empty, half-learned, illiterate, unread, uninformed, empty-headed)

kowtow-v bow, depress, lower, take-down, subvert, prostrate, level, fell, cast, genuflection, obeisance, surrender, succumb, submit, yield, bend, resign, (elevate, raise, lift, sublimation, exaltation, prominence, heighten, erect)

L

labor-n work, action, performance, perpetration, movement, operation, evolution, procedure, execution, handicraft, business, deed, act, transaction, job, doings, dealings, proceeding, measure, achieve, inflict, (indolent, lazy, slothful, idle, lust, remiss, slack, inert, torpid, sluggish, languid, supine, heavy, dull leaden, lumpish, listless, dilatory, laggard)

lack-n insufficient, inadequate, impotence, deficiency, imperfection, shortcoming, paucity, stint, scantiness, scarcity, dearth, want, need, poverty, exigency, inanition, starvation, famine, drought, dole, pittance, short-allowance, (sufficient, adequate, enough, satisfaction, competence, fullness, abundance, copiousness, galore, lots, profusion, full measure, rich, luxuriant, ample)

lackadaisical-adj indifferent, cold, frigid, lukewarm, cool, unconcerned, insouciant, phlegmatic, easy-going, devil-may care, careless, listless, half-hearted, unambitious, unaspiring, unsolicitous, inactive, dilatory, laggard, lagging, slow, tottering, irresolute, (active, briskness, liveliness, animation, life, vivacity, spirit, dash, eager, quick, prompt, instant, ready, alert, spry, sharp, spry)

ladle-n receptacle, shovel, trowel, spoon, spatula, watch-glass, thimble, receiver, cup, goblet, chalice, soup, decant, draft off, transfuse, spoon, hod, paddle, hoe, spade, spud

lag-v linger, slow, retard, relax, slacken, check, moderate, slack, tardy, dilatory, inactive, gentle, easy, leisurely, deliberate, gradual, insensible, imperceptible, languid, sluggish, slow-paced, tardigrade, snail-like, creeping, follow, attendant, shadow, dangler, get behind, (lead, in advance, before, ahead, precede, forerun, introduce)

lame-adj incomplete, imperfect, defective, deficient, wanting, failing,

meager, half and half,
perfunctory, sketch, crude,
mutilated, garbled, lopped,
truncated, helplessness,
prostration, paralysis,
palsy, apoplexy, syncope,
collapse, exhaustion,
emasculation, (ability,
ableness, togetherness,
faculty, quality, attribute,
endowment, virtue, gift,
property, qualification,
susceptibility, valid,
effective)
lampoon-*n* censure, scoff
at, point at, twit, taunt,
satirize, defame,
depreciate, find fault with,
criticize, disparaging,
condemnatory, damnify,
denunciatory, reproachful,
abusive, objurgatory,
clamorous, vituperative,
defamatory, satirical,
sarcastic, sardonic, cutting,
severe, hypercritical,
(applaud, praise, laud,
good work, homage,
blessing, benediction,
plaudit, shout, approval)
lance-*n* pierce, perforate,
tap, bore, drill, mine,
tunnel, enfilade, impale,
spike, spear, gore, spit,
stab, puncture, stick, prick,
riddle, punch, shooter,
shot, archer, propel,
project, throw, dart, tilt,
fling, cast, pitch, chuck,
toss, jerk, heave,
(repulsion, repulse,
abduction, dispel, abduct,
repellent, keep at arms's

length, send away)
land-*n* arrive, reach, attain,
get to, come to, overtake,
light, alight, dismount,
debark, disembark, here,
hither, detrain, welcome,
converge, meet,
completion, earth, ground,
continent, coast, shore,
mainland, peninsula, delta,
soil, globe, clay, loam,
acres, real estate, (ocean,
brine, water, waves,
departure, cessation,
decampment,
embarkation, outset, start,
exit, egress, exodus,
farewell)
landscape-*n* agriculture,
management of plants,
cultivation, husbandry,
farming, gardening,
horticulture, floriculture,
ornamental, flower garden,
vineyard, till, scenery,
dress the ground,
undeformed, undefaced,
unspotted, (deformed,
defaced, ugly, uninviting)
languid-*adj* weak, poor,
infirm, fantasia, sickly, dull,
slack, spent, short-winded,
effete, weatherbeaten,
decayed, rotten, worn,
seedy, wasted, washy, laid
low, pulled down, frail,
fragile, shatter,
decrepit,feeble, debilitate,
impotent, soft, effeminate,
femininity, womanly,
colorless, (strength, power,
stoutness, strong, might,
vigorous, forcible, hard,

adamantine, stout, robust,
sturdy, hardy)
lap-*n* abode, dwelling,
lodging, domicile,
residence, address,
habitation, berth, seat,
sojourn, housing, quarters,
head-quarters, residence,
tabernacle, throne, ark,
supporter, aid, prop, stand,
anvil, stay, shore, skid, rib,
truss, bandage, sleeper,
stirrup, stilts, shoe, heel,
splint, bar, rod, (suspend,
loose, flowing, hang, slip,
hitch, fasten to, append)
lapidate-*v* kill, homicide,
manslaughter, murder,
assassination, attack,
assault, onset, onslaught,
charge, aggression,
offense, incursion, inroad,
cut, thrust, fire, volley,
platoon, (defend, protect,
guard, ward, shield,
preservation, guardianship,
fortify, resistance)
lapse-*n* elapse, course,
progress, process,
succession, flow, flux,
stream, tract, current, tide,
march, run, expire,
duration, past, gone, gone
by, over, passed away,
bygone, foregone, expired,
exploded, forgotten,
former, pristine, (future,
hereafter, approaching,
prospectively, hereafter,
tomorrow, eventually,
ultimately)
large-*adj* quantity, vast,
immense, enormous,

extreme, inordinate,
excessive, extravagant,
exorbitant, outrageous,
preposterous,
unconscionable, swinging,
monstrous, big, great,
considerable, bulky,
voluminous, ample,
massive, mass, capacious,
comprehensive, spacious,
might, towering, fine,
magnificent, (dwarf,
pygmy, chit, minute,
diminutive, microscopic,
inconsiderable, exiguous,
puny)
lash-*v* enforce, force, impel,
push, propel, whip, goad,
spur, prick, urge, hurry-on,
exhort, advise, advocate,
impulsive, seductive,
attractive, fascinating,
provocative, exciting,
violent, vehement, warm,
acute, sharp, rough, rude,
ungentle, bluff, boisterous,
impetuous, rampant,
turbulent, (moderation,
lenitive, gentleness, quiet,
mental calmness, sobriety,
relaxing, remission,
mitigation, tranquilization,
pacification)
last-*n* final, end, close,
termination, dissonance,
conclusion, period, term,
extreme, verge,
consummation, finish,
conclude, expire, definitive,
ending, durable, lasting,
standing, permanent,
chronic, long-standing,
macrobiotic, perpetual,

lingering, (transient,
impermanence, temporary,
brief, quick, brisk,
extemporaneous,
summary, sudden,
momentary)
laud-*v* praise,
commendation, approval,
sanction, advocacy,
esteem, good opinion,
admiration, love, worship,
benediction, blessing, clap,
cheer, hosanna,
compliment,
complimentary, uncritical,
lavish of praise,
(disapprove, dislike,
lament, reprehension,
remonstrance,
expostulation, admonition,
reproach, rebuke,
reprimand, castigation,
lecture, curtain lecture,
blow up)
laugh-*v* ridicule, derision,
sardonic, smile, grin,
scoffing, mockery, quiz,
banter, irony, squib, satire,
skit, quip, quibble, grin,
parody, burlesque, satirize,
caricature, travesty, giggle,
titter, snigger, cheer,
chuckle, shout, (lament,
wail, complaint, plaint,
murmur, mutter, grumble,
groan, moan, whine,
whimper, sob, sigh,
suspiration, mourning,
condolence, deplore,
grieve)
launch-*v* beginning,
commencement, opening,
outset, incipience,

inception, introduction,
initial, inauguration,
embarkation, outbreak,
fresh start, origin, source,
rise, bud, germ, egg,
genesis, birth, nativity,
cradle, start, (end, close,
termination, dissonance,
conclusion, period, term,
extreme, consummation,
finish)
lavish-*adj* profuseness,
redundance, too much,
super abundance,
inordinate, excessive,
replete, prodigal,
overweening, extravagant,
overcharged,
supersaturated, drenched,
overflowing, superfluous,
(receive, take, catch,
miser, waste, scrubby,
touch, acquire, reception,
susceptibility, release)
law-*n* statute, rule, canon,
code, rubric, stage,
regulation, technicality,
precept, direction,
instruction, prescription,
receipt, golden rule,
maxim, permit, give
permission, grant,
empower, charter,
enfranchise, privilege,
license, authorize, warrant,
sanction, entrust,
(disallowance, interdiction,
injunction, embargo, ban,
taboo, proscription,
restriction, hindrance,
forbid, disallow, bar,
forefend)
lax-*adj* slackness, loose,

toleration, anarchy,
interregnums, loosening,
remission, dead, letter,
misrule, dethrone, depose,
abdicate, careless, weak,
free rein, unbridled,
unauthorized, (authority,
influence, patronage, hold,
rasp, grip, reach, clutch,
talons, power,
preponderance, credit,
jurisdiction)

lazy-*adj* inactive, inertness,
obstinacy, idle, remiss,
sloth, indolence,
indulgence, dawdling,
languor, sluggishness,
procrastination, torpidity,
somnolence, drowsiness,
drone, droll, nothingness,
slow, slack, moderate,
linger, loiter, tortoise,
(active, brisk, liveliness,
animation, life, vivacity,
spirit, dash, energy,
nimbleness)

lead-*v* direct, management,
government, gubernatorial,
conduct, legislate,
regulate, guide, steer, pilot,
administer, prescribe, cut
out work for, head, show
the way, authority,
influence, patronage,
power, jurisdiction,
despotism, command, (lax,
loose, slackness,
toleration, freedom,
loosening, remission,
misrule, relax, unbridled,
unauthorized, dethrone,
depose, abdicate)

leak-*n* crack, interval,

interspace, separation,
break, gap, opening, hole,
chasm, interruption, cleft,
mesh, crevice, chink,creek,
cranny, chap, slit, fissure,
scissure, rift, flaw, breach,
gorge, defile, transude, run
out, strain, distill, perspire,
sweat, filter, filtrate,
dribble, gush, spout, flow,
(excretion, discharge,
emanation, exhalation,
exudation, extrusion,
contiguity, contact,
proximity, apposition, join,
adjoin, graze, meet,
osculate, coincide, adhere,
touching)

lean-*adj* thin, narrowness,
closeness, exiled, exiguity,
tenuity, emaciation,
shaving, slip, skeleton,
shadow, anatomy, spindle,
meager, gaunt, tendency,
aptness, proneness,
proclivity, bent, turn, tone,
bias, set, (breadth, width,
latitude, amplitude,
diameter, bore, caliber,
radius, superficial,
thickness, corpulence,
dilation, wide, broad,
ample, extended, thick)

leap-*v* sudden change,
revolution, subversion,
break up, destruction,
radical, sweeping,
transilience, jump, plunge,
jerk, start, explosion,
spasm, convulsion, throe,
revulsion, storm, ascent,
ascension, rising, rise,
upgrowth, acclivity, hill,

rocket, lark, sky-rocket,
ascend, rise, mount, climb,
clamber, ramp, scramble,
(descent, dissension,
declination, fall, drop,
cadence, subsidence)

leave-*v* fissure, breach,
rent, split, rift, crack, slit,
incision, fission, dissection,
anatomy, disjoin,
disconnect, disengage,
sunder, divide, sever,
abscind, relinquish,
abandon, defection,
secession, withdrawal,
discontinuance,
renunciation, abrogation,
resignation, (arrive,
reunion, remain,
confinement, restrict,
forbid, hindrance, taboo,
embargo, ban)

leaven-*n* component,
integral, element,
constituent, ingredient, part
and parcel, contents,
appurtenance, feature,
member, to be implicated
in, cause, origin, source,
principle, element, agent,
groundwork, foundation,
(effect, consequence,
result, upshot, issue,
produce, work, handiwork,
fabric, performance,
creature)

ledge-*n* shelf, support,
ground, foundation, base,
basis, bearing, fulcrum,
footing, prop, stand, anvil,
shore, skid, rib, truss,
bandage, stirrup, stilts,
tower, pillar, column,

obelisk, monument,
steeple, spire, escarpment,
edge, brae, height,
(lowness, neap, debased,
nether, flat, level with the
ground)

left-*adj* residuary,
remaining, remainder,
residue, remnant, rest,
relic, leavings, heel-tap,
odds and ends, surplus,
overplus, excess,
complement, sinistrality,
left-handed, port, (dextral,
right-handed,
ambidextrous, adjunct,
affix, appendage,
reinforcement,
accompaniment, adjective)

leg-*n* support, travel,
wayfaring, journey,
excursion, expedition, tour,
trip, grand tour, circuit,
peregrination, discursion,
ramble, pilgrimage, course,
ambulation, march, step,
tread, pace, plod, wend,
promenade

legal-*adj* permit, leave,
allow, sufferance,
tolerance, liberty, law,
license, concession, grace,
indulgence, favor,
dispensation, exemption,
release, connivance,
vouchsafement,
authorization, warranty,
accordance, admission,
warrant, sanction, (forbid,
prohibit, disallowance,
injunction, embargo, ban,
taboo, hindrance, bar,
forefend)

legend-_n_ record, trace, vestige, transactions, proceedings, debates, chronicles, annals, history, biography, tabulation, entry, booking, signature, identification, recorder, journalism, register, (efface, obliteration, erasure, cancellation, circumscribe, deletion, expunge, cancel, blot, deface)

legion-_n_ multitude, numerousness, multiplicity, profusion, host, enormous number, array, sight, army, sea, galaxy, scores, peck, bushel, shoal, armed force, troops, soldiery, military, standing army, volunteers, (few, paucity, small number, small quantity, rarity, infrequency, handful, minority, thin)

leisure-_n_ spare time, slow, deliberate, quiet, calm, undisturbed, slack, tardy, dilatory, gentle, easy, gradual, insensible, imperceptible, languid, sluggish, slow-paced, tardigrade, creeping, (speed, velocity, celerity, swiftness, rapidity, expedition, eagle speed, haste, spurt, dash, race, lively)

lend-_v_ loan, advance, accommodation, federation, mortgage, investment, pawnbroker, money lender, usurer, advance, intrust, invest, let, lease, demise, aid, assistance, help, support, lift, patronage, countenance, favor, interest, advocacy, (prevention, preclusion, obstruction, stoppage, interruption, restriction, borrow, pledge, hire, rent, farm brace, touch, hold up)

lenient-_adj_ moderate, temperateness, gentleness, sobriety, quiet, mental calmness, relaxation, remission, mitigation, tranquilization, assuagement, contemplation, pacification, measure, (violence, inclemency, vehemence, might, impetuosity, boisterousness, uproar, riot, severity)

lessen-_v_ decrease, subtraction, reduction, abatement, declination, shrinking, abridgment, diminish, abridge, shrink, fall away, waste, wear, wane, ebb, decline, subside, compression, compactness, collapse, emaciation, atrophy, (expansion, enlargement, extension, augmentation, growth, development, increase, additional, undiminished, exaggerate, exasperate)

let-_v_ permit, leave, allow, tolerance, liberty, law, license, concession, grace,

indulgence, favor,
dispensation, exemption,
release, connivance,
vouchsafement,
authorization, warranty,
lend, advance,
accomodate, (prohibition,
disallowance, borrow,
interdict, injunction,
embargo, ban, taboo,
restriction, release,
hindrance, exclusive)

lethargic-adj inactivity,
inaction, inertness,
obstinacy, drowsiness,
nodding, hypnotism,
heaviness, sleep, coma,
trance, nap, doze, snooze,
relaxation, idle, drone,
droll, dawdle, insensibility,
(active, briskness,
liveliness, animation, life,
vivacity, spirit, dash,
energy, nimbleness, agility,
quickness)

letter-n mark, character,
hieroglyphic, writing,
printing, abc's, consonant,
vowel, diphthong, mute,
liquid, labial, dental

levity-n lightness,
imponderability, buoyancy,
volatility, feather, dust,
mote, down, thistle down,
flue, cobweb, gossamer,
straw, cork, bubble, float,
ether, air, leaven ferment,
barm, yeast, (gravity,
weight, heaviness, specific
gravity, ponderous,
pressure, load, burden,
ballast, counterpoise, lead)

libation-n drunkenness,

intemperance, drinking,
inebriety, insobriety,
intoxication, tipsy, sot,
potable, draught, carousel,
nourishment, sustenance,
nurture, (excretion,
discharge, exhalation,
exudation, extrusion,
secretion, sobriety,
teetotaler)

liberty-n freedom,
independence, immunity,
exemption, emancipation,
franchise, liberalism,
permission, leave, allow,
sufferance, tolerance, law,
concession, grace,
indulgence, favor,
dispensation, release,
(prohibit, disallowance,
interdict, unlicensed,
contraband, subjection)

lick-v eat, feed, fare,
devour, swallow, take,
gulp, bolt, snap, dispatch,
pick, peck, crunch, chew,
masticate, nibble, gnaw,
mumble, strike, deal a
blow to, smite, slap, face,
smack, (discharge,
emanation, exhalation,
exudation, extrusion,
secretion, effusion, saliva,
outpour)

limbo-n purgatory, hell,
bottomless pit, place of
torment, everlasting fire,
torment, Gehenna, abyss,
inferno, mental suffering,
pain, ache, smart,
displeasure, vexation of
spirit, (pleasure,
gratification, enjoyment,

fruition, relish, zest,
satisfaction, heavenly,
paradise, eden, celestial)
limit-*n* restrain, hindrance,
restraint, coercion,
constraint, repression,
discipline, control,
confinement, durance,
duress, imprisonment, end,
close, termination,
conclusion, finish, (begin,
commence, originate,
conceive, initiate, open,
dawn, liberation,
disengagement, free,
deliverance)
linear-*adj* continuity,
consecutive, progressive,
gradual, serial, successive,
immediate, unbroken,
entire, uninterrupted,
unremitting, perennial,
paternity, parentage,
consanguinity, maternal,
family, ancestral,
patriarchal, (discontinue,
pause, interrupt, intervene,
break, disconnect, break)
liniment-*n* ointment,
linseed, unguent,
glycerine, stearin, grease,
suet, remedy, help,
redress, antidote,
antiseptic, corrective,
restorative, sedative,
physic, medicine, drug,
potion, (bane, curse, evil,
hurtfulness, painfulness,
scourge, sting, fang, thorn)
link-*n* pin, nail, bolt, hasp,
clasp, clamp, screw, rivet,
impact, solder, set, weld,
fuse-together, wedge,

rabbet, mortise, mire, jam,
dovetail, encase, graft,
ingraft, inosculate, close,
tight, taut, (sunder, divide,
subdivide, sever, dissever,
abscind, saw, snip, nib,
nip, cleave, rive, rend, slit)
lion-*n* courage, hero,
demigod, tiger, panther,
bull-dog, prowess,
heroism, chivalry,
manliness, nerve, pluck,
mettle, game, spunk, face,
virtue, prodigy,
phenomenon, potent,
(coward, timidity,
effeminacy, poltroonery,
baseness, dastardliness,
sneak, recreant, shy)
liquid-*n* fluid, inelastic,
liquor, humor, juice, sap,
serum, blood, serosal,
succulent, sappy, flowing,
soluble, lymph,
(atmospheric, airy, aerial,
meteorological weather-
wise, ventilate, climate)
list-*n* catalog, inventory,
schedule, register,
account, file, index, book,
ledger, synopsis, bill of
lading, prospectus,
statistics, directory, score
listless-*adj* inattentive,
inconsiderateness, absent,
abstracted, lost,
preoccupied, engrossed,
napping, dreamy,
disconcerted, (attention,
mindfulness, observance,
consideration, notice,
regard)
literary-*adj* lingual, dialectic,

vernacular, polyglot, book,
writing, work, volume,
publication, portfolio,
periodical, style, diction,
phraseology, wording,
manner, strain, literary
litigation-*n* citation,
arraignment, prosecution,
impeachment, accusation,
apprehension, arrest,
committal, writ, summons,
subpoena, strife, warfare,
outbreak, disagreement,
variance, difference,
(concord, accord,
harmony, symphony,
agreement, sympathy,
response, union, unison)
litter-*n* disorder, irregularity,
anomaly, unconformity,
anarchy, confusion,
disarray, jumble, huddle,
lumber, mess, mash,
hodgepodge, (order,
regularity, uniformity,
symmetry, gradation,
progression, series,
subordination, routine,
method, disposition)
little-*adj* small, quantity,
vanishing,diminutive,
minute, inconsiderable
paltry, faint, unimportant,
weak, slender, light, slight,
scanty, scant, limited,
mere, simple, sheer, stark,
bare, dwarf, pygmy, chit,
(corpulent, stout, fat,
plump, squab, full, lusty,
strapping, bouncing, portly,
burly, huge, immense)
live-*v* exist, being, entity,
subsistence, reality,

actuality, positiveness,
fact, matter of fact, real,
actual, absolute, true,
permanence, persistence,
endurance, standing,
maintenance, present,
occupying, inhabiting,
dwell, reside, stay, sojourn,
abide, lodge, (absence,
inexistent, empty, void,
vacant, inexistent,
extinction, annihilate,
nullify, abrogate, destroy,
negative, blank, missing)
livery-*n* outfit, equipment,
uniform, regimentals,
canonical, gear, harness,
turn out, accouterment,
caparison, suit, rigging,
trappings, traps, slops,
masquerade, color, hue,
tint, tinge, dye,
complexion, shade,
tincture, cast, coloration,
glow, flush, tone, key,
(hueless, pale, pallid,
muddy, leaden, nudity,
bareness, undress,
dishabille, molting,
exfoliation, divest, uncover,
denude)
load-*n* cargo, contents,
lading, freight, shipment,
bale, shipload, stuff,
oppress, care, anxiety,
solicitude, trouble, trial,
fiery ordeal, shock, blow,
dole, fret, burden,
(pleasure, gratification,
enjoyment, fruition, relish,
zest, gusto, satisfaction,
complacency, well-being)
loadstar-*n* motion toward,

attraction, pulling toward,
adduction, magnetism,
gravity, siderite, beacon,
cairn, seamark, lighthouse,
guide, address, direction, ·
heliograph
loathe-v dislike,
repugnance, disgust,
queasiness, turn, nausea,
averseness, antipathy,
abhorrence, horror, hatred,
detestation, animosity,
hydrophobia, insulting,
irritating, provoking,
abomination, aversion,
(love, fondness, liking,
inclination, affection,
sympathy, tenderness)
local-adj location,
lodgement, reposition,
stow, package, settlement,
installation, fixation,
insertion, anchorage,
mooring, encampment,
plantation, colony, place,
situate, locate, localize,
station, house,
(displacement,
transposition, eject, exile,
removal, dislocation,
unload, empty)
lock-v fasten, attach, fix,
affix, bind, secure, clinch,
twist, string, strap, firm,
close, knot, shackle, rein,
padlock, rivet, stake, hook,
latchet, resistance, stand,
front, oppugnant,
opposition, reluctant,
(separate, parting,
detachment, segregation,
divorce, divide, unlock,
detach, isolate)

locomotion-n moving,
stream, flow, flux, run,
course, evolution,
kinematics, step,
transitory, shifting,
movable, mobile,
mercurial, restless,
nomadic, erratic, cadence,
(quiet, tranquility, calm,
repose, peace, dead calm,
immobility, fixed, stay,
stagnate, rest, pause, lull)
lodge-n location, place,
situate, locate, localize,
put, lay, set, seat, station,
quarter, post, install,
house, stow, establish, fix,
pin, root, graft, plant,
people, inhabit, dwell,
reside, stay, sojourn, live,
abide, nestle, present,
(absent, missing, empty,
void, vacant, devoid,
truant, displacement)
lofty-adj height, altitude,
elevation, eminence, pitch,
sublimity, colossus, tall,
gigantic, Patagonian,
vehement, impassioned,
poetic, eloquent, petulant,
(feeble, tame, meager,
vapid, trashy, cold, frigid,
dull, dry, monotonous,
weak, careless, inexact)
log-n fuel, firing,
combustible, coal,
anthracite, culm, coke,
carbon, charcoal, turf,
peat, firewood, bobbing,
faggot, cinder, record,
note, minute, register, roll,
list, entry, memorandum,
document, deposition,

affidavit, certificate,
(efface, obliterate, erase,
expunge, cancel, blot,
scratch)
long-*adj* durable, lasting,
permanent, chronic, long-
standing, protracted,
prolonged, lengthy, drawn
out, profuse, verbose,
copious, exuberant,
rambling, broad, wide,
ample, extended, thick,
dumpy, streak,
outstretched, elongate,
extend, stretch, (short,
little, abbreviated, brief,
curt, compact, stubby,
temporary, cursory, short-
lived, deciduous, mortal,
summary, concise, terse)
longevity-*n* age, oldness,
senility, anility, climacteric,
declining years,
decrepitude, caducity,
seniority, eldership,
matronly, anile, ripe,
mellow, wrinkled, (youth,
juvenility, cradle, nursery,
green, budding)
longitude-*n* situation,
position, locality, status,
footing, standing,
standpoint, post, stage,
aspect, attitude, posture,
place, site station, seat,
length, span, linear,
measure of length,
(shortness, brevity,
littleness, shortening,
abbreviation, abridgment,
concision, retrenchment,
curtailment)
look-*v* see, vision, sight,

view, glance, glimpse,
peep, gaze, stare, leer,
contemplation, squint,
visual, ocular, optic,
appear, aspect, phase,
guise, complexion, color,
image, apparent, seeming,
ostensible, (invisible,
imperceptible, conceal,
blind, sightless)
loop-hole-*n* hole,
perforation, opening, vent,
orifice, path, thoroughfare,
escape, avocation,
elopement, flight, evasion,
retreat, narrow, hair-
breadth, impunity,
reprieve, livery, liberation,
refugee, elude, (closure,
occlusion, blockade,
shutting up, obstruction,
plug, block, shut, bolt,
stop, seal, unopened)
loose-*adj* detach, sunder,
divide, subdivide, sever,
dissever, abscind, saw,
snip, nib, nip, cleave,
rupture, shatter, shiver,
lacerate, scramble,
mangle, gash, hash, slice,
whittle, carve, dissect,
liberate, disengagement,
release, enlargement,
emancipation,
enfranchisement,
discharge, dismissal,
(restraint, hindrance,
coercion, compulsion,
constraint, repression,
discipline, control)
lose-*v* loss, depredation,
forfeiture, lapse, privation,
bereavement, deprivation,

dispossession, riddance,
lost, irretrievable,
hopeless, farewell, adieu,
failure, miscarriage,
repulse, rebuff, defeat, fall,
downfall, defeat, rout,
overthrow, (success,
fulfillment, advance,
progress, surmount,
overcome, triumph,
proficiency, gain, attain,
carry, acquire, obtainment,
purchase, descent, inherit)
love-*v* desire, wish, fancy,
fantasy, want, need,
exigency, longing,
hankering, inkling,
solicitude, anxiety,
yearning, coveting,
aspiration, liking, fondness,
relish, passion, rage,
mania, ambition,
eagerness, zeal, ardor,
breathless, impatience,
impetuosity, (indifferent,
cold, frigid, lukewarm, cool,
careless, listless,
lackadaisical, half-hearted,
apathy, insensibility)
lucid-*adj* luminous, lighten,
enlighten, shine, glow,
glitter, glisten, twinkle,
gleam, flare, glare, beam,
shimmer, glimmer, flicker,
sparkle, scintillate, dazzle,
transparent, pellucid,
diaphanous, limpid, clear,
serene, crystalline, glassy,
hyaline, (opacity,
opaqueness, film, cloud,
dim, turbid, thick, muddy,
opaques, obfuscated,
cloudy, hazy, misty, foggy,

vaporous, dark, black,
shade, shadow, extinction)
lush-*adj* vegetation, rank,
drunkenness,
intemperance, drinking,
inebriety, insobriety,
intoxication, tipsy, guzzle,
swill, soak, sot, lush, bib,
carouse, (sobriety,
teetotaler, abstainer)
luxury-*n* enjoyment,
pleasure, gratification,
relish, complacency,
comfort, ease, cushion,
joy, gladness, delight, glee,
cheer, sunshine,
happiness, felicity, bliss,
paradise, ecstasy,
Elysium, indulgence, high
living, excess, sensuality,
(temperance, moderation,
forbearance, self-denial,
frugality, total abstinence,
sufficient, care, anxiety,
solicitude, concern)
lymph-*n* fluid, liquid, liquor,
humor, juice, sap, serum,
blood, transparent,
pellucid, lucid, relucent,
limpid, clear, serene,
crystalline, vitreous,
watery, aqueous, aquatic,
lymphatic, drenching,
diluted, week, wet, moist,
(airy, ventilate, flatulent,
effervescent, windy,
opaque, smoky, murky,
dirty, opaque)

M

maceration-*n* saturation,
water, serum, serosal,

lymph, rheumy, delude,
dilution, dip, immerse,
submerge, plunge, souse,
duck, drown, soak, steep,
pickle, sprinkle,
atonement, reparation,
compromise, composition,
compensation, quitting,
expiation, redemption,
(atmospheric, airy)

mad-*adj* insane, disordered,
lunacy, madness, mania,
mental alienation,
aberration, demented,
frenzy, raving,
incoherence, wandering,
delirium calenture of the
brain, delusion,
hallucination, vertigo,
dizziness, fanaticism,
(sanity, soundness,
rationality, sobriety,
lucidity, senses, sound
mind)

madcap-*n* buffoon,
humorist, wag, with,
repartee, life of the party,
wit-snapper, joker, jester,
farceur, tumbler, acrobat,
harlequin, clown, motley,
motley fool, zany, dandy,
caricaturist, lunatic,
maniac, dreamer,
excitable, impetuosity,
boisterousness,
impatience, (passive,
coolness, calmness,
serene)

madrigal-*n* solo, duet, duo,
trio, quartet, descant, glee,
catch, round, chorus,
antiphon, accompaniment,
composer, musician,

perform, attune,
instrumental, vocal, choral,
lyric, operatic, harmonious,
poetry, versification,
rhyming, (unpoetical,
unrhymed)

magistrate-*n* authority,
influence, patronage,
power, preponderance,
credit, prestige,
jurisdiction, divine right,
despotism, command,
empire, auspicious,
propitious, master,
padrone, paramount,
(servant, subject, retainer,
follower, henchman,
menial, attendant, squire,
usher, page, footboy)

magnetism-*n* power,
potency, puissance, might,
force, energy,
almightiness,
omnipotence, authority,
strength, ability, ableness,
competency, efficiency,
validity, cogency,
enablement, pressure,
elasticity, gravity,
electricity, galvanism,
(impotence, disability,
disablement, impiousness,
imbecility, incapacity)

magnificent-*n* grand,
ostentation, display, show,
flourish, parade, pomp,
array, state, solemnity,
dash, splash, glitter, strut,
pomposity, magnificence,
splendor, demonstration,
celebration, pageant,
spectacle, form, elegance,
brace, beauty, unadorned,

symmetry, refined,
delicate, (ugly, graceless,
inelegant, ungraceful,
ungainly, uncouth, stiff,
rugged, rough, gross, rude,
awkward, clumsy)

magnify-v increase,
augment, enlargement,
extension, expansion,
increment, accretion,
accession, development,
intensify, enhance,
redouble, exaggerate,
exasperate, heighten,
overestimate,
oversensitive, vanity, over-
rate, (underestimate,
depreciate, detraction,
undervalue, modesty)

magnitude-n size, quantity,
dimension, amplitude,
mass, amount, quantum,
measure, substance,
strength, more or less,
greatness, multitude,
immense, enormity,
infinity, might, volume,
heap, (minimum, particle,
molecule, corpuscle, small,
diminutive, minute,
inconsiderable)

main-adj important,
consequence, moment,
prominence, consideration,
mark, materialistic, import,
significance, concern,
emphasis, interest, gravity,
seriousness, solemnity,
conduit, channel, duct,
(unimportant, insignificant,
nothingness, immaterial,
triviality, levity, frivolity,
minor detail, nonsense)

maintain-v sustain, act
upon, perform, play,
support, strain, take effect,
quicken, strike,
preservation, safe keeping,
conservation, keep,
prophylactic, unimpaired,
unbroken, continue,
persist, perpetuate,
undying, unvaried,
(discontinue, cease, desist,
stop, slacken, decay,
deteriorate, suspend,
interrupt)

major-adj greater, supreme,
higher, exceeding,
distinguished, vaulting,
utmost, paramount,
foremost, crowning, first-
rate, excellent,
transcendent, sovereign,
superlative, inimitable,
incomparable, potentate,
lord, sovereign, monarch,
autocrat, despot, tyrant,
(servant, subject, flunky,
inferior)

make-v constitute,
composition, combination,
inclusion, admission,
comprehension, reception,
form, compose, contain,
embrace, embody, involve,
implicate, produce, create,
fabricate, manufacture,
establish, perform,
achievement, (destruction,
waste, dissolution, ruin,
annihilation)

makeshift-n substitute,
supplanting, supersession,
stop-gap, jury-mast,
dummy, scapegoat,

double, alternative,
representative, supersede,
replace, ostensible motive,
ground, plea, pretext,
pretense, lame, excuse,
(interchanged, reciprocal,
mutual, communicative,
intercurrent)

malaise-*n* pain, suffering,
bodily, physical pain, dolor,
ache, smart, twinge, twitch,
ripe, headache, hurt, cut,
sore, discomfort, spasm,
mental suffering,
annoyance, irritation,
infliction, plague, (happy,
blest, blessed, blissful,
beatified, comfortable,
overjoyed, entranced,
enchanted)

malaria-*n* contagious,
infectious, catching, taking,
epidemic, insalubrious,
noxious, deleterious,
pestilent, poisonous, bane,
curse, evil scourge,
leaven, virus, mephitis,
(remedy, help, restorative,
corrective, tonic,
therapeutic, sedative)

malformation-*n* distortion,
twist, crookedness,
grimace, deformity,
monstrosity, misproportion,
contort, twist, warp, writhe,
irregular, unsymmetrical,
awry, askew, ugliness,
misshape, (symmetry,
shapeliness, finish, beauty,
proportion, uniformity,
regular, uniform, balanced,
parallel, coextensive)

malign-*v* bad, hurtful,

virulence, bane,
malevolence, ill-treatment,
annoyance, molestation,
abuse, oppression,
persecution, outrage,
misusage, injury, damage,
wrong, aggrieve,
(goodness, excellence,
merit, virtue, value, worth,
price, beneficial, profitable,
edifying, healthful,
salutary)

man-*n* adult male, he,
manhood, gentlemen, sir,
master, yeoman, swain,
fellow, blade, beau, chap,
gaffer, good man,
husband, masculine,
manly, hero, demigod,
bully, courageous, lion-
hearted

manager-*n* director,
manager, governor, rector,
comptroller,
superintendent, over-seer,
inspector, surveyor,
moderator, monitor,
taskmaster, leader,
conductor, property man,
machinist, prompter, call-
boy, (unmanaged,
abandoned, without
direction)

mangle-*v* separate, part,
detachment, segregation,
divorce, fissure, breach,
split, rift, crack, slit,
incision, sunder, divide,
haggle, lacerate, gash,
hash, slice, scramble,
whittle, impairment, injury,
damage, infect, (improve,
mend, revise, refine,

rectify, enrich, mellow,
elaborate, fatten)

mania-_n_ disordered,
abnormal, unsound,
derangement, insanity,
lunacy, madness, mental
alienation, aberration,
demented, frenzy, raving,
incoherence, wandering,
hallucination, dizziness,
kleptomania, dipsomania,
hypochondriasis, hysteria,
(sane, rational,
reasonable)

manifold-_adj_ multiform,
variety, diversity,
multifariousness, many-
sided, omnifarious,
irregular, diversified,
different, all sorts and
kinds, many, several,
sundry, divers, various,
profusion, populous,
numerous, (fewness,
paucity, small number,
rarity, infrequency, handful,
maniple, minority,
scattered)

manner-_n_ description,
denomination, designation,
character, stamp,
predicament, sort, genus,
species, variety, family,
race, tribe, clan, type, kit,
sect, assortment, feather,
kidney, suit, range, style,
mode of expression,
method, way, manner,
wise, gait, form, mode,
fashion, tone, guise

mannerism-_n_ special,
particular, individual,
specific, proper, personal,

original, private,
respective, definite,
determinate, especial,
characteristic, ideocracy,
distinctive feature,
(general, universal,
miscellany, collective,
common, prevalent,
transcendental)

many-_adj_ frequent,
repetition, many times,
incessant, perpetual,
continual, constant,
numerous, multiplicity,
profusion, plenty, majority,
huge numbers, several,
sundry, various, manifold,
multiplied, thick, studded,
(fewness, reduction,
weeding, elimination,
decimation, scanty, thin)

marble-_n_ hard, rigid,
stubborn, stiff, firm,
starched, stark, unbending,
unlimber, unyielding,
inflexible, tense, indurate,
adamantine, concrete,
stony, granitic, vitreous,
(soft, tender, supple, pliant,
lithe)

march-_v_ advance,
precession, leading,
heading, precedence,
priority, forerun, proceed,
progress, roving, vagrancy,
countermarching, nomad,
vagabondism, (regression,
withdrawal, retirement,
recession, follow, pursue,
shadow, trail, lag)

margin-_n_ edge, verge,
brink, brow, brim, border,
skirt, rim, flange, side,

space extension, extent,
expanse, room, field, way,
expansion, compass,
sweep, play, swing,
spread, capacity, stretch,
range, latitude, scope,
(center, interior, surface,
climate, zone, meridian)
mark-*n* indication, sign,
symbol, type, figure,
emblem, cipher,
representation, epigraph,
motto, characteristic, —
pointer, note, token, line,
stroke, dash, score,
witness, voucher, position,
place, period, pitch, stand,
(insignificant, disregard,
non-representative, without
affirmation)
market-*n* purchase, buying,
shopping, bribery, patron,
client, customer, invest in,
procure, rent, spend, mart,
place, bazaar, staple,
exchange, hall, stall,
booth, wharf, office,
chambers, warehouse,
establishment, (sale,
seller, vendor, dispose of,
dispense, merchant, vent)
marry-*v* combine, unite,
incorporate, amalgamate,
embody, absorb, re-
embody, blend, merge,
fuse, melt into one,
consolidate, cement in a
union, impregnate,
matrimony, wedlock,
union, nuptial, tie, match,
betrothment, bridal,
spouse, join, couple,
betroth, (divorce, separate,

widowhood,
decomposition, dissection,
resolution, dissolution,
corruption, dispersion)
martial-*adj* warfare, fighting,
hostilities, war, arms, battle
array, campaign, crusade,
expedition, mobilization,
battle, campaigning,
service, havoc, tribunal,
court, board, bench, law,
arbitration, inquisition,
(pacification, conciliation,
reconciliation,
accommodation, terms,
compromise, amnesty)
martyrdom-*n*
unselfishness, self-
denying, sacrificing,
devoted, generous, liberal,
benevolence, elevation,
loftiness of purpose,
exaltation, magnanimity,
chivalry, heroism,
sublimity, (selfishness,
indulgence, worldliness,
self-seeking, mean,
narrow-minded,
mercenary, earthly,
mundane)
marvelous-*adj* great,
wonderful, admire,
surprise, astonish, amaze,
astound, dumbfound,
dazzle, wondrous,
overwhelming,
stupendous, indescribable,
inexpressible, awesome,
aghast, agape, spellbound,
(common, ordinary,
expected, foreseen,
astonished at nothing)
mash-*v* mix, blend, tincture,

sprinkle, cross, alloy,
amalgamate, compound,
adulterate, infect, instill,
infiltrate, confusion,
disorder, disarray, jumble,
huddle, litter, lumber,
mess, muddle, hash,
hodgepodge, (uniformity,
symmetry, orderly, neat,
tidy, well regulated,
correct, methodical)
mask-v conceal, hide,
mystification, seal of
secrecy, screen, disguise,
masquerade, stealthiness,
reticence, reserve,
evasion, suppression,
white lie, cover, blind,
gauze, veil, mantle, cloud,
mist, shade, shadow,
(inform, acquaint,
announce, tell, impart,
mention, make known,
enlighten, specify)
master-v understand,
comprehend, take in,
catch, grasp, follow,
collect, make out, easily
understood, clearness,
simplify, explain, plain,
distinct, explicit, positive,
precise, graphic,
expressive, conceive,
accomplished, profound,
book-learned, (shallow,
superficial, rude, empty,
illiterate, uninformed)
mate-n similar,
resemblance, likeness,
affinity, approximation,
parallelism, sameness,
fellow, analog, pair, twin,
double, counterpart,

likeness, wife, espouse,
marry, join, spousal, bridal,
helper, auxiliary, recruit,
assistant, associate,
midwife, colleague,
(opposition, enemy,
adversary, dissimilar,
unlike, unmatched,
unlikeness, diversity,
dissemblance, difference)
matter-n substance, body,
flesh and blood, thing,
object, article, tangible,
material, essential,
physical, sensible,
ponderable, palpable,
objective, impersonal,
neuter, unspiritual, subject,
idea, argument, text, sum
and substance, gist,
suggestive, (immaterial,
unextended, disembodied,
personal, subjective,
groundless, nothingness,
nonentity, unsubstantial)
mature-adj old, age,
antiquity, decline, decay,
seniority, eldership,
tradition, custom,
venerable, time-honored,
prime, adolescent,
pubescent, of age, grown
up, virile, adult, (new,
novel, recent, fresh, young,
green, immature, virgin,
modern, late, neoteric)
maze-n convolution,
winding, circumvolution,
wave, undulation,
tortuosity, coil, roll, curl,
buckle, spiral, helix,
corkscrew, worm, volute,
tendril, dilemma,

embarrassment, perplexity, intricacy, entanglement, awkwardness, mesh, (ease, feasibility, flexibility, smoothness, round, rounded, oval)

meager-*adj* small, little, tenuity, paucity, few, mediocrity, moderation, minute, slight, limited, sparing, incomplete, insufficient, immature, deficit, omission, lack, hollow, (complete, large, entirety, full, sufficiency, replenish, whole, quantity, volume, unlimited, vast, immense, enormous, extreme)

mean-*adj* contemptible, wretched, vile, scrubby, pitiful, sorry, trashy, worthless, medium, intermediate, average, balance, mediocrity, generality, compromise, neutrality, commonplace, (gravity, seriousness, solemnity, pressure, urgency, stress, matter of life and death)

meander-*v* winding, convolution, sinuosity, undulation, tortuosity, twirl, snake-like, involved, intricate, complicated, perplexed, stray, straggle, sidle, diverge, trailing, digress, wander, twist, rove, drift, go astray, adrift, (bearing a straight course, set, directly, straight, point blank, straightforward)

measure-*n* compute, survey, valuation, appraisement, assessment, estimate, reckoning, gauging, standard, rule, compass, calipers, gage, meter, scale, coordinates, degree, extent, amount, ratio, intensity, strength, quantity, mass, comparative, gradual, limits

mediocrity-*n* mean, medium, average, generality, intermediate, neutral, compromise, imperfect, deficiency, inadequacy, fault, defect, weak point, flaw, blemish, indifferent, middling, ordinary, passable, secondary, limited, (perfect, faultless, model, standard, complete, intact, inimitable, harmless, immaculate, impeccable)

medley-*n* alloy, mixture, jumble, sauce, mash, instill, infiltrate, blend, cross, amalgamate, compound, infect, complex, intricacy, perplexity, disarrange, entangled, deranged, haphazard, random, luck, (orderly, regularity, subordination, methodical, unconfused, arranged)

meet-*v* assemble, crowd, throng, flood, rush, deluge, rabble, mob, horde, body, tribe, crew, gang, group,

cluster, muster, convene,
gather, converge, concur,
come together, unite,
concentrate, expedite,
convenient, due, proper,
eligible, seemly, (exit,
emergence, burst,
evacuation, diverge, repel,
push, dispel, leave, depart,
disperse, dismember)
mellow-*adj* advance,
ascend, increase, fructify,
ripen, pick up, come about,
rally, better, improved,
enrich, cultivate, enhance,
render, elaborate, season,
bring to maturity, mature,
nurture, (crude, raw, virgin,
unprepared, improvise,
coarse, deteriorate,
degenerate, impair,
weaken)
melt-*v* convert, pervert,
render, mold, form, merge,
liquefy, dissolve, solvent,
boil, heat, calcination,
ignite, inflammation, adust,
incendiary, caustic, smelt,
digest, stew, cook, seethe,
simmer, (cool, fan,
refrigerate, refresh,
congeal, freeze, glaciate,
benumb, starve, quench,
extinguish)
memory-*n* remembrance,
retention, tenaciy,
readiness, reminiscence,
recognition, recurrence,
recollection, retrospect,
reminder, memento,
souvenir, keepsake, relic,
memorandum,
memorabilia, tenacious,

(oblivion, forgetfulness,
short, efface, mindless,
insensible, escape, failing
memory)
menagerie-*n* collection,
clan, brotherhood,
association, gang, swarm,
shoal, school, covey, flock,
herd, drove, array, bevy,
vivarium, zoological
garden, aviary, aquarium,
domestication, breeding,
(disperse, scatter,
disseminate, diffuse, shed,
spread)
mendicant-*adj* beggar,
sturdy, cadger, canvasser,
touter, loss of fortune,
pauper, poor, indigent,
penniless, insolvency,
(wealth, richness, fortune,
affluence, sufficiency,
livelihood)
mental-*adj* intellect,
understanding reason,
rationality, cogitative,
faculties, senses,
consciousness,
observation, percipience,
under consideration,
thought, reflect, consider,
deliberate, (unendowed
with reason, imbecility,
vacant, thoughtless,
diverted, irrational)
mercy-*n* leniency,
moderation, tolerance,
mildness, gentleness,
favor, clemency,
forbearance, compassion,
tolerance, pity,
commiseration, sympathy,
ruthful, humane, exorable,

melt, thaw, relent,
unhardened, (severity,
strictness, harshness,
rigor, stringency, austerity,
inclemency, relentless)
merge-v combine, mixture
union, unification,
synthesis, incorporation,
amalgamation,
embodiment, coalescence,
fusion, blending,
absorption, centralization,
impregnate, ingrained,
(decompose, analysis,
dissect, catalysis,
dissolution, corruption,
unravel, disperse)
merit-n goodness,
excellence, virtue, value,
worth, price, perfection,
prime, flower, cream,
champion, beneficial,
profitable, advantageous,
salutary, favorable, good,
superior, fine, genuine,
admirable, praiseworthy,
(vile, oppressive,
burdensome, malign,
corrupting, corrosive,
destructive, destroy)
merriment-n cheerful,
geniality, gaiety, cheer,
good humor, high spirits,
liveliness, vivacity,
animation, joviality, jollity,
jocularity, mirth, hilarity,
exhilaration, laughter,
rejoicing, elate, exhilarate,
gladden, inspire, perk up,
delight, (dejection,
depression, lowness,
heaviness, melancholy,
sadness, dismal)

mesh-v interval, interspace,
separation, break, gap,
opening, hole, chasm,
interruption, interstice,
cleft, crevice, chink, rime,
creek, cranny, crack, chap,
slit, flaw, breach, rent,
gash, cut, crossing,
intersection, transversely,
network, web, twill, skein,
chain, braid, entanglement,
(coexist, adhere, graze,
touch, meet, osculate,
contact, proximity,
meeting)
mess-n mixture, combine,
intermix, mingle, shuffle,
knead, brew, impregnate
with, instill, imbue,
infiltrate, compound, infect,
among, amongst, amid,
amidst, miscellaneous,
dilemma, embarrassment,
perplexity, intricacy,
entanglement,
awkwardness, delicacy,
maze, vexed, quandary,
(ease, facilitate, smooth,
emancipate, free,
manageable, light, simple,
eliminate, single, pure,
clear)
messenger-n envoy,
emissary, legate,
ambassador, diplomat,
marshal, flag-bearer,
herald, crier, trumpeter,
courier, runner, errand-
boy, reporter, mail,
telephone, wireless,
heliograph, subject,
retainer, follower,
henchman, menial, help,

attache, handmaid,
secretary, assistant,
(master, lord, padrone,
paramount, commander,
captain, chief, authority,
corporal)

meteor-*n* heavenly body,
cosmically, mundane,
terrestrial, solar, heliacal,
lunar, celestial, sphere,
starry, stellar, luminary,
light, flame, spark,
phosphorescence, star,
blazing, (shade, sunshade,
gauze, veil, mantle, mask,
cloud, mist, umbrageous)

mettle-*n* sensible,
impressionable,
susceptive, impassion,
gushing, warm-tender,
soft-hearted, romantic,
enthusiastic, highflying,
spirited, vivacious, lively,
expressive, mobile,
trembling, excitable,
fastidious, (insensible,
inertness, apathy, dull,
frigid, cold-hearted,
indifferent, lukewarm,
careless)

middle-*n* midst, half-way,
navel, equidistance,
bisection, half-distance,
equator, diaphragm,
midriff, intermediate,
equatorial, midship,
compromise,
compensation, middle
term, meet one half way,
give and take, arrange,
adjust, agree, moderate,
average, mediocrity

midst-*n* centrality, center,
core, kernel, nucleus,
heart, pole, axis, navel,
backbone, marrow,
symmetry, center of
gravity, bring to focus,
intermediate, intervention,
introduce, (surround,
beset, encompass)

mild-*adj* moderate,
temperate, relaxation,
remission, mitigation,
tranquilization, pacification,
gentleness, sobriety, quiet,
contemplation, appease,
soothe, lull, swag, calm,
cool, hush, quell, tame,
(violent, fury, storm, rough,
vehement, warm, acute,
sharp, rude, impetuous,
rampant)

mill-*v* reduce, grind,
pulverize, comminute,
granulate, triturate,
levigate, scrape, file,
abrade, rub down, grate,
rasp, pound, bray, bruise,
contuse, beat, crush,
crunch, crumble,
disintegrate, (lubricate, oil,
glycerine, lather, grease,
lather, smooth)

millennium-*n* period,
second, minute, hour, day,
week, month, quarter,
year, decade, lifetime,
generation, century, age,
prospectively, hereafter,
eventually, ultimately,
whereupon, (lapse, elapse,
advance, progress,
succession, proceed, slip,
slide, past, gone, foregone,
extinct, forgotten, over)

mince-v cut up, separate, sunder, divide, subdivide, rescind, segregate, keep apart, sever, abscind, chop, chip, crack, snap, break, tear, burst, rend, wrench, rupture, shatter, shiver, hack, slash, mangle, slice, tear, whittle, (join, unite, annex, attach, hinge, seam, suture, stitch, link, miter, close, combine)

mind-n intellect, understanding, reason, thinking, rationality, cogitative, faculties, senses, consciousness, observation, percipience, intuition, association of ideas, instinct, conception, judgment, wits, capacity, genius, ability, thoughtful, reflect, speculate, contemplate, consider

mine-n sap, destroy, waste, dissolution, breaking up, disruption, consumption, disorganization, fall, downfall, ruin, perdition, annihilation, demolition, overthrow, subversion, suppress, abolish, ruinous, incendiary, deleterious, (produce, perform, operate, form, construct, fabricate, frame, contrive, forge)

minister-n subserve, mediate, intervene, instrumental, useful, give, bestow, donation, presentation, accordance, delivery, consignment, dispensation, communication, endowment, award, generosity, liberality, offering, bequest, legacy, devise, deliver, present, (receive, acquire, accept, assign, admit)

minor-adj inferior, shortcoming, deficiency, minimum, smallness, less, lesser, minus, lower, subordinate, second-rate, least, lowest, diminished, decrease, infant, babe, youth, youngster, master, (veteran, old, seer, patriarch, superior, supreme, major, great, noble, higher, exceeding)

minute-adj small, little, diminutive, inconsiderable, paltry, faint, slender, light, slight, scanty, limited, sparing, inappreciable, infinitesimal, mere, simple, sheer, stark, bare, period of time, duration of, moment, instant, second, twinkling, flash, breath, burst, sudden, instantaneous, hasty, quick, lightning, (perpetuity, eternity, ever, everlasting, great, magnitude, considerable, ample)

mirror-n imitate, copy, repetition, duplication, quotation, reproduction, mimicry, simulation, reflector, speculum, looking glass, pier, model,

standard, pattern, best,
inimitable, paragon,
unparalleled, supreme,
perfect, (imperfect, faulty,
unsound, deficient,
unimitated, original,
unmatched)

misbehave-v coarse,
indecorous, ribald, gross,
unseemly, unpresentable,
ungraceful, ill-mannered,
underbred, ungentlemanly,
unladylike, unpolished,
uncouth, heavy, rude,
awkward, (good taste,
cultivated, delicacy,
refinement, gust, finesse,
nicety, polish, elegance,
grace, connoisseur)

miscalculate-v misjudge,
prejudgment, foregone
conclusion, narrow-
minded, intolerant,
besotted, dogmatic,
opinioned, unreasonable,
false judgment, weak,
feeble, poor, flimsy, loose,
vague, irrational, foolish,
frivolous, (logical
sequence, good sense,
deduce, conclusive)

mischief-n evil, harm hurt,
nuisance, disaster,
accident, casualty, mishap,
calamity, bale, mental
suffering, outrage, wrong,
injury, foul play, grievance,
disastrous, bad, aggrieve,
oppress, persecute, inflict,
maltreat, abuse,
(goodness, admirable,
estimable, praise-worthy,
satisfactory, favorable)

misconduct-n mismanage,
misapplication, absence of
rule, bungling, blunder,
unskillful, quackery,
mistake, misguided,
foolish, inconsistent,
ignorant, (accomplished,
expert, skillful, competent)

miserable-adj suffering,
pain, dolor, ache, smart,
displeasure,
dissatisfaction, discomfort,
discomposure, malaise,
uneasiness, dejection,
annoyance, irritation,
worry, infliction visitation,
care, anxiety, solicitude,
trouble, trial, ordeal, shock,
burden, unhappiness,
misery, tribulation,
(pleasure, gratification,
enjoyment, well-being,
comfort, ease, joy,
gladness, delight, mind at
ease)

misfortune-n adversity, evil,
failure, bad fortune,
trouble, hardship, curse,
blight, blast, load,
pressure, mishap, disaster,
calamity, catastrophe,
accident, casualty, ruin,
failure, affliction,
(prosperity, welfare, well-
being, affluence, wealth,
success, thrift, roaring,
prosper, thrive)

mishap-n source of
irritation, annoyance,
grievance, nuisance,
vexation, mortification,
bore, bother, plague, pest,
infestation, molestation,

(pleasant, inviting,
attractive, lovely,
enchantment, seduction)
misjudgment-*n* bias, warp,
twist, hasty conclusion,
preconceived,
partisanship, partial,
narrow, blind side,
confined, error, fallacy,
laxity, mistake, fault,
blunder, (accuracy,
exactness, honest,
precise)
mismatch-*v* different,
diverse, varied, modified,
various, dissimilarity,
disagreement, disparity,
discord, unconformity,
conflict, unfitness,
inaptitude, impropriety,
inconsistency, disjoining,
(conformity, uniformity,
concert, relevancy,
admissibility, compatibility,
relation)
misrepresent-*v* lie,
falsehood, deception,
untruth, guile, mendacity,
perjury, forgery, invention,
fabrication, suppression of
truth, perversion,
distortion, exaggeration,
misinterpretation,
misconstrue, mistake,
parody, equivocation,
evasion, fraud, (veracity,
truthfulness, frankness,
sincerity, honesty)
miss-*v* girl, lass, wench,
damsel, maiden, virgin,
fail, unsuccessful, labor,
toil in vane, miscarry,
omission, oversight, slip,

trip, stumble, mess,
mishap, misfortune,
collapse, (success,
advance, lucky, fortunate,
prosperity, triumph, gain,
advantage, conquest,
victory)
mist-*n* cloud, bubble, foam,
froth, head, spume, lather,
spray, surf, yeast, barm,
vapor, fog, haze, stream,
effervescence,
fermentation, nebulous,
(semi-fluid, stickiness,
viscidity, adhesiveness)
mistake-*n* error, fallacy,
misconception, miss, fault,
blunder, oversight,
misprint, slip, blot, flaw,
trip, stumble, heresy,
hallucination, laxity,
miscount, untrue, false,
unreal, ungrounded,
failure, unsuccessful,
mishap, split, collapse,
(true, infallible, successful,
fortunate, prosperous)
mitigate-*v* abate, moderate,
soften, temper, mollify,
leniency, dull, take off the
edge, blunt, obtund,
sheathe, subdue, chasten
sober, tone, smooth down,
lessen, palliate, tranquilize,
assuage, appease,
(violent, sharpen, quicken,
excite, explode, convulse,
infuriate, madden, lash)
mix-*v* combine, instill,
imbue, transfuse, join,
intermix, mingle, shuffle,
knead, brew, impregnate,
infiltrate, dash, stir-up,

together, compound,
adulterate, (simple, purity,
homogeneity, eliminate)
mob-n crowd, assemblage,
throng, flood, rush, press,
crush, horde, body, tribe,
crew, gang, knot, squad,
band, party, swarm,
school, covey, flock, herd,
drove, array, bevy, galaxy,
company, troop, group,
cluster, clump, (disperse,
scatter, sow, disseminate,
diffuse, shed, spread,
disembody)
mobile-adj motion,
movement, going, unrest,
stream, flow, run, coarse,
stir, evolution, kinematics,
step, transitional, motor,
motive, shifting, mercurial,
unquiet, restless, nomadic,
inconstancy, versatility,
mobility, unstable,
restlessness, fidget,
disquiet, agitation, (stable,
constant, immobility, stand,
established, fixture,
foundation, permanence,
durable)
mock-v imitate, copy,
mirror, reflect, reproduce,
repeat, echo, catch,
transcribe, match, mimic,
ape, simulate,
impersonate, counterfeit,
parody, modeled after,
verbatim, word for word,
repetition, sameness, pair,
mate, double, parallel,
(dissimilar, unlike,
unmatched, originality,
different kind)

mode-n state, condition,
category, estate, lot, case
trim, mood, plight, aspect,
schuss, tone, tenor, trim,
guise, light, complexion,
style, character, structural,
organic, method, way,
manner, fashion, form,
habit, (infraction of usage,
unaccustomed, leave off,
unusual, unaccustomed)
model-n represent,
imitation, illustration,
delineation, depiction,
imagery, portraiture,
design, art, personation,
impersonation, image,
likeness, (misrepresent,
distort, exaggerate, daub)
moderate-adj small, allay,
slow, sufficient, cheap,
temperate, low,
reasonable, inexpensive,
depreciated, nominal,
bargain, sufficient,
adequate, enough,
satisfactory, competent,
mediocrity, fill, (scarcity,
want, need, lack, poverty,
insufficient, inadequate)
modesty-n humility, timidity,
diffidence, bashfulness,
blushing, self-knowledge,
shy, nervous, skittish, coy,
sheepish, shamefaced,
unpretending, reserved,
constrained, demure,
private, without ceremony,
(vanity, conceit, self-
confidence, airs,
pretension, egotism,
gaudery, elation,
ostentation)

multifarious-adj disconnections, independence, strange, alien, foreign, outlandish, exotic, diverse, variety, diversity, manifold, motley, mosaic, indiscriminate, irregular, (regularity, uniformity, constant, punctual, routine, normal, natural, ordinary, steady)

multitude-n numerous, multiplicity, profusion, legion, host, great, enormous, quantity, number, array, army, sea, galaxy, scores, peck, bushel, shoal, swarm, many, several, sundry, various, (few, small quantity, rarity, infrequency, handful, maniple, minority, reduction)

musical-adj melody, rhythm, measure, rhyme, pitch, tone, modulation, temperament, syncopation, song, glee, madrigal, compose, perform strains, (discord, harshness, tuneless, unmusical, dissonance)

mute-adj silent, stillness, peace, hush, lull, solemn, dead, render, hold one's tongue, stifle, muffle, muzzle, inaudible, faint, suppress, smother, dumb, (vocal, cry, utter, exclaim, pronounce)

mysterious-adj obscure, dark, muddy, dim, nebulous, undiscernible, invisible, indefinite, perplexed, confused, undetermined, vague, loose, ambiguous, mystic, transcendental, occult, recondite, undefinable, (intelligent, clear, explicit, lucid, perspicuity, legibility, plain speaking, understandable)

N

name-n imprint, label, indicate, symbolize, mark, note, stamp, earmark, ticket, docket, score, dash, trace, print, appoint, nominate, return, charter, ordinate, install, inaugurate, investiture, accession, coronation, enthronement, (countermand, disclaim, abolish, dissolve, dismiss, nullify, annul, cancel)

napping-v dull, unentertaining, depress, humdrum, monotonous, inactive, heaviness, absent, bemused, dreaming, unreflective, (attentive, observant, absorption of mind)

native-adj inhabitant, resident, dweller, occupier, householder, lodger, inmate, tenant, incumbent, sojourner, settler, squatter, indigent, aborigines, free, plain, outspoken, blunt, downright, (cunning, craft, artful, skillful, subtle, alien, foreign)

naught-n nothing, zero,

cipher, none, nobody, complete absence, insubstantiality, vacant, vacuous, empty, blank, hollow, nominal, null, inane, (numerous, many, several, some, profuse, multiple)

near-adv loom, impending, destined, about to happen, coming, eventually, prospective, approaching, future, precipitation, anticipation, premature, soon, shortly, (now, occurring, happening, immediate)

necessity-n requirement, need, want, have occasion for, needful, essential, indispensable, prerequisite, demanding, urgent, obligatory, involuntary, compulsive, inevitable, (willing, volition, free-will, voluntary, optional, discretionary, intentional, spontaneous)

neglect-v abandon, negligent, careless, omit, default, thoughtless, remiss, perfunctory, inconsiderate, reckless, (care, watchful, vigilant, survey, alert, regardful, cautious, considerate, prepared)

negotiate-v mediate, intervene, peacemaker, diplomat, moderate, arbitrate, intercede, bargain, agree, promise, stipulate, barter,

compromise, settle, conclude, come to an understanding

net-n remainder, residue, remains, remnant, rest, relic, leavings, result, left, unconsumed, sedimentary, surviving, exceeding, over and above, outlying, superfluous, (adjunct, addition, addendum, affix, appendage, augment, increment)

neutralize-v opposition, contrariety, antagonism, polarity, clashing, compensation, cross, interfere, conflict with, jostle, antagonize, withstand, counterpoise, retroactive, reactionary, contrary, (concur, conspire, cooperate, agree, consent)

nice-adj pleasing, savory, good, fastidious, agreeable, delectable, lovely, beatify, satisfy, refreshing, comfortable, genial, glad, sweet, luxurious, voluptuous, sensual, attractive, enticing, appetizing, charming, (annoying, painful, grievance, vexation, mortification, bother, displeasing, disturbing)

nightmare-n fright, affright, alarm, dread, awe, terror, horror, dismay, consternation, panic, scare, stampede,

intimidation, terrorism,
reign of terror, demonic,
scarecrow
nil-*n* inexistent, negative,
annihilation, extinction,
destruction, abrogate,
destroy, take away, perish,
blank, missing, omitted,
absent, exhausted, gone,
lost, departed, defunct,
dead, (subsist, presence,
positive, realty, actuality,
live, breathe, real, actual,
positive, substantial)
nip-*v* cut, destroy, shorten,
sunder, divide, subdivide,
sever, dissever, abscind,
saw, snip, nib, cleave, rive,
rend, slit, split, splinter,
crack, snap, carve, dissect,
hinder, impede, obstruct,
stop, (attach, join, hinge,
seam, suture, stitch, link,
miter, close, combine, fix,
affix, fasten)
noble-*adj* great,
virtuousness, morality,
ethical, rectitude, integrity,
cardinal virtues, merit,
worth, desert, excellence,
credit, self-control,
resolution, self-denial,
exemplary, saintly,
seraphic, godlike,
commendable,
praiseworthy, (wicked,
immoral, impropriety,
weak, fault, deficient,
vicious, sinful)
nod-*v* signal, wag, gesture,
wink, glance, leer, shrug,
beck, touch, nudge,
oscillate, undulate, wave,

beat, waggle, bob, curtsy,
play, dangle, assent,
acquiescence, admission,
accordance, agreement,
recognition,
acknowledgment, avowal,
(dissent, discordance,
contradiction, protest, noncompliance)
nomination-*n* commission,
delegation, assignment,
procuration, deputation,
legation, mission,
embassy, agency,
appointment, return,
charter, ordination,
installation, inauguration,
investiture, accession,
coronation, enthronement,
(dismiss, abolish, dissolve,
cancel, repeal, revocation,
annul)
nonsense-*n* absurdity,
vagary, tomfoolery,
mummery, imbecility,
blunder, muddle, farce,
absence of meaning,
meaningless, empty,
jargon, gibberish,
balderdash, insanity,
(significant, expression,
substantial, literal, plain,
simple, suggestive,
convey, imply, indicate)
nook-*n* limited space, lieu,
spot, pint, dot, niche, hole,
compartment, premises,
station, abode, angle,
cusp, bend, fold, notch, for,
corner, recess, oriel
noose-*n* snare, trap, pitfall,
decoy, bait, cobweb, net,
meshes, mouse-trap,

mine, scaffold, block, axe,
guillotine, stake, cross,
gallows, gibbet, drop, rope,
halter, bowstring
normal-*adj* regular, intrinsic,
fundamental, implanted,
inherent, essential, natural,
innate, inborn, inbred,
radical, incarnate,
thoroughbred, immanent,
instinctive,
(extraneousness,
incidental, accidental)
note-*n* remark, examine,
scan, scrutinize, consider,
revise, pour over, inspect,
review, indication, observe,
look, see, view, notice,
regard, give, heed,
contemplate, attentive,
mindful, watchful,
(inattentive, blind, deaf,
inconsiderate, absent,
abstracted, lost, overlook,
disregard, dismiss)
noteworthy-*adj* exceptional,
non-conformity,
unconventional, unusual,
uncommon, extraordinary,
unparalleled, fantastic,
exceptional, (conventional,
usual, common, ordinary,
natural)
notorious-*adj* famous,
notability, notoriety, vogue,
celebrity, renown, popular,
glory, honor,
illustriousness, regard,
respect, reputable,
respectable, dignity,
stateliness, solemnity,
grandeur, splendor, noble,
majesty, sublime,

(shameful, disgrace,
tarnish, blot, taint,
discredit, degrade, vilify)
null-*adj* powerless,
impotent, disable,
impiousness, invalidity,
inefficiency, incompetence,
disqualification,
helplessness, prostration,
paralysis, palsy, apoplexy,
exhaustion, emasculation,
(power, potency, ability,
ableness, energy, force,
control, authority, strength,
influence, magnetism)
nurture-*n* feed, food,
nourishment, nutriment,
sustenance, fodder,
provision, ration, keep,
commons, board,
commissariats, pasture,
dietary, eatable, edible,
culinary, succulent,
potable, (starve, excrete,
deject, perspire, sweat,
diarrhea, salivation,
discharge)

O

oak-*n* strong, mighty,
vigorous, forcible, hard,
adamantine, stout, robust,
sturdy, hardy, powerful,
potent, puissant, valid,
courage, brave, valor,
resolute, bold, gallant,
intrepid, defiant, (coward,
timid, poltroonery,
baseness, dastard, sneak,
weak, relaxed, frail, fragile,
shatter, flimsy)
oar-*n* paddle, navigate, fin,

flipper, natation, handle,
hilt, haft, shaft, heft, shank,
blade, trigger, tiller, helm,
treadle, key, turn screw,
screwdriver

oasis-_n_ separation, parting,
detachment, segregation,
divorce, supposition,
deduction, discerptible,
unconformable,
exceptional, abnormal,
continent, mainland,
peninsula, delta, isthmus,
(attach, fix, affix, fasten,
bind, secure, clinch, twist,
pinion)

obdurate-_adj_ obstinate,
tenacious, stubborn, case-
hardened, inflexible,
immovable, inert,
unchangeable, severe,
strictness, harshness,
rigor, stringency, austerity,
inclemency, (lenitive,
moderation, tolerance,
mildness, gentleness,
favor, indulgence,
clemency, mercy)

obey-_v_ rules, observance,
compliance, submission,
subjection, resignation,
allegiance, loyalty, fealty,
homage, deference,
devotion, complying,
(violate, infringe, shirk,
insubordination,
disobedient)

object-_n_ thing, matter, body,
substance, stuff, element,
principle, material, article,
something, still life,
decision, determination,
resolve, purpose,

ultimatum, resolution,
motive, intention, advise,
(speculation, venture,
stake, game of chance,
risk, hazard, fortuitous,
indiscriminate)

oblige-_v_ accommodate,
consult the wishes of,
humor, cheer, encourage,
nurture, cultivate, foster,
cherish, support, sustain,
uphold, bolster,
compulsive, coercion,
coaction, constraint,
duress, enforcement,
press, conscription,
(prevention, preclusion,
obstruction, interruption,
hindrance)

obnoxious-_adj_ source of
irritation, annoyance,
grievance, nuisance,
vexation, mortification,
bore, bother, burdensome,
oppressive, sinister,
maltreat, abuse,
persecute, abomination,
(excellence, merit, virtue,
value, worth, beneficial,
advantageous, edifying,
pleasant, agreeable,
enchanting)

obscure-_adj_ dark, murky,
gloomy, extinguish, cloudy,
confused, indistinct,
shadowy, indefinite, ill-
defined, opaque, (visible,
conspicuousness, distinct,
exposure, discernible,
apparent, perceptible)

observation-_n_
understanding, reason,
rationality, cogitative,

intelligence, intuition, association of ideas, instinct, conception, judgment, wits, capacity, ability, attention, mindfulness, intentness, thought, consideration, (abstraction, absorption, preoccupation, distraction, disregard)

obstruct-v hinder, prevent, preclude, stoppage, interruption, retard, embarrassment, restriction, impede, obstacle, drag, stay, stop, shut, blockage, bar, bolt, seal, choke, occlusion, (open, vent, vomiter, perforate, pierce, puncture, support, lift, advance, assist, promote, favor, relief, rescue)

obtain-v get, acquisition, gaining, procuration, purchase, descent, inheritance, gift, recover, retrieval, redemption, salvage, gain, remuneration, proceeds, harvest, benefit, (deprived, loss, lapse, bereft)

obtrude-v interfere, intervention, introduce, import, insinuate, smuggle, infiltrate, ingrain, partition, interpenetrate, permeate, insert, implantation, inoculation, immersion, imbed, (removal, elimination, extrication, eradication, evolution, wrench, evulsion)

occasion-n opportunity, opening, room, suitable, proper, tempestuous, crisis, turn, juncture, conjuncture, turning point, given time, timely, providential, lucky, fortunate, happy, favorable, propitious, auspicious, critical, (unsuitable, ill timed, intrude, premature, intrusion)

occult-adj concealed, hidden, secret, recondite, mystic, cabalistic, dark, cryptic, private, privy, auricular, clandestine, close,inviolate, stealthy, skulking, surreptitious, (informant, enlightenment, case, specification, communicative, advice, monition, statement, affirmation)

occupation-n business, employet, pursuit, affair, concern, matter, case, task, work, job, errand, commission, mission, charge, care, duty, vocation, calling, profession, industry, trade, officiate, serve, capacity, handicraft

occupy-v presence, attendance, where, permeation, pervasion,diffusion, dispersion, omnipresence, inhabit, dwell, reside, stay, sojourn, live, abide, lodge, nestle, roost, perch, locate,

fill, domiciled, (truant,
absent, absence,
inexistent, emptiness, void,
vacant, deserted, devoid)
occur-v eventuality, event,
occurrence, incident, affair,
transaction, proceeding,
phenomenon, advent,
concern, circumstance,
casualty, accident,
adventure, passage, crisis,
pass, emergency,
contingency,
consequence, (impending,
threaten, loom, await,
approach, destined,
approaching)
odd-adj individuality,
idiosyncrasy, originality,
mannerism, exception,
peculiarity, infraction,
violation, infringement,
eccentricity, bizarre,
monstrosity, rarity, freak,
remainder, residue,
remains, relic,
(supplement, continuation,
rider, off-shoot, conformity,
symmetry, conventionality,
pattern, specimen)
ode-n poetry, poetics,
versification, rhyming,
making verses, prosody,
song, ballad, lullaby,
anthology, assonance,
accentuation, laureate,
lyrist, (prose, unpoetical,
unrhymed)
offensive-adj unsavory,
repulsive, nasty, acrid,
acrimonious, rough,
sickening, nauseous,
loathsome, unpleasant,

displease, annoy,
discompose, trouble,
disquiet, disturb, cross,
perplex, molest,
(refreshing, comfortable,
cordial, genial, glad, sweet,
delectable, good,
palatable, nice, dainty)
offer-v proposal,
presentation, tender, bid,
overture, motion, invitation,
candidature, move, start,
gift, donation, present,
fairing, favor, benefaction,
grant, oblation, sacrifice,
(receive, acquire,
reception, acceptance,
release, admission,
refusal, rejection, denial,
decline, repulse, rebuff,
discountenance)
official-adj authoritative,
influence, patronage,
power, preponderance,
absolute, command,
empire, rule, dominion,
sovereign, hold, grasp,
certain, necessity, surety,
unerring, infallible,
reliability, (uncertainty,
doubt, dubiety, hesitation,
precariousness,
unfortunate, fallible,
adverse, disastrous)
offset-n compensate,
equate, commutation,
indemnification,
compromise,
neutralization, nullification,
counteraction,
counterpoise, equivalent,
consideration, offshoot,
ramification, descendant,

often-_adv_ repetition,
iteration, reiteration,
harping, recurrence,
succession, monotony,
rhythm, repeat, echo,
frequent, many times,
repeatedly, perpetually,
continually, constantly,
incessantly, (sometimes,
occasionally, at times,
rarity, fewness, seldom,
scarcely)

ogle-_v_ look, view, espial,
glance, ken, glimpse,
peep, gaze, stare, leer,
contemplation, survey,
speculation, watch, sight-
seeing, longing, hankering,
inkling, solicitude, anxiety,
yearning, coveting,
(indifferent, cold, frigid,
lukewarm, cool,
unconcerned, blind,
hoodwink, dim sighted)

oil-_n_ lubricate, anointment,
glycerine, grease, lather,
grease, soap, wax,
ointment, unctuous,
slippery, oleaginous,
adipose, sebaceous, fatty,
(pulpy, paste, dough, curd,
jam, poultice, watery)

old-_adj_ age, ancient,
antique, long standing,
time-honored, venerable,
elder, prime, primitive,
igneous, primordial,
seniority, maturity, decline,
decay, senility, ripe,
mellow, longevity,
decrepitude, (young,
youthful, juvenile, green,
callow, budding, new,

novel, recent, fresh,
modern, recent, immature)

omission-_n_ exclusion,
exception, rejection,
repudiation, exile,
seclusion, separation,
segregation, supposition,
elimination, bar, leave,
shut, reject, repudiate,
blackball, banish, (include,
admit, consist of, embrace,
embody, involve, implicate,
contain, constitute,
complete, entire,
supplement)

one-_adj_ whole, total,
integrity, collectiveness,
unity, complete,
indivisibility, integration,
aggregate, main, essential,
identity, sameness,
monotony, identical,
(inversion, contrariety,
contrast, part, portion,
division, segment, fraction,
parcel, piece, morsel)

oneself-_n_ identity,
sameness, coincidence,
facsimile, similar, alter ego,
identification, self,
monotony, exactness,
identical (opposite,
reverse, inverse, converse)

only-_adj_ small, unity,
individual, sole, single,
solitary, apart, alone,
unaccompanied, isolation,
seclusion, lone, lonely,
desolate, dreary, simple,
purity, homogeneity,
uniform, neat, (mixture,
tinge, tincture, compound,
infusion, combination,

matrimony, accompany,
coexist, attend, part)
ooze-v emerge, exit, issue,
emersion, burst,
emanation, evacuation,
perspiration, sweating,
leakage, percolation,
distillation, gush,
outpouring, effluence,
effusion, disclose, divulge,
split, acknowledge, allow,
(screen, cover, mask,
masquerade, ingress,
enter, influx, invasion,
import)
opalescent-adj
semitransparent,
opalescence, milkiness,
pearliness, gauze, muslin,
film, mist, cloud,
variegation, iridescence,
play of colors, polychrome,
maculation, spottiness,
spectrum, rainbow,
(transparent, pellucid,
lucid, diaphanous,
relucent, limpid, clear,
serene, crystalline,
vitreous)
open-adj divulge, reveal,
break, split, disclose,
resection, unveiling,
deterred, revelation,
exposition,
acknowledgement, avowal,
confession, disclose, allow,
concede, grant, admit,
(ambush, screen, cover,
shade, blinker, veil,
curtain, blind, cloak, cloud,
mask, visor, disguise,
masquerade, dress)
operate-v cause,

groundwork, foundation,
support, spring, genesis,
descent, produce, perform,
fabricate, frame, construct,
manufacture, contrive,
forge, coin, carve, build,
raise, edify, rear, erect,
constitute, (extinction,
annihilation, destroy, ruin,
demolish, over-turn,
sacrifice, subvert)
operator-n agent, doer,
actor, agent, performer,
perpetrator, executor,
practitioner, worker,
stager, bee, ant, artisan,
handicrafts, workman,
artisan, craftsman,
mechanic, operative,
maker, journeyman,
pursuit, pursuing,
prosecution, (abstain,
refrain, spare, eschew,
maintain, spare)
opinion-n persuasion,
conviction, convince, self-
conviction, certainty, mind,
view, conception,
impression, surmise,
conclusion, judgment,
tenet, dogma, principle,
popular belief, (misbelief,
discredit, miscreant,
infidelity, dissent,
retraction, doubt,
skepticism, misgiving,
demur, mistrust)
opponent-n antagonist,
adversary, adverse party,
opposition, enemy,
assailant, obstructive,
brawler, wrangler,
disputant, malcontent,

demagogue, reactionary, rival, competitor, (helper, recruit, assistant, midwife, colleague, partner, mate, collaborator, ally, friend, confidant)

opportunity-*n* occasion, opening, room, suitable time, proper time, crisis, turn, juncture, turning point, timely, lucky, fortunate, happy, providential, favorable, propitious, auspicious, suitable, (untimely, intrusive, inopportune, unlucky, inauspicious)

oppose-*v* contrary, contrast, antithesis, contradiction, antagonism, inversion, opposite, invert, diverse, conflicting, hostile, diametrically opposite, crossfire, clashing, collision, conflict, resistance, restraint, hindrance, (cooperation, association, alliance, conference, coalition, fusion)

oppressor-*n* tyrant, severe, strictness, harshness, rigor, stringency, austerity, inclemency, arrogance, arbitrary power, despotism, dictatorship, autocracy, tyranny, domineering, assumption, usurpation, inquisition, reign of terror, disciplinarian, despot, inquisitor, extortioner, (lenient, mild, gentle, clement, tolerant,

indulgent, easy-going, forbearing)

oral-*adj* voice, vocal, organ, lungs, bellows, cry, utterance, breathe, ejaculate, rap out, articulate, distinct, stertorous, melodious, enunciate, pronounce, accentuate, aspirate, deliver, (stammer, hesitation, impediment, titubation, whisper, lisp, drawl, twang, accent, stutter, mumble, mutter, whisper)

oratory-*n* speaking, speech, locution, talk, parlance, verbal intercourse, oral communication, oration, recitation, delivery, lecture, harangue, sermon, formal speech, rhetoric, declamation

orb-*n* region, sphere, ground, soil, area, realm, hemisphere, quarter, district, beat, circuit, circle, department, domain, tract, territory, country, canton, county, shire, province, parish, township, arena, precincts, walk, clime, climate, zone, meridian, (spacious, roomy, extension, extent, superficial extent)

orbit-*n* world, creation, nature, universe, earth, globe, wide world, cosmos, sphere, heavens, sky, firmament, celestial spaces, stars, asteroids,

nebulae, galaxy, milky
way, path, way, manner,
method, gait, form, mode,
fashion, tone, guise,
procedure

orchestra-*n* music, concert,
strain, tune, air, melody,
instrumental music, full
score, minstrels, band,
concerted, piece, stringed
instruments, wind
instruments, vibrating
surfaces

ordain-*v* appointment,
nomination, return, charter,
installation, inauguration,
investiture, accession,
coronation, enthronement,
vicegerency, regency,
regentship, viceroy,
consignee, commission,
accredit, (abrogate, annul,
cancel, destroy, abolish,
revoke, repeal, rescind,
reverse, retract, recall)

ordeal-*n* concern, grief,
sorrow, distress, affliction,
woe, bitterness, heartache,
broken hearted, anxiety,
solicitude, trouble, fiery
ordeal, shock, blow, dole,
fret, burden, load,
(happiness, felicity, bliss,
beatitude, enchantment,
transport, rapture,
ravishment, ecstasy,
paradise, pleasing)

order-*n* regular, uniformity,
symmetry, gradation,
progression, routine,
method, disposition,
arrangement, array,
system, economy,
discipline, orderliness,
rank, place, methodically,
systematically, periodically,
(disorder, derangement,
irregularity, confusion,
complexity, perplexity)

ordinary-*adj* indifferent,
middling, mediocre,
average, tolerable, fair,
passable, decent,
admissible, bearable,
secondary, inferior,
second-rate, second-best,
typical, normal, orthodox,
regular, steady, (irregular,
abnormal, unconventional,
unusual, perfect,
impeccability, model,
paragon)

organize-*v* arrange, plan,
preparation, distribution,
allocation, sorting,
assortment, allotment,
apportionment, taxis,
graduation, organization,
analysis, classification,
division, digestion, atlas,
(disorder, disturbance,
dislocation, perturbation,
interruption, shuffling,
inversion, misplace,
mislay)

original-*n* prototype, model,
pattern, precedent,
standard, scanting, type,
protoplasm, module,
exemplar, example,
ensample, text, (imitation,
copy, transcription,
repetition, duplication,
mimicry)

orthodox-*adj* conformity,
observance, symmetry,

naturalization,
conventionality, custom,
agreeable, example,
quotation, exemplification,
illustration, typical normal,
formal, canonical, sound,
strict, rigid, positive,
uncompromising, (unusual,
unaccustomed,
uncommon, remarkable,
extraordinary, curious)

oscillation-*n* motion,
vibration, liberation, motion
of a pendulum, nutation,
undulation, pulsation,
pulse, alternate, wave,
rock, swing, pulsate, beat,
waggle, fluctuate, dance,
curvet, reel, change,
inconstancy, vicissitude,
(stable, constant,
established, fixture,
permanence, solidity, firm,
steadfast)

osculation-*n* contact,
contiguity, proximity,
apposition, juxtaposition,
touching, abutment,
meeting, coincidence,
adhesion, (gorge, defile,
ravine, crevice, separation,
interval, opening, leak)

ostensible-*adj* probable,
likely, hopeful, to be
expected, in a fair way,
plausible, specious,
colorable, well-founded,
reasonable, credible,
presumable, presumptive,
apparent, apparently,
seemingly, (improbability,
unlikelihood, unfavorable,
possibility, incredibility,

rare, infrequent,
inconceivable)

oust-*v* eject, emit, exit,
dispatch, exhale, excerpt,
excrete, secrete, secern,
extravagate, shed, void,
evacuate, effuse, spend,
expend, pour forth, squirt,
spurt, spill, slop, perspire,
exude, (admit, receive,
import, introduce, ingest,
absorb, suction, sucking,
insertion)

outburst-*n* violence,
inclemency, vehemence,
might, impetuosity,
effervescence, turbulence,
ferocity, rage, fury,
exacerbation,
exasperation, (moderation,
lenitive, gentleness,
sobriety)

outcome-*n* profit, earnings,
winnings, innings, pickings,
net profit, proceeds, return,
harvest, benefit, get back,
recover, regain, retrieve,
redeem

outlandish-*adj* ridiculous,
ludicrous, comic, droll,
funny, laughable,
grotesque, farcical, odd,
whimsical, fanciful,
fantastic, queer, eccentric,
strange, awkward,
(tasteful, unaffected,
cultivated, refined)

outline-*n* origin, source,
rise, but, germ, egg,
rudiment, genesis, birth,
title page, heading,
rudiments, elements,
grammar, alphabet, begin,

commence, inchoate,
arise, originate, conceive,
initiate, open, (end, close,
finish, terminate, conclude,
expire, consummation,
definitive)

outlying-*adj* remaining,
unconsumed, sedimentary,
surviving, net, exceeding,
over and above,
outstanding, cast off,
superfluous, redundant,
surplus, overplus, excess,
(augment, appendage,
adjunct, addition, affix,
reinforcement,
supernumerary,
accessory)

outmaneuver-*v* deception,
falseness, fraud, deceit,
guile, fraudulence,
knavery, cunning,
misrepresentation,
delusion, gullible, juggling,
trick, cheat, feint, juggle,
defeat, conquer, vanquish,
over come, silence, quell,
checkmate, (fruitless,
ineffectual, inefficient,
impotent, efficacious)

outrage-*n* bad turn, affront,
disrespect, atrocity, ill
usage, intolerance,
persecution, malevolent,
grudge, abolish, malign,
molest, worry, harass,
haunt, wreck, impair,
wane, (benevolent, kind,
well meaning, amiable)

outrageous-*adj* violent,
vehement, warm, acute,
sharp, rough, rude,
ungentle, bluff, boisterous,

wild, brusque, abrupt,
impetuous, excite, incite,
urge, lash, stimulate,
irritate, inflame, kindle,
(tranquilize, assuage,
appease, swag, lull,
soothe, compose, still,
calm, cool, quiet, hush,
quell)

outrival-*adj* superior,
exceed, excel, transcend,
out-do, out-weigh,
dominate, prevail, come
first, culminate,
distinguished, vaulting,
greatest, paramount,
foremost, crowning,
excellent, important,
(inferior, minority,
subordinate, short-coming,
deficiency, minimum,
smallness, diminish)

outset-*n* beginning,
commencement, opening,
incipience, inception,
inchoation, introduction,
alpha, initial, inauguration,
embarkation, outbreak,
onset, brunt, initiative,
fresh start, (end, close,
finish, terminate, conclude,
be all over with, expire,
final, crowning, complete,
hinder)

outside-*n* exterior, surface,
eccentricity, face,
superficial, skin-deep,
frontal, external, outward,
covering, extramural,
(interior, inside, interspace,
innermost, indoor, inward,
enclosed)

outstanding-*adj* remainder,

residue, remains, remnant,
rest, relic, leavings, heel-
tap, odds and ends, left,
unconsumed, sedimentary,
surviving, exceeding,
outlying, (adjunct, addition,
affix, appendage,
augment, increment,
reinforcement,
supernumerary, accessory,
item, garnish, sauce)
outweigh-v exceed, excel,
transcend, out-balance,
out-do, pass, surpass, get
ahead of, cap, beat,
eclipse, preponderate,
predominate, prevail,
proceed, take precedence,
come first, render larger,
(inferior, smaller,
decrease, contract, hide,
lower, minor, less, lesser,
deficient, minus)
ovation-n celebration,
solemnization, jubilee,
commemoration, triumph,
jubilation, keep, signalize,
rejoice, (nonobservance,
evasion, failure, omission,
neglect, laxity, informality)
overburden-adj redundant,
luxury, excess, surplus,
margin, remainder,
duplicate, surplusage,
extravagance, lavishness,
superfluous, unnecessary,
needless

P

pack-v arrange, dispose,
place, form, collocate,
marshal, size, rank, group,

parcel out, allot, distribute,
dispose of, assign, assort,
classify, divide, file, string,
assembled, closely
packed, dense, swarming,
(dispersion, divergence,
scattering, dissemination,
misplace, mislay, disorder)
paddle-v walk, march, step,
tread, pace,plod, wend,
promenade, trudge, tramp,
stalk, stride, straddle, strut,
stump, bundle, handle, hilt,
haft, shaft, heft, shank,
blade, trigger, tiller, helm,
treadle, key
padlock-n fasten, bolt,
latch, latchet, tag, tooth,
hook, holdfast, rivet,
anchor, grappling, stake,
post, tie, strap, tackle,
rigging, brace, girder
page-n numeration,
numbering, pagination,
tale, recension,
enumeration, summation,
reckoning, computation,
check, prove, demonstrate,
balance, audit, part, issue,
number, album, portfolio,
periodical, serial,
magazine, circular, paper,
bill, sheet, broadsheet
pair-n couple, duality,
duplicity, two, deuce,
brace, cheeks, twins,
duplex, analog, the like,
match, similarity,
resemblance, likeness,
affinity, pendant, fellow,
mate, double, counterpart,
(dissimilar, unlike,
disparate, of a different

kind, unmatched, nothing
of the kind)
palatable-*adj* savoriness,
zest, dainty, delicacy,
ambrosia, nectar, appetite,
relish, like, smack the lips,
well-tasted, good, nice,
dainty, delectable, gusty,
appetizing, lickerish,
delicate, delicious,
exquisite, rich, luscious,
(offensive, repulsive,
nasty, sickening,
nauseous, loathful,
unpleasant)
pale-*adj* dimness, darkness,
half-light, glimmer,
nebulosity, aurora, dusk,
twilight, shades, moonlight,
lackluster, dingy, dark,
pallid, tallow-faced, faint,
dull, cold, muddy, leaden,
discoloration, neutral tint,
monochrome, (pigment,
color, dye, tinge,
illuminate, emblazon,
bright, vivid, intense, deep)
pall-*n* cloak, mantle,
mantlet, mantua, shawl,
wrapper, veil, cape, tippet,
kirtle, plaid, muffler,
comforter, coffin, shell,
sarcophagus, urn, bier,
hearse, catafalque,
offensive, repulsive, nasty,
sickening, nauseous,
loathful, unpleasant,
(dainty, delicacy,
ambrosia, nectar, game,
relish, like)
palpable-*adj* material,
bodily, corporeal, physical,
somatic, sensible, tangible,

ponderable, substantial,
objective, impersonal,
neuter, unspiritual, plain,
distinct, definite, well
defined, marked, in focus,
recognizable, (invisible,
non-appearance,
concealment, dim,
confused, indistinct)
palpitate-*v* tremble,
agitation, stir, tremor,
ripple, jog, jolt, jar, jerk,
shock, succussion,
trepidation, tingle, thrill,
heave, pant, throb, quiver,
flutter, twitter, shake
pamper-*v* indulge, high,
living, self-indulgence,
voluptuousness,
dissipation, sensuality,
animalism, carnality,
pleasure, effeminacy,
silkiness, luxury, piggish,
gluttony, greed, epicurism,
gorge, overfed,
omnivorous, (fast, starve,
clam, famish, perish,
Lenten, unfed, frugality,
moderation)
panel-*n* partition, septum,
diaphragm, midriff, party-
wall, vail, between, betwixt,
sandwich, parenthesis, list,
catalog, inventory,
schedule, register,
account, bill, calendar,
index, table, contents,
(surround, beset,
compass, encompass,
environ, inclose, enclose,
encircle, embrace)
paper-*n* write, pen, copy,
engross, write out, fair,

transcribe, scribble, scrawl, scrabble, scratch, interline, stain paper, write down, record, sign, compose, indite, draw up, dictate, inscribe

paradox-*n* absurdity, imbecility, nonsense, inconsistency, blunder, muddle, bull, farce, rhapsody, farrago, extravagance, romance, obscure, dark, muddy, dim, nebulous, shrouded in mystery, invisible, (plain, distinct, explicit, positive, definite, graphic, expressive, illustrative, lucid)

parallel-*adj* similarity, resemblance, likeness, similitude, semblance, affinity, approximation, agreement, analogy, brotherhood, repetition, uniformity, imitation, copying, transcription, duplication, quotation, (unimitated, unmatched, unparalleled, original, dissimilar, unlike, disparate)

paramount-*adj* supreme, essential, vital, all-absorbing, radical, cardinal, chief, main, prime, primary, principal, leading, capital, foremost, over-ruling, of vital importance, significant, telling, trenchant, emphatic, pregnant, urgent, pressing, critical,

(poor, paltry, pitiful, contemptible, sorry, mean, meager)

paraphrase-*n* explanatory, expository, explicative, exegetical, polyglot, literal, significative, synonymous, equivalent, interpret, explain, define, construe, translate, phrase, expression, set phrase, sentence, paragraph, figure of speech, periphrase, (misrepresent, pervert, garble, falsify)

parody-*n* ridicule, derision, sardonic, smile, grin, scoffing, mockery, quiz, banter, irony, raillery, chaff, joke, twit, quiz, satirize, caricature, burlesque, travesty, servile, copy, imitation, counterfeit, deception, faithful, (prototype, original, model, pattern, precedent, standard, scanting, type, paradigm)

paroxysm-*n* passion, excitement, flush, heat, fever, fire, flame, fume, blood boiling, tumult, effervescence, ebullition, boiling, whiff, gust, storm, tempest, scene breaking out, agony, explosion, burst, (submission, resignation, suffer, forbearance, fortitude, compose, appease)

part-*n* divide, portion, dose, item, particular, aught, any, division, ward, subdivision,

section, chapter, verse,
article, clause, count,
paragraph, passage,
sector, segment, fraction,
fragment, parcel, (whole,
totality, integrity, entirety,
aggregate, gross amount,
sum total, bulk, mass,
lump, altogether)
particular-*adj* exact,
accurate, definite, precise,
well defined, just right,
correct, strict, close, rigid,
rigorous, punctual,
genuine, authentic,
legitimate, orthodox, pure,
natural, sound, sterling,
(error, fallacy,
misconception, mistake,
miss, fault, blunder,
oversight, misprint, slip,
blot, flaw, loose thread)
partner-*n* companion,
accompany, coexist,
attend, fellow associate,
escort, consort, spouse,
colleague, satellite,
concomitant, accessory,
spouse, mate, yokefellow,
husband, man, consort,
goodman, squaw, lady,
matron, wedded pair,
husband, wife, (separation,
divorce, unity, oneness)
pass-*v* move through,
transmission, permeation,
transudation, infiltration,
endosmose, ingress,
egress, opening, journey,
perforate, penetrate,
thread, conduit, gone, last,
latter, bygone, foregone,
elapsed, lapsed, expired,

(future, prospectively,
impending, next, stay,
eventual)
passion-*n* emotion,
character, qualities,
disposition, nature, spirit,
tone, temper, idiosyncrasy,
soul, pervading, spirit,
humor, mood, grain,
mettle, sympathy, desire,
wish, fancy, fantasy, want,
need, exigency, inclination,
leaning, (indifferent, cold,
frigid, lukewarm,
unconcerned, careless,
listless)
passive-*adj* inert, dullness,
inactivity, torpor, languor,
quiescence, latency,
inaction, sloth, sluggish,
heavy, flat, slack, tame,
slow, blunt, lifeless, dead,
uninfluential, dormant,
(strong, energetic, forcible,
active, intense, severe,
keen, vivid, sharp, acute,
incisive, trenchant, brisk,
poignant, caustic)
paste-*n* bond, tendon,
tendril, fiber, ribbon, rope,
cable, line, hawser, painter,
mooring, wire, chain,
fasten, tie, strap, tackle,
rigging, adhere, fuse
pat-*v* blow, stroke, knock,
tap, rap, slap, smack dab,
fillip, slam, bang, hit,
whack, thwack, cuff,
squash, dowse, whop,
swap, punch, thump, pelt,
kick, cut, thrust, lunge,
hammer, batter, (recoil,
retroaction, revulsion,

rebound, rebuff, reflux,
reverberation, return)

patch-*n* plot, enclosure,
close, arena, precincts,
tract, territory, country,
canton, county, shire,
domain, blemish,
disfigurement, deformity,
defect, flaw, injury, stain,
blot, spot, speck, freckle,
mole, blotch, disfigure,
pitted, (spacious, roomy,
extensive, expansive,
capacious, ample,
boundless)

patience-*n* perseverance,
resolution, determination,
desperation, devotion,
tenacity, obstinacy, self-
control, submission,
resignation, forbearance,
longanimity, fortitude,
(ruffle, hurry, fuss, stew,
ferment, fit, violence, rage,
fury, desperation,
madness, distraction,
raving, delirium, frenzy,
hysterics)

patter-*v* rap, snap, tap,
knock, click, clash, crack,
crash, pop, slam, bang,
clap, rustle, loquacity,
talkativeness, garrulity,
eloquent, jaw, gabble,
jabber, chatter, orate,
fluent, (silence, mute,
mum, still, reserved,
reticent, conceal, hush)

pause-*v* rest, lull, respite,
truce, drop, interregnums,
abeyance, cessation,
resistance, intermission,
interruption, stop, halt,

arrival, closure,
discontinue, quiet, tranquil,
calm, repose, stand still,
stagnate, quell, stationary,
anchor, (move, motion,
transitorily, restless,
changeable, nomadic)

pay-*v* remunerate, reward,
recompense, meed,
quitting, compensation,
reparation, redress,
retribution, reckoning,
acknowledgment, requital,
amends, salvage,
perquisite, allowance,
salary, (penalty, fine,
forfeit, escheat, amerce,
sconce, confiscate,
punishment, penalty,
atonement)

peace-*n* concord, accord,
harmony, symphony,
agreement, love,
response, union, unison,
unity, assent, unanimity,
friendship, alliance,
understanding,
conciliation, fraternize,
(dissension, odds, discord,
disagreement, division,
split, quarrel, squabble,
altercation, wrangling,
strife, embroilment)

peak-*n* summit, top, vertex,
apex, zenith, pinnacle,
acme, culmination,
meridian, utmost height,
pitch, maximum, climax,
tip, crown, garret, ceiling,
pediment, (bottom, base,
basement, foundation,
substructure, ground,
earth, pavement, floor)

perform-v achieve, accomplish, completion, fulfillment, execution, dispatch, consummation, culmination, finish, conclusion, close, issue, (incomplete, shortcoming, unfulfilled, neglect)

perhaps-adv possibly, potentiality, feasibility, conceivable, credible, compatible, achievable, chance, contingency, practicable, within reach, accessible, surmountable, (impossible, absurd, contrary)

perish-v die, death, decease, demise, dissolution, departure, release, rest, loss, bereavement, end, cessation, extinction, death rattle, (life, vitality, animation, vivification, alive, respire, subsist, revive)

permeate-v pervade, fill, present, occupy, inhabiting, moored, domiciled, omnipresent, dwell, reside, diffusion, haunt, revisit, sojourn, abide, lodge, nestle, roost, (empty, vacuum, truant, absent, vacate)

perplex-v distressing, bothersome, afflicting, unlucky, uncomfortable, disheartening, depressing, distasteful, unpleasant, unpopular, thankless, (refreshing, comfortable, cordial, genial, glad, pleasant delightful, lovely, felicitous)

persecute-v oppress, wrong, aggrieve, trample, tread, overburden, weigh down, victimize, molest, maltreat, abuse, ill-use, ill-treat, harm, injure, (goodness, merit, beneficial, valuable, profitable)

persist-v continue, last, endure, go on, remain, intervene, elapse, continue, seize an opportunity, permanent, duration, pending, interval, (never, nevermore, at no time, hesitant, doubtful)

persuade-v induce, prevail, overcome, carry, bring round, procure, enlist, engage, invite, court, tempt, seduce, entice, allure, captivate, fascinate, (discourage, dampen, restrain, reluctance)

pertinent-adj relative, bearing, reference, connection, concern, correlative, cognate, association, nearness, interest, relevancy, comparison, correlation, (incidental, parenthetical, remote, far fetched)

pervert-n misrepresent, garble, distort, travesty, retort, stretch, strain, misinterpreted, hardening, backsliding, declination, reprobation, (elected, adopted, regenerated, inspired, consecrated, converted)

pessimism-*n* underestimate, depreciate, detract, undervalue, modest, under rate, disparage, minimize, (over-estimation, oversensitive, vanity)

petrify-*v* density, solidity, solidness, constipation, solidified, compact, thickset, substantial, massive, impenetrable, impermeable, (rare, subtile, thin, fine, tenuous, compressible, flimsy, slight, spongy)

phantom-*n* imaginary, fancy, conceive, deal, realize, create, originate, devise, invent, fabricate, improvise, fertile, unreal, ideal, legendary, whimsical, fairy-like, mythological, illusory, fallacious

photography-*n* representation, illustration, delineation, depiction, portraiture, engraving, daguerreotype, image, likeness, facsimile, (misrepresent, distort, exaggerate, daub)

physical-*adj* materialistic, substantiality, condition, matter, body, substance, stuff, element, principle, object, article, (immaterial, disembody, spiritualize,

extramundane, earthy, pneumatolysis)

pick-*v* select, choice, option, discretion, volition, alternative, dilemma, adoption, decision, judgment, election, poll, ballot, exception, preference, (indifferent, neutral, abstain, refrain)

picket-*n* place, situate, locate, moor, tether, pack, tuck in, imbed, vest, make a place for, put, lay, set, seat, station, lodge, quarter, post, sentinel, watch, patrol, vedette, bivouac, scout, spy, spiel

pickle-*n* preserve, maintain, keep, embalm, dry, cure, salt, season, bottle, pot, tin, can, macerate, dilution, humectant, dilemma, embarrassment, perplexity, (easy, facile, feasible, easily managed)

picture-*n* description, set forth, portray, represent, characterize, particularize, narrate, relate, recite, recount, graphic, appearance, aspect, color, image, (vanish, disappear, missing, lost, departure)

piercing-*v* shrill, harsh sounds, acute, high note, scream, discordant, cry, roar, shout, hoop, whoop, yell, bellow, howl, scream, screech, shriek (muffled, dead silence, melodious)

pile-*v* heap, exaggerate, magnify, aggravate,

amplify, overestimate,
hyperbolize, overestimate,
accumulation, congeries,
lump, mass, pyramid, drift,
acervate, conglomeration,
quantity, greatness,
(disperse, scatter,
disseminate, diffuse, shed,
spread, overspread,
distribute, dispel)

pilot-n guide, direct,
manage, govern, conduct,
order, prescribe, regulate,
steer, take the helm,
superintend, sailor,
mariner, navigator,
skipper, gondolier,
steersman, seaman

pin-v fasten, restraint,
hindrance, coercion,
compulsion, constraint,
repression, discipline,
control, confinement,
durance, duress,
imprisonment, (liberate,
disengagement, release,
dismissal)

pinch-v requirement, need,
want, necessities, stress,
exigency, essential,
indispensability, urgency,
pain, suffer, ache, smart,
bleed, tingle, hurt, chafe,
(pleasure, bodily
enjoyment, gratification,
luxury)

pioneer-n precursor,
antecedent, precedent,
predecessor, forerunner,
van-courier, prodrome,
outrider, leader, herald,
prelude, prior, groundwork,
(sequel, suffix, successor,

tail, train, wake, rear)

pitch-v degree, grade,
extent, measure, amount,
ratio, stint, standard,
reach, amplitude, range,
scope, gradation, shade,
tenor, station, comparative,
gradual, limit, height

pith-n gist, intrinsically,
inherence, inhesion,
subjectiveness, ego,
essence, essential part,
quintessence, incarnation,
quiddity, marrow, sap,
lifeblood, backbone, heart,
soul, (outward, incidental,
extrinsic, extraneous,
accidental, objective,
derived from without)

place-v arrange, prepare,
plan, disposal, distribute,
sort, assort, allotment,
apportionment, analysis,
classification, division,
digest, (disorder,
misarrange, disturb,
confuse, perturb, jumble,
muddle)

placid-adj passive, tranquil,
collness, calmness,
composure, serenity, quiet,
peace of mind

plagiarism-n steal, theft,
thievery, borrowed,
forgery, imitator, echo,
transcribe, match, parallel,
simulate, impersonate,
represent, counterfeit,
parody, travesty,
caricature, burlesque

plain-adj simple, plain,
homeliness, undress,
chastity, unaffected,

chaste, severe, bald, flat,
dull, unvaried,
monotonous,
unornamented, blank,
(ornate, florid, rich, flowery,
elegant)

platform-*n* pulpit, desk,
reading, theater,
amphitheater, forum,
stage, rostrum, hustings,
tribune, plan, scheme,
design, project, proposal,
suggestion, sketch,
skeleton, outline, draught,
draft

plausible-*adj* probable,
likelihood, hopeful,
specious, ostensible,
founded, reasonable,
credible, presumable,
presumptive, apparent,
most-likely, (improbable,
unlikely, long odds,
unfavorable)

plea-*v* vindication,
justification, warrant,
exoneration, exculpation,
acquittal, whitewashing,
extenuation, softening,
mitigation, reply,
(accusation, charge,
imputation, slur, libel)

pleasant-*adj* flatter,
adulator, eulogist,
euphemism, optimist,
encomiast, laudatory,
whitewasher, toady,
sycophant, courtier, puffer,
touter, amuse, entertain,
diversion, relaxation,
solace, fun, frolic,
merriment, laughter, labor
of love, (weariness,

lassitude, disgust, nausea,
loathing)

pledge-*v* promise,
undertaking, word, troth,
plight, parole, word of
honor, vow, oath,
affirmation, assurance,
warranty, guarantee,
insurance, contract,
borrow, (demise, lease,
advance, loan,)

plenty-*n* sufficient,
adequate, enough, withal,
satisfaction, ample,
copious, abundant,
abounding, replete, rich,
luxuriant, affluent,
inexhaustible, liberal,
(scarcity, want, need, lack,
poverty, dole)

plod-*v* slow, languor, slow-
goer, linger, loiter,
sluggard, snail, dawdle,
creep, crawl, lag, drawl,
saunter, trudge, stump
along, retard, slacken,
(move quickly, trip, speed,
hasten, scuttle, scud)

pluck-*v* take, catch, hook,
nab, bag, sack, pocket,
receive, accept, assume,
possess, take possession
of, ravish, seize, pounce,
assault, intercept,
scramble for, snatch,
(return, restore,
recuperate, reinvest,
reparation, remit,
rehabilitate)

plump-*adj* huge, immense,
enormous, might, vast,
stupendous, monstrous,
colossal, gigantic, infinite,

large as life, hulky,
unwieldy, lumpish,
whopping, (dwarf, pygmy,
atom, microscopic, gaunt,
molecular, thin,
inconsiderable)

pocket-*n* receptacle,
compartment, hole, corner,
niche, recess, nook, crypt,
stall, chest, box, coffer,
caddy, case, basket,
pouch, sack, wallet, scrip,
poke, knit, knapsack,
haversack, satchel

point-*v* mark, topic, food for
thought, subject matter,
theme, thesis, text,
business, affair, argument,
motion, resolution, inquiry,
problem, question, (notion,
conception, reflection,
observation, idea)

polemic-*n* combatant,
disputant, controversial,
litigant, belligerent,
competitor, rival,
contention, strife,
opposition, rivalry,
handicap, contest, match,
race, (peace, amity,
friendship, harmony)

polished-*adj* polite,
courtesy, respect, good
manners, good behavior,
good breeding, urbanity,
presence, obeisance,
politeness, amiability,
complacency, (impudence,
disrespect, sternness)

pommel-*v* rotund, round,
circular, cylindrical,
columnar, spherical, ball,
boulder, oblong, oblate,

drop, vesicle, bulb, bullet,
barrel, drum, rolling pin,
rundle, cone

ponderous-*adj* judgment,
result, conclusion, upshot,
deduction, inference,
egotism, illation, corollary,
porism, estimation,
valuation, appreciation,
assessment, (detection,
discovery, find, determine,
trace)

poor-*adj* poverty, indigence,
penury, pauperism,
destitution, want, need,
lack, necessity, distress,
difficulties, bad,
embarrassed, reduced,
circumstances, slender,
stricken, (wealth, rich,
fortunate, opulence,
affluence, provision,
livelihood, maintenance,
dowry, means, resources)

pop-*v* abruptly,
unexpectedly, plump,
unaware, without notice,
startle, take aback,
electrify, stun, stagger,
astonish, surprise,
(expected, anticipating,
reckoning, suspense,
waiting, abeyance)

popular-*adj* celebrated,
distinction, mark, name,
figure, repute, reputation,
fame, renown,
approbation, notoriety,
illustriousness, hero,
nobility, glory, honor,
(disgrace, shame,
humiliation, tarnish,
scandal)

portable-*adj* transit,
transition, passage,
removal, conveyance,
relegation, portage,
carting, shoveling, freight,
convoy, bring, fetch, reach,
send, consign, deliver,
transpose, movable,
contagious
portfolio-*n* book, part,
issue, number, album,
magazine, periodical,
serial, annual, journal,
paper, bill, broadsheet
positive-*adj* certain,
necessity, certitude,
surety, assurance,
infallibleness, reliability,
gospel, scripture, absolute,
unqualified, inevitable,
infallible, unchangeable,
impeachable, conclusive,
authoritative, (uncertain,
doubtful, dubious,
indecisive, value,
ambiguous, undefined,
confused)
possess-*v* ownership,
tenure, occupancy,
holding, tenancy, heritage,
inheritance,enjoy, labor
under, come to pass,
conditional, (circumstance,
situation, phase, position)
posthumous-*adj* late, tardy,
slow, behind, belated,
unpunctual, backward,
slowly, leisurely,
deliberately, delay,
postponement,
adjournment, prorogation,
retardation, (punctual,
promptitude, prematurity)

posture-*n* form, figure,
conformation, make,
formation, feature,
lineament, turn, phase,
aspect, situation, locality,
latitude, footing, standing,
standpoint, stage, aspect,
attitude
potentiality-*n* possibility,
compatibility, agreement,
practicability, feasibility,
feasible, performable,
achievable, accessible,
superable, surmountable,
obtainable, contingent,
(impossibility, absurd,
unreasonable, incredible,
inconceivable, improbable,
prodigious, impervious)
potpourri-*n* fragrant,
aromatic, redolent, spicy,
balmy, scented, sweet-
smelling, perfumed,
muscadine, ambrosial,
scent, mixture, join,
combine, intermix, mingle,
instill, compound, medicate
pout-*v* moody,
discourteous, displacency,
grim, sullen, peevish,
acrimonious, surly, rough,
blunt, gruff
poverty-*n* indigence -
penury, pauper,
destitution, want, need,
necessity, privation,
distress, needy, difficulties,
beggar, (wealth, riches,
fortune, opulence,
affluence, livelihood)
practical-*adj* operative,
efficient, efficacious,
effectual, maintaining,

practice, procedure,
practical joking, ridicule,
sarcasm, mockery,
discourtesy

praiseworthy-*adj*
commendable, praise,
laud, good work, tribute,
eulogy, homage,
benediction, blessing,
applause,complimentary,
uncritical, (frown upon,
reprehend, admonish,
reprimand, chastise,
castigate, lash out,
trounce)

precedent-*n* coming before,
lead, superiority,
antecedent, anterior, prior,
former, foregoing,
prefatory, introductory,
precursor, (sequence,
coming after, succeed,
follow, ensure, alternate)

precious-*adj* valuable, dear,
extravagance, exorbitance,
superiority, goodness,
excellence, worth, rare
expensive, costly,
beneficial, serviceable,
advantageous, edifying,
(cheap, depreciated,
bargain)

precipice-*n* slope, obliquity,
inclination, slant, crooked,
leaning, bevel, tilt, bias,
twist, swag, cant, lurch,
rise, ascent, gradient,
rising ground, dip, fall
downhill, steepness, cliff,
escarpment

precocious-*adj* flippant,
pert, cavalier, saucy,
forward, impertinent,

malapert, assuming, bluff,
brazen, shameless,
aweless, unblushing,
unabashed, bold, bare,
impudent, audacious,
presumptuous, (servile,
obsequious, supple,
soapy, oily, groveling,
sniveling, mealy-mouthed,
beggarly, prostrate)

pregnant-*adj* productive,
fertility, luxuriance,
puberty, pullulating,
fructify, multiplication,
propagation, procreation,
superfetation, generate,
(sterile, waste, barren,
addle, unfertile, arid)

prejudice-*adj* misjudgment,
miscalculation, hasty
conclusion, foregone
conclusion, narrow-
minded, confined, illiberal,
intolerant, besotted,
infatuated, fanatical,
positive, dogmatic, bias,
underestimate,
overestimate, (solve,
resolve, render right, be
near the truth, recognize,
realize, verify, make
certain)

prepense-*v*
predetermination,
premeditation, deliberation,
foregone conclusion,
resolve, propend, intention,
project, redesigned,
advised, calculated, well-
laid, (impulse, sudden)

prerogative-*n* right,
privilege, prescription, title,
claim, pretension, demand,

birthright, immunity,
license, liberty, franchise,
vested interest, sanction,
authority, (impropriety,
emptiness, illegality)
prescribe-v advice,
counsel, suggestion,
recommendation,
advocacy, instruction,
charge, direct, manage,
govern, conduct, order,
lead
present-v bestowal,
donation, delivery,
consignment,
dispensation, endowment,
investment, almsgiving,
generosity, liberality,
charity, dispensation,
(receive, acquire,
admission, benefactor)
pretend-v feign, assume,
make believe, false,
simulate, counterfeit,
sham, malign, deceitful,
dishonest, evasive, hollow,
insincere, forsworn,
fabricate, prevaricate,
(veracity, truth, frankness)
primary-adj important,
significant, concern,
emphasis, greatness,
superiority, notability,
gravity, seriousness,
solemnity, no laughing
matter, urgent,
prominence, (trivial,
frivolous, paltry, small)
privacy-n seclusion,
exclusion, retirement,
reclusion, recess,
snugness, solitude,
solitary, isolation,

loneliness, voluntary exile,
aloofness, convent, exile,
ostracism, (social,
companionship,
association, acquaintance,
conversable, convivial,
jovial, hospitable)
probation-n verification,
test, assay, proof,
diagnostic, crucial test,
check, ordeal, experiment,
answerable, prove,
establish, make good,
show, conclusiveness,
(refutation, answer,
disproof, conviction,
invalidation, retort,
negative, parry, argument)
procreate-v productive,
prolific, teeming, fertile,
fruitful, frugivorous,
luxuriant, pregnant,
generative, life-giving,
spermatic, multiparous,
(sterility, infertility, waste,
desert, unprofitable)
profession-n part, cue,
province, function, look-
out, department, capacity,
sphere, orb, field, line,
routine, career, race,
vocation, calling, craft,
trade, actively employed,
employment
promise-v undertaking,
work, troth, plight, pledge,
parole, affirmation, vow,
oath, profession,
assurance, warranty,
guarantee, insurance,
obligation, contract,
(release, liberation,
absolute, free)

purpose-*n* intent, project, predetermination, design, ambition, contemplation, mind, view, proposal, study, decision, resolve, settled, resolution, wish, motive, deliberate, (speculation, venture, chance)

pursue-*v* continue, persist, keep, stick to, maintain, carry on, uninterrupted, sustain, uphold, hold up, perpetuate, preserve, harp upon, repeat, (cease, discontinue, desist, pause, rest, respite)

push-*v* propulsion, ejaculation, ejection, throw, fling, toss, shot, discharge, missile, projectile, motion, dart, lance, flirt, flip, shoot, launch, send forth, (draw, pull, haul, lug, rake, drag, tug, tow, trail)

Q

quackery-*n* unskillful, incompetency, inability, disqualification, folly, stupidity, indiscretion,neglect, thoughtless, absence of rule, blunder, (skill, dexterity, clever, talent, ability)

quadrant-*n* angular measurement, elevation, distance, velocity, sextant, miter, obtuse, salient, fusiform, wedge-shaped, cuneiform, triangular, rectangular, multilateral, cubical, pyramidal

quagmire-*n* marsh, swamp, morass, moss, fen, bog, slough, sump, wash, mud, squash, slush, embarrassing, awkward, unwieldy, unmanageable, intractable, (ease, feasibility, smooth)

quake-*v* flutter, trepidation, fear and trembling, perturbation, tremor, quivering, shaking, trembling, throbbing, palpitation, fright, affright, quiver, quaver, twitter, twirl, writhe, toss

qualify-*v* change, mutate, permutation, variation, modification, modulation, innovation, metastasis, deviation, turn, diversion, beat, transform, transfigure, metamorphosis, convert, alter, vary, diversity, (stable, permanent, persist, endure, standing, maintain, preserve, conserve)

qualm-*n* misbelief, discredit, infidelity, dissent, change of opinion, doubt, uncertainty, skepticism, misgiving, demure, suspicion, jealousy, scruple, unbeliever, (credence, assurance, faith trust)

quantity-*n* magnitude, amplitude, mass, amount, quantum, measure,

substance, strength,
quantitative, some, any,
more or less,
(comparative, gradual,
shading, range, scope,
caliber)

quantum-_n_ dividend,
portion, contingent, share,
allotment, lot, measure,
dose, dole, meed, pittance,
ration, ratio, proportion,
quota, mess, allowance,
(insufficient, inadequate,
scarce, lack, famine)

quarrel-_n_ dispute, tiff,
squabble, altercation,
words, big words,
wrangling, jangle, babble,
cross questions, strife,
broil, brawl, row, racket,
embroilment, (accord,
peace of mind, comfort,
harmony, unison,
agreement)

quarter-_n_ quadratic,
quartile, tetracid, four,
tetrad, quartet, abode,
dwelling, lodging, domicile,
residence, address,
habitation, berth, seat, lap,
sojourn housing,
headquarters, throne

quasi-_adj_ imitate, copy,
mirror, reflect, reproduce,
repeat, do like, echo,
catch, transcribe, match,
parallel, mock, mimic,
simulate, impersonate,
counterfeit, (original,
unique, unimitated)

quell-_v_ becalm, hush, lull to
sleep, lay an embargo on,
remain, stay, stand, resting

place, bivouac, anchor,
rest, cast, quiet, tranquility,
repose, (motion, stream,
flow, restlessness,
nomadic)

quench-_v_ dissuade, deport,
cry out against,
remonstrate, expostulate,
warn, contraindicate,
disincline, repel, damp,
cool, calm, quiet,
deprecate, (persuade,
prevail, overcome, carry,
procure)

question-_n_ inquiry,
examination, review,
scrutiny, investigation,
exploration, sifting,
calculation, analysis,
dissection, resolution,
induction, (answer,
respond, reply, rebut,
retort, rejoin)

questionable-_adj_ doubtful,
mistrust, suspect, raise a
question, unbeliever,
refuse to admit, harbor,
demure, suspicious, have
one's doubts,
inconceivable, (belief,
credence, credit, reliability,
assurance)

quibble-_v_ sophism,
solecism, paralogism,
quirk, fallacy, subterfuge,
subtlety, quilled,
inconsistency, mockery,
pervert, equivocate,
mystify, evade, elude, the
absence of reason,
evasion, (logical
sequence, good cause,
sound, valid)

quick-*adj* hurry, hasten, accelerate, quicken, swift, rapid, eagle speed, acceleration, spurt, rush, dash, fast, speedy, nimble, agile, expeditious, express, (slow, dawdle, retard, slacken, falter)

quid-*n* barter, exchange, truck system, tit for tat, give and take, blow for blow, measure for measure, recrimination, accusation, revenge, (resist, rebuff, opposition, reluctant, withstand)

quiet-*adj* moderation, lenitive, temperate, gentle, tranquilize, assuage, appease, hush, quell, sober, soothe, compose, lull, calm, pacify, (loud, violent, ear-breaking, blast, fury)

quip-*n* cranks, jest, joke, conceit, quirk, merry, bright, happy, flash of wit, scintillation, witticism, work-play, riddle, smartness, retort, repartee, ridicule, (dull, uninteresting, unlively, stupid, slow, flat)

quirk-*n* amusement, entertainment, reaction, relaxation, solace, pastime, sport, labor of love, fun, frolic, merriment, jollity, heyday, laughter, (weariness, lassitude, fatigue, disgust, loathing)

quit-*v* relinquish, abandon, desertion, defection

secession, withdrawal, break off, desist, stop, vacate, renounce, forego, discard, abandon, discontinue, resignation, retirement

quiz-*v* question, interrogate, interpolation, challenge, examination, cross-examination, inquire, investigate, seek, search, rummage, explore, (answer, respond, reply, rebut, unriddle)

quota-*n* apportionment, dividend, contingent, allotment, measure, dose, dole, meed, pittance, ration, proportion, allowance, share, portion, assign, appropriate

quote-*v* example, instance, specimen, sample, exemplification, illustration, case in point, pattern, agreement, illustrative, invariable, instance, cite

R

rabid-*adj* longing, hankering, inkling, solicitude, anxiety, yearning, coveting, aspiration, ambition, eagerness, zeal, ardor, breathless, impatience, over-anxiety, (indifferent, cold, frigid, lukewarm)

race-*v* run, spurt, rush, dash, steeplechase, lively, gallop, cantor, trot, round trot, scamper, lightening,

rocket, arrow, dart, torrent,
hustler, gazelle, (creep,
crawl, shuffle, saunter,
delay, sluggish)

rack-n care, anxiety,
solicitude, trouble, trial,
ordeal, shock, blow, dole,
fret, burden, load, vessel,
vase, bushel, barrel,
canister, utensil, hamper,
crate, cradle (well-being,
good, snugness)

racket-n loudness, power,
loud noise, din, clang,
clatter, bombination, roar,
uproar, peal, swell, blast,
boom, resonance,
vociferation, hullabaloo,
thunder, resound,
(whisper, inaudible, low,
dull, muffled)

radical-adj cause, original,
primary, aboriginal,
embryonic, germinal,
having a common,review,
improve, refine upon,
rectify, enrich, mellow,
elaborate, fatten, promote,
cultivate, advance

rage-n resentment,
displeasure, animosity,
anger, wrath, indignation,
exasperation, violence,
vehemence, impetuosity,
boisterousness,
effervescence, row, (calm,
moderate, gentle, sobriety)

raise-v increase, augment,
enlarge, extend, expand,
increment, accretion,
accession, develop,
aggravate, ascent,
acerbate, spread, exalt,

deepen, (decrease,
diminution, lessen,
subtraction)

rake-v drag, draw, pull,
haul, lug, tug, tow, trail,
train, take in tow, wrench,
jerk, twitch, tousle, traction,
rascal, scoundrel, villain,
miscreant, wretch, reptile,
viper, scamp, (model,
paragon, good example)

rampant-adj influential,
important, weighty,
prevailing, prevalent, rife,
dominant, regnant,
predominant, run through,
pervade, (impotence,
inertness, irrelevant,
uninfluential, powerless)

random-adj indiscriminate,
aimless, promiscuous,
undirected, drift,
causeless, without
purpose, casually, by the
way, accidental, speculate,
unintentional, (intentional,
purpose, decision, motive)

ransack-v plunder, pillage,
rifle, sack, loot, spoil,
spoilt, despoil, strip, steal,
abstract, appropriate,
plagiarize, seize, poach,
swindle, peculate,
embezzle

rapid-adj advance, proceed,
progress, move quickly,
trip, speed, hasten, spank,
scuttle, hurry, accelerate,
quicken, fast, swift, quick,
nimble, agile, expeditious,
express, (relax, slow,
regress, retreat,
retrograde, withdraw,

short, halt)

rapture-_n_ love, fondness, liking, inclination, regard, admiration, affection, sympathy, yearning, tender passion, flame, devotion, (hate, detest, abominate, abhor, loathe, revolt against)

rare-_adj_ unusual, extraordinary, singular, unique, curious, odd, strange, monstrous, unexpected, remarkable, noteworthy, queer, quaint, nondescript, original, (typical, normal, ordinary, conventional)

rate-_v_ estimation, valuation, appreciation, judicature, result, conclusion, upshot, deduction, ponderous, assessment, deduce, derive, gather, collect, (result, discover, find, determine, evolve)

ratio-_n_ degree, grade, extent, measure, amount, stint, standard, height, pitch, reach, amplitude, range, scope, caliber, gradation, shade, rate, sort, comparative, (absolute, quantity, mass)

rational-_n_ intellect, mind, understanding, reason, thinking, principle, rationality, cogitative, faculties, senses, consciousness, observation, intuition, soul, spirit, (imbecility, brutality, brute-instinct)

rattle-_v_ repeated noise, roll, drum, rumble, clatter, patter, clack, hum, trill, shake, chime, peal, toll, tick, beat, ding-dong, tantara, whir, rat-a-tat, rub-a-dub, racket, clutter, cuckoo, repetition, devil's tattoo

ravenous-_adj_ appetite, sharp appetite, keenness, hunger, stomach, twist, thirst, avidity, greed, covetous, grasping, craving, voracity, gluttony, (earnestness, anorexia, inappetence, apathy)

raw-_adj_ immaturity, crudity, abortion, disqualification, improvisation, dismantle, extemporize, non-preparation, neglect, improvidence, (preparation, ripen, maturation, evolution, elaboration, gestation)

reaction-_n_ counteraction, opposition, contrariety, antagonism, polarity, clashing, collision, interference, resistance, renitency, friction, neutralization, recoil, compensation, hindrance, (concurrence, cooperation, cogency, union, agreement, consent)

ready-_adj_ prepare, providing, provision, anticipation, foresight, precaution, rehearsal, note of preparation, arrangement, clearance,

tuning, array, ripening,
(extemporize, improvise,
undress)

reap-v acquire, get, gain,
win, earn, obtain, procure,
gather, collect, assemble,
find, receive, replevy,
redeem, advantageous,
gainful, remunerative,
paying, lucrative, (loss,
privation, bereavement,
deprivation, dispossession,
riddance, deprived, bereft,
irretrievable)

reason-n wisdom, sapience,
sense, common sense,
rationality, judgment,
solidity, depth, profundity,
caliber, enlarged views,
genius, inspiration,
aptitude, (shallow, wanting,
weak, idiotic, vacant,
blatant)

reassure-v hope, confident,
trust, rely on, presume,
optimism, enthusiasm,
aspiration, secure,
encouraging, cheering,
inspiriting, looking up,
bright, roseate, (hesitate,
falter, funk, cower, crouch)

rebuff-v repulse, defeat,
rout, overthrow,
discomfiture, beating,
drubbing, nonsuit,
subjugation, fall, downfall,
ruin, perdition, wreck, fail,
unsuccessful, (success,
speed, advance, progress,
good fortune)

recede-v recession, move
from, retirement,
withdrawal, retreat,

retrocession, departure,
recoil, flight, avoidance,
remove, shunt, shun,
shrink, depart, (approach,
approximate, near, access)

receive-v acquisition,
exception, introduction,
susceptibility, acceptance,
admission, assignee,
devisee, donor, grantee,
take in, (give, gift,
donation, delivery,
dispensation, generosity)

recess-v regress, retreat,
withdrawal, retirement,
recession, refluence, ebb,
return, reflection, recoil,
deterioration, recede,
retrograde, (progression,
advance, improvement,
proceed, forward, onward)

reciprocate-v interchange,
exchange, transposition,
shuffling, castling, barter,
retaliation, bandy, shuffle,
permute, in exchange, vice
versa, (consideration,
substitute, supersede,
replace, redeem)

reckon-v discharge, settle,
quit, acquit, account,
balance, square up,
disgorge, make
repayment, repay, refund,
reimburse, retribute, make
compensation, (default,
defalcation, protest,
repudiation)

recognize-v see, behold,
discern, perceive, have in
sight, descry, sight, make
out, discover, distinguish,
spy, witness, contemplate,

speculate, cast, (blind,
hoodwink, dazzle, screen
from sight)
recommend-v approval,
approbation, sanction,
advocacy, esteem,
estimation, good opinion,
admiration, appreciation,
regard, account,
popularity, credit, repute,
(reprehension, admonition)
reconcile-v forgiveness,
pardon, condonation,
grace, remission,
absolution, amnesty,
oblivion, indulgence,
reprieve, conciliation,
excuse, exonerate,
(revenge, ruthless,
avenging, retaliation, feud)
recovery-n restitution,
restoration, return,
reinvestment,
recuperation, rehabilitation,
reconstruction, reparation,
atonement, release,
regurgitate,
(dispossession, relapse,
deterioration, return,
retrogression, confiscate,
eviction)
rectify-v restoration,
renovation, revival, refresh,
renaissance, redress,
recovery, restitution, return
to original state, curable,
heal, repair, (deterioration,
relapse, retrograde,
recidivism)
redeem-v recover, retrieval,
replevin, salvage, trove,
find, foundling,
compensate, equate,

indemnity, compromise,
neutralization, nullification,
retaliation, equalize
reduce-v decrease,
diminish, lessen, abridge,
shorten, shrink, contract,
discount, depreciate,
extenuate, lower, weaken,
fritter away, subtract,
(increase, enlarge, extend,
augment, magnify, gain)
reek-v unclean, impurity,
defilement, contamination,
abomination, taint, decay,
corruption, mold, must,
mildew, dirty, filthy, grimy,
soiled, stink, rank, (clean,
immaculate, spotless,
neat, tidy, trim)
refinement-n improvement,
betterment, melioration,
amendment, mend,
advancement, cultivate,
reformation, correction,
elaboration, purification,
repair, (deterioration,
impairment, injury,
damage)
reflux-v recoil, refluent,
react, spring, rebound,
revulsion, ricochet,
elasticity, reflection,
reverberation, resonance,
boomerang, (impulse,
impetus, momentum, push,
thrust, hammer, punch)
refrain-v avoidance,
forbearance, inaction,
abstention, neutrality,
evasion, elusion,
seclusion, avocation, flight,
escape, retreat, recoil,
departure, (pursuit,

prosecution, enterprising, undertaking)

refresh-v restoration, rehabilitation, reproduce, renovation, revival, resuscitation, renaissance, second youth, rejuvenescence, new birth, regeneration, (relapse, fall back, retrograde, return)

regard-v view, look, espial, glance, point of view, see, behold, discern, perceive, descry, make out, discover, distinguish, recognize, contemplate, speculate, (blindness, undiscerning)

register-v digest, synopsis, compendium, table, analysis, classification, division, atlas, classify, methodize, regulate, systematize, coordinate, settle, fix, (litter, scatter, mix, entangle, ravel, dishevel)

regret-v self-reproach, penitence, contrition, compunction, repentance, remorse, self-accusation, be sorry for, confess, reclaimed, disclose, (induration, obduracy, impenitence, uncontrite, shiftless)

rehabilitate-v restore, reinstatement, renovation, revival, refreshment, renaissance, redress, retrieval, reclamation, recovery, convalescence, resumption, recuperate,

curative, remedial, recover

rehearse-v repetition, iteration, reiteration, harping, recurrence, succession, monotony, rhythm, chimes, imitation, reverberation, recur, reappear, renew, repeated, often, again, over again, ditto

reinforce-v aid, assist, help, appellation, support, lift, advance, furtherance, promotion, relief, sustenance, nutrition, ministry, accommodation, supply, (prevent, preclude, obstruct, stop, block)

rejoice-v bless, beatify, satisfy, gratify, desire, slake, satiate, quench, indulge, humor, flatter, regale, refreshing, comfortable, cordial, glad, cheering, exciting, (annoyance, grievance, nuisance, bother)

relax-v loose, incoherence, immiscibility, looseness, laxity, loosening, freedom, disjunction, slacken, detach, disheveled, segregated, unconsolidated

relentless-adj resolved, determined, strong-willed, resolute, self-possessed, decided, definitive, peremptory, obstinate, persevering, (fickleness, levity, weakness, demur, hesitating, vacillation)

relief-n aid, assist, oblige,

accommodate, humor,
cheer, encourage, rescue,
deliverance, refreshment,
easement, softening,
alleviation, mitigation,
palliation, soothing,
consolation, (aggravate,
embitter)
relish-*n* desire, wish, fancy,
want, need, exigency,
mind, inclination, bent,
longing, hankering, inkling,
solicitude, anxiety,
yearning, coveting,
aspiration, (indifference,
cold, frigid, halfhearted,
neutrality)
remarkable-*adj* paramount,
essential, vital, all-
absorbing, radical,
cardinal, chief, main,
prime, primary, principal,
leading, foremost, vital,
significant, emphatic,
(ordinary, petty, frivolous,
insignificant)
remiss-*adj* careless,
neglect, trifling, omission,
default, supineness,
reckless, inconsiderate,
slovenly, erroneous,
nonchalant, inactive,
abandoned, disorderly,
(care, heed, watchful,
exact, attentive, vigil)
remote-*adj* distant, far,
elongation, background,
removed, telescopic,
yonder, farther, further,
beyond, apart, asunder,
wide apart, (nearness,
nigh, close, adjacent,
intimate, adjoin)

remove-*v* extract,
elimination extrication,
eradication, evolution,
extermination, ejection,
egress, extirpation, export,
evolve, squeeze out,
(insertion, introduction,
insinuation, injection,
immersion)
render-*v* restitution, return,
restoration, reinvestment,
recuperation, rehabilitation,
reparation, release,
replevin, redemption,
remit, revert, (take, catch,
capture, seizure,
subtraction, reception)
renovate-*v* restore,
reinstate, cure, repair,
reparation, recruit,
disinfection, redemption,
deliverance, restitution,
relief, recover, return to
original state,
(deterioration, retrogress,
fall back, relapse)
repair-*v* improve, amend,
betterment, mend,
advancement, progress,
ascent, promotion,
elevation, increase, reform,
correct, refinement,
elaborate, (deteriorate,
impair, injure, damage,
loss, detriment)
repel-*v* depart, cessation,
removal, exit, egress,
valediction, farewell,
outward bound, repulsive,
abduction, chase, dispel,
(attract, magnetism,
gravity, draw, adduce)
replace-*v* substitute,

commutation, supplant,
supersession, make-shift,
alternative, supersede, in
lieu of, redeem, change,
equivalent, shift,
(exchange, reciprocation,
transposition, shuffling,
barter, swap)
report-v description,
account, statement,
expose, disclosure,
specification, particulars,
abstract, narrative, history,
memoir, memorials,
annals, chronicle, relate,
recount, descriptive
repose-v rest, sleep,
relaxation, breathing time,
halt, pause, respite,
unbend, slacken, lie down,
recline, unstrained,
cessation, vacation,
recess, holiday, (exertion,
effort, strain, tug, pull)
represent-v express,
exposition, demonstration,
exhibition, production,
display, showing,
indication, publicity,
disclosure, indicate,
manifest, proclaim,
(allusive, dormant, hidden,
invisible, imply, conceal)
repress-v restraint,
hindrance, coercion,
compulsion, repression,
discipline, control,
confinement, durance,
duress, imprison, restrict,
(liberate, disengage,
release, enlarge, dismiss)
reprieve-v forgive, pardon,
condonation, grace,

remission, absolution,
amnesty, oblivion,
indulgence, conciliation,
reconciliation, pacification,
excuse, exonerate,
(revenge, vindictive,
unforgiving, ruthless,
retaliation, rancorous)
repudiate-v dissent,
discordance,
disagreement, difference,
diversity of opinion, non-
conformity, protest,
contradiction, rejection,
demur, (ratification,
confirmation,
corroboration, approval)
require-v need, want,
necessary, essential,
indispensable, urgent,
requisition, exactness,
demanding, compel, force,
make, drive, coerce,
enforce, oblige, (depletion,
vacancy, low, empty,
insolvency)
rescind-v abrogation,
annulment, canceling,
repeal, dismiss, depose,
abolish, retraction, destroy,
ignore, repudiate,
reconsecrate, divest,
(commission, delegate,
assign, ensign, entrust)
resist-v refuse, reject,
denial, decline,
peremptory, repulse,
rebuff, discountenance,
protest, dissent,
revocation, disclaim,
(present, bid, propose,
move, advance, start,
invite)

resolute-adj determined, strong-willed, decided, definitive, peremptory, obstinate, steady, intense, serious, relentless, inflexible, persistent, stability, (vacillating, changeable, weak, fluctuate, hesitate)

resolve-v interpret, explain, define, construe, translate, render, find out, illustrate, exemplify, unfold, expound, comment upon, annotate, popularize, disentangle, (misrepresent, garble, distort)

respect-n courtesy, good manners, behavior, breeding, politeness, gentility, polish, presence, humor, humility, obeisance, (disrespect, rude, insult, repulsive, bitter, acrimonious, sarcastic)

respire-v breathe, puff, gasp, wheeze, snuff, sniff, sneeze, cough, fan, ventilate, blow-up, air pump, lungs, bellows, hiccup

response-n answer, reply, replication, rejoinder, rebut, retort, repartee, rescript, examination, acknowledgement, password, discover, solution, explanation, rationale, respond, (question, analysis, query, problem, exploration, review, exploitation,

ventilation, sifting, search, inquire, calculation, analysis)

restless-adj disturbance, fidget, disquiet, agitation, unstable, vacillation, fluctuate, vicissitude, alteration, oscillation, unrest, agitation, (stable, stand, keep, remain firm, establish, settled, solid)

restore-v repair, reparation, recruit, reaction, redemption, restitution, relief, reconstruct, redeem, redress, resuscitate, renovate, renew, reestablish, (deteriorate, mutilate, disfigure, blemish, deface)

result-n conclusion, upshot, deduction, inference, corollary, estimation, valuation, appreciation, estimate, deduce, derive, gather, collect, settle, (discover, detect, find, determine, evolve)

retain-v retention, keep, detention, custody, tenacity, firm hold, grasp, gripe, grip, clinch, clench, secure, withhold, detain, hold, reserve, possess, entail, settle, (relinquish, abandon, dispense)

retire-v seclusion, privacy, reclusion, recess, snugness, sequestered, delitescent, hermit, estrangement, voluntary exile, solitude, isolation, loneliness, (social,

companionship,
comradeship, hospitality)
retort-v retaliation, reprisal,
retribution, reciprocation,
recrimination, accusation,
revenge, reaction, turn
upon
retreat-v regress,
retirement, withdrawal,
recede, counter-motion, remigration, recession,
recidivation, deterioration,
(progression, advance,
improvement, proceed,
forward, forth)
return-v succession,
revolve, pulsate, alternate,
intermit, steady, punctual,
arrive, disembark, advent,
reception, welcome,
recursion, remigration,
(departure, cessation,
removal, exit)
revenge-n vengeance,
avenged, rancor,
vindictiveness,
implacability, malevolence,
ruthlessness, unforgiving,
rankling, (forgiveness,
pardon, conciliate,
condone, acquit, pacify)
reverse-v contrary,
opposite, counter, differing,
diametrically opposed,
inverse, antipodal, against,
annulment, dismissal,
remission, abolish, retract,
recall, dissolve.
(inaugurate, accredit,
engage)
revolt-v resistance, stand,
front, oppugnant,
opposition, renitency,

reluctant, repulse, rebuff,
insurrection, against,
strong, obstinate,
stubborn, (retaliate, retort,
turn upon, reciprocate)
rich-adj sufficient,
adequate, enough,
satisfaction, competence,
ample, abundant, wealthy,
luxuriant, fertile, affluent,
pregnant, inexhaustible,
(insufficient, deficiency,
incomplete, shortcoming)
rid-v liberate, disengage,
release, free, disband,
discharge, unfetter, untie,
loose, relax, escape,
redeem, deliver, extricate,
emancipate, acquit,
escape, (confine, imprison,
repress, control, hinder)
riddle-n instrument for
sorting, sieve, screen,
arrange, dispose, place,
form, put, collocate, pack,
marshal, range, size, rank,
group, enigma, puzzle,
charade, maze, (news,
information, advice, word)
ride-v chase, give chase,
course, hunt, hound, tread,
rush upon, run, direct,
pursue, quest, follow,
prosecute, prowl, engage
in, endeavor, search,
(retreat, recoil, depart,
avoid, evade, seclude)
ridiculous-adj folly, frivolity,
irrationality, trifling,
ineptitude, negaters,
inconsistency, conceit,
giddiness, inattention,
eccentricity, absurd, idiotic,

imbecile, (wise, sapient,
reasonable, rational,
sensible)

rift-*n* fissure, breach, rent,
split, crack, slit, incision,
dissection, decomposition,
cutting instrument, sharp,
divorce, part, detach,
separate, rescind,
segregate, (attach, fix,
bind, secure, join, hinge)

right-*n* privilege, allow,
sanction, warrant,
authorize, ordain,
prescribe, constitute,
charter, enfranchise,
prescribe, presume,
absolute, indefeasible,
unalienable, merit,
(infringe, encroach)

rigid-*adj* obstinate,
tenacious, stubborn,
obdurate, case-hardened,
inflexible, hard,
immovable, inert, arbitrary,
dogmatic, positive,
bigoted, prejudiced,
(recant, retract, revoke,
rescind, recall, withdraw)

rile-*v* annoy, grieve,
nuisance, vexation, bore,
bother, blow, distressing,
afflicting, disheartening,
depressing, deplorable,
undesirable, causing pain,
haunt, (pleasant,
charming, fascinating)

ring-*n* resonance, loud,
clang, clatter, noise, roar,
uproar, racket, sonorous,
powerful, thundering, ear-
splitting, deafening,
(inaudible, scarcely, low,

dull, faint, soft, soothing,
melodious)

riot-*n* violence, row,
rumpus, inclemency,
vehemence, impetuosity,
boisterousness, rage,
ferocity, fury, exacerbation,
turbulent, disorderly,
uproarious, frenzied,
(tranquil, mild, reasonable,
cam, still)

ripen-*v* completion,
accomplish, achieve,
fulfillment, performance,
execution, dispatch,
consummation,
culmination, conclusion,
close, final, finished,
(incomplete, neglect,
undone)

rise-*v* ascend, grow, begin,
slope, progress, stir, revolt,
rocket, climb, clamber,
mount, aspire, tower, soar,
hover, spire, excelsior, up
hill, flight, (decline, fall,
drop, lapse, tumble, dip,
descend, sink)

risk-*v* danger, chance,
speculation, venture,
stake, blind bargain,
gamble, fate, hazard,
wager, game, accidental,
indiscriminate, random,
(decision, determination,
purpose, resolution)

ritual-*n* rite, ceremony,
observance, duty,
solemnity, sacrament,
service, worship, duty,
officiate, transfiguration,
consecration, ostentation,
showy, pretentious,

pompous, palatial,
theatrical, dramatic
rival-n competition, contest,
opposition, strive, struggle,
scramble, wrestle, spar,
square, exchange,
belligerent, combative,
unpeaceful, quarrelsome,
pugilistic, (harmony,
peace, concord, tranquil)
rivet-v attach, join, close,
tight, taut, taught, secure,
set, intervolved, hinge,
unite, connect, fix, bind,
tie, string, pin, nail, bolt,
hasp, clasp, fuse-together,
jam, (separate, rupture,
shatter, carve, cut)
roast-v heat, calefaction,
increase of temperature,
melt, burn, combustion,
ignition, warm, chafe,
stove, kindle, toast,
inflame, stew, cook,
seethe, simmer, (cool, fan,
refrigerate, refresh,
congeal)
robust-adj strong, mighty,
vigorous, forcible, hard,
adamantine, stout, sturdy,
hardy, powerful, potent,
puissant, valid, resistless,
invincible, impregnable,
able-bodied, (weak,
delicate, soft, limp, feeble)
rogue-n cheat, knave,
scamp, bad man, wrong-
doer, evil doer, sinner,
rascal, scoundrel, villain,
wretch, viper, serpent,
monster, devil incarnate,
(paragon, hero, demigod,
saint, benefactor, angel)

rollick-v cheerful, genial,
gaiety, good humor,
liveliness, vivacity,
animation, jovial, pleasing,
laughter, amusement,
rejoicing, smile, rejoice,
enliven, exhilarate,
(depressed, dejected,
gloom, weariness)
romantic-adj
impressionable, sensitive,
gushing, impassioned,
tender, warm, enthusiastic,
highflying, spirited,
mettlesome, vivacious,
lively, expressive,
excitable, (nonchalance,
unconcern, callousness)
room-n spacious, extensive,
expansive, capacious,
ample, wide-spread, vast,
world-wide,
uncircumscribed,
boundless, capacity,
stretch, absence
root-n base, basement,
plinth, dado, wainscot,
foundation, support,
substructure, substratum,
ground, earth, pavement,
floor, paving, flag, carpet,
fundamental, built-on,
(summit, apex, zenith,
pinnacle)
rose-n fragrant, aroma,
redolence, perfume,
bouquet, sweet, aromatic
perfume, sachet, scent,
spicy, balmy, muscadine,
ambrosial, fragrant as a
rose, (stench, stick,
unclean, offensive, rank)
rot-v deteriorate, debase,

wane, ebb, recess,
retrogradation, decrease,
degenerate, impairment,
injury, damage, loss,
detriment, outrage,
pollution, poison, (relieve,
refresh, infuse, reform,
enhance)
rotation-*n* periodically,
intermittent, beat,
oscillation, bout, round,
revolution, turn, cycle,
stated time, routine,
succession, return,
revolve, pulsate, alternate,
(uncertain, capricious,
flicker, ramble, spasmodic)
rough-*adj* uneven,
scabrous, knotted, gnarled,
unpolished, rugged, grain,
texture, ripple, corrugated,
ruffle, crisp, crumble,
(smooth, even, plane,
shave, level)
round-*adj* circle, rotund,
circlet, ring, areola, hoop,
roundlet, annulet, bracelet,
armlet, ringlet, eye, loop,
wheel, cycle, orb, orbit,
ellipse, oval, necklace,
collar, noose
rouse-*v* stimulate, excite,
inspirit, animate, incite,
provoke, instigate, induce,
move, prompt, attract,
beckon, bribe, lure, inspire,
encourage, solicit,
(discourage, dampen,
hinder, restraint, repel)
routine-*n* custom, habit,
rule, standing order,
precedent, red-tape, rut,
groove, usual, general

accustom, naturalize,
repeat, prevalent, vogue,
etiquette, order of the day,
(breached, spontaneous)
row-*v* discord,
disagreement, jar, clash,
shock, broil, brawl, racket,
hubbub, embroilment,
disturbance, commotion,
quarrel, dispute, embroil,
entangle, (harmony,
agreement, conciliation,
peace, accord)
rub-*v* friction, attrition,
rubbing, scratch, scrape,
scrub, fray, graze, curry,
scour, polish, rub out,
gnaw, file, grind, difficult,
hard, tough, laborious,
awkward, unwieldy,
(lubricate, smooth, pat,
gentle touch)
rude-*adj* graceless,
inelegant, harsh, abrupt,
dry, stiff, cramped, formal,
forced, labored, artificial,
mannered, ponderous,
turgid, affected, barbarous,
uncouth, (graceful, easy,
temperate, gentle)
ruin-*n* waste, destroy,
dissolution, breaking up,
consumption, fall, downfall,
perdition, crash, smash,
havoc, extinct, annihilation,
demolish, suppress,
abolish, ravage, devastate,
(rectify, flower, evolve)
rumple-*v* disorder,
derangement, confusion,
disarray, jumble, huddle,
litter, lumber, mash,
muddle, complex, intricate,

unsymmetrical,
unsystematic, untidy,
slovenly, (order, uniform,
symmetry, arranged)
runagate-n absence of
pursuit, abstention,
forbearance, refrain,
inaction, neutrality,
avoidance, evasion,
elusion, seclusion, flight,
escape, retreat, departure,
rejection, (pursuit, chase,
hunt, follow)
rush-v haste, urgency,
acceleration, spurt, spurt,
forced, march, dash,
velocity, precipitancy,
impetuosity, hurry, drive,
scramble, bustle, fuss,
fidget, flurry, (leisurely,
slow, deliberate, quiet,
calm)
rusty-adj moldy, musty,
mildewed, moth-eaten,
mucid, rancid, bad, gone
bad, touched, effete,
rotten, corrupt, tainted,
unclean, dirty, filthy, sooty,
turbid, (wash, clean, pure,
disinfect, neat)
ruthless-adj revenge,
vengeance, vendetta,
retaliation, rancor,
vindictiveness,
implacability, malevolence,
avenge, unrelenting,
rigorous, (forgive, pardon,
conciliation, reconciliation,
absolution)

S

sack-n bag, receptacle,
enclosure, recipient,
receiver, reservoir, sac,
knapsack, satchel, take,
catch, hook, gain, acquire,
procure, collect, assemble,
bring home, secure,
derive, draw
saintly-adj piety, religious,
holiness, sanctimony,
reverence, humility,
veneration, devotion,
prostration, worship, grace,
unction, edification,
consecration, spiritual
existence, (hypocrisy,
irreverence, sin)
salute-v respect, regard,
consideration, courtesy,
attention, deference,
reverence, honor, esteem,
estimation, veneration,
admiration, homage,
command, (dishonor,
desecrate, insult, affront,
outrage)
salvage-v get back,
recover, regain, retrieve,
replevy, redeem, come by
one's own, come by,
receive, inherit, succeed,
realize, treasure up, clear,
produce, (loss, incur, rid,
forfeit, lapse)
sanctify-v moral, ethical,
casuistical, conscientious,
amenable, liable,
accountable, responsible,
answerable, allegiance,
(exempt, release, acquit,
discharge, remise, remit,
free)
satiate-v satisfy, saturate,
replete, glut, surfeit,

weariness, cloy, quench,
slake, pall, gorge, tire,
enough, complete,
altogether, wholly, totally,
laden, (exhaustive, regular,
consummate, sheer)
saunter-v creep, ramble,
dawdle, drawl, slacken,
mincing steps, linger,
loiter, sluggard, tortoise,
snail, move slowly, crawl,
lag, plod, lumber, drag,
grovel, waddle, shuffle
(move quickly, speed,
hasten)
savage-adj cruel, brutal,
inhuman, barbarous, fell,
untamed, truculent,
incendiary, bloodthirsty,
murderous, atrocious,
fiendish, demoniacal,
diabolic, devilish,
(benevolent, consideration,
kind)
save-v economy, frugality,
thrift, care, husbandry,
retrenchment, prevention
of waste, parsimony,
sparing, invest, miserly,
tightfisted, mercenary,
venal, greedy, (liberal,
generous, charitable,
bounty)
say-v speech, locution, talk,
parlance, verbal
intercourse, oral
communication, spoken,
lingual, phonetic,
unwritten, eloquent,
talkative, mouthpiece,
language, (stammer,
stutter, falter, mumble)
scaffold-n support,

foundation, base, bearing,
footing, hold, place,
platform, block, rest,
sustentation, aid, prop,
stand, truss, stilt, staff,
shaft, pediment, (pendant,
hanging, dependent,
suspended, loose)
scatter-v dispersion,
disjunction, divergence,
dissemination, diffusion,
dissipation, distribution,
apportionment, spread,
sow, strew, dismember,
interspersion, (accumulate,
heap, lump, pile, stack)
scold-v execrate, beshrew,
anathematize, denounce,
execration, proscribe,
excommunicate, fulminate,
threaten, abuse, cross,
grumpy, glum, morose,
(hug, cuddle, address with
affection, serenade)
scourge-v rod, cane, stick,
switch, truncheon, ship,
last, strap, thong, cowhide,
pillory, stocks, whipping-
post, brank, triangle,
wooden horse,
thumbscrew, guillotine
(reward, satisfy,
compensate)
scratch-v mark, line, stroke,
dash, score, stripe, streak,
tick, dot, point, notch, nick,
asterisk, red letter, jotting,
print, imprint, note,
annotation, maltreat,
abuse, bruise, hurtful,
injurious
scruple-n probity, integrity,
rectitude, uprightness,

honesty, faith, honor, good
faith, purity, clean,
fairness, fidelity, loyalty,
trustworthiness, candor,
dignity, (dishonesty, moral
turpitude, disloyalty)
scrutiny-*n* attention,
mindfulness, intentness,
thought, observance,
consideration, reflection,
heed, notice, regard,
circumspection, study,
(abstract, absence,
preoccupation, reverie)
scuttle-*n* destroy, move
quickly, trip, fisk, speed,
hasten, accelerate,
quicken, whisk, bolt,
bound, scamper, run,
spank, scour, scamper, run
like mad, fly, race, (slow,
slack, tardy, gentle, easy,
leisurely)
secure-*v* hope, desire,
sanguine expectation,
trust, confidence, reliance,
faith, belief, affiance,
assurance, reassurance,
promise, well-grounded,
presumption, anticipation,
(despair, lose, desperate)
seduction-*n* desire, wish,
fancy, fantasy, want, need,
exigency, mind, inclination,
attraction, magnet,
allurement, temptation,
fascination, devotee,
solicitant, (indifferent, cold,
frigid, half-hearted)
see-*v* view, vision, sight,
optics, look, espial, glance,
ken, glimpse, peep, gaze,
stare, leer, point of view,

demonstrate, eye, field of
view, contemplation,
regard, survey, (close,
blind, shut, cataract)
seethe-*v* hot, glow, flush,
sweat, swelter, bask,
smoke, reek, stew,
simmer, boil, burn, broil,
blaze, flame, smolder,
parch, fume, pant, sunny,
torrid, tropical, estival,
canicular, sultry,
oppressive
seize-*v* reception, carry,
bear sway, abstract, hurry
off, abduct, steal, ravish,
size, pounce, spring upon,
swoop, assault, confiscate,
sequester, despoil,strip,
(restitution, return,
restoration, atonement)
send-*v* delegate, consign,
relegate, turn over to,
deliver, ship, embark, waft,
shunt, transpose, propel,
project, throw, fling, cast,
pitch, chuck, toss, jerk,
heave, shy, (draw, pull,
haul, lug, rake, drag, tug)
sensation-*n* pleasure,
bodily enjoyment, animal
gratification, luxuriousness,
dissipation, titillation,
gusto, comfort ease,
refreshment, voluptuous,
cozy, snug, agreeable,
(torment, torture, rack,
agonize)
senseless-*adj* absurd,
imbecility, nonsense,
paradox, inconsistency,
blunder, muddle, bull, slipslop, anticlimax, farce,

rhapsody, farrago, jargon, fustian, twaddle, no meaning, (wise, perception, belief)

sensuous-*adj* feeling, warmth, glow, unction, gusto, fervor, heartiness, cordiality, earnestness, eagerness, ardor, zeal, passion, enthusiasm, blush, flush, penetrating, absorbing, impetuous

sequence-*n* coming after, going after, order, following, consecutive, succession, posteriority, continuation, sequential, alternate, latter, posterior, subsequently, (litter, scatter, confound, tangle)

service-*n* useful, utility, efficacy, efficiency, adequacy, use, stead, avail, help, applicability, subservience, instrumentality, function, value, worth, productive, (worthless, inefficient, unskillful)

settle-*v* pay, discharge, clearance, liquidation, satisfaction, reckoning, arrangement, reimbursement, retribution, reward, expenditure, defray, quit, acquit, (repudiate, protest, dishonor, nullify)

several-*adj* many, numerous, multitude, profusion, large, enormous, array, scores, bushel, majority,

multiplication, diverse, various, populous, crowd, manifold, (few, small, handful, paltry, minority)

severe-*adj* strict, harsh, rigor, stringent, austere, inclemency, absolute, tyrant, disciplinarian, stickler, despot, hard master, oppressor, inquisitor, extortioner, vulture, (moderate, lenient, tolerant, mild, soft)

shabby-*adj* poor, paltry, pitiful, contemptible, sorry, meager, miserable, wretched, vile, scrubby, scrannel, weedy, scurvy, putrid, beggarly, worthless, cheap, trashy, (essential, vital, prime, main)

shade-*n* cover, screen, cloak, veil, shroud, screen from sight, draw close, curtain, eclipse, mask, disguise, ensconce, muffle, smother, whisper, conceal, (enlighten, open, impart)

shake-*v* oscillate, vibrate, liberate, nutation, undulation, pulsation, alternation, flow, flux, wave, swing, beat, wag, dance, lurch, dodge, fluctuate, to and fro, brandish, (steady, unfurl, unfold, without motion)

shame-*n* disgrace, dishonor, tarnish, stain, discredit, degrade, debase, defile, expel, punish, stigmatize, vilify, defame, slur, reprehend,

despicable, unworthy,
(worthy, glorification, hero,
elevate)
shape-n form, figure,
fashion, carve, cut, chisel,
hew, cast, sketch, block,
hammer, frame, stamp,
build, mold, contour,
phase, posture, attitude,
sculpt, type, (destroy,
shapeless, unformed,
deface, mutilate)
shield-n defend, protect,
guard, ward, preservation,
resistance, safeguard,
shelter, fortification, hold,
armed, screen, shroud,
fence, ward off, hinder,
asylum, (attack, invade,
outbreak, assault, siege)
shift-v deflect, divert, shunt,
wear, draw aside, crook,
warp, stray, straggle, sidle,
diverge, digress, drift,
wander, twist, meander,
veer, rove, adrift, yaw,
(direct, aligned, straight,
straightforward)
shock-n false expectation,
disappointment,
miscalculation, surprise,
sudden burst, thunderclap,
blow, wonder, bolt of the
blue, electrify, astonish,
abrupt, startling, (foresight,
anticipate, reckon, waiting)
shoot-v death blow,
finishing stroke, execution,
gallows, fast, speedy,
rapid, quick, fleet, nimble,
agile, expeditious, express,
active, swift, (slow,
languor, drawl, retard,

relax, slow, slack, tardy)
short-adj concise, brief,
terse, close, to the point,
exact, neat, compact,
laconic, curt, pithy,
trenchant, summary,
compendious, compress,
summarize, (amplify,
profuse, drawn out,
ramble)
shrewd-adj cunning, crafty,
subtle, sharp, diplomatic,
artful, skillful, feline,
profound, designing,
contriving, intriguing,
strategic, underhanded,
hidden, (free, outspoken,
direct, downright, candid)
shrivel-v reduce, lessen,
shrink, consume,
condense, compress,
compact, squeeze,
strangle, corrugate,
astringent, dwindle,
narrow, collapse,
deteriorate, (expand, swell,
wide, fat, bulbous)
shudder-v cold, shiver,
gooseflesh, quake, shake,
tremble, diddle, quiver,
chill, frigid, nipping,
piercing, icy, glacial, frosty,
freezing, wintry, bitter,
(sunny, torrid, tropical,
seethe, broil)
shut-v close, enclose,
surround, imprison, enfold,
buy, encase, enshrine,
confine, desist, stop, give
over, break, relinquish,
abandon, renounce,
defect, withdraw,
renounce, desert, forsake

sick-*adj* ill, disease, ailing, infirmity, seizure, stroke, atrophy, disorder, malady, sore, fever, ulcer, corruption, abscess. consumption, eruption, rash, (healthy, sound, vigor, staunch, robust)

siege-*n* attack, assault, assail, aggression, offense, incursion, invasion, outbreak, storming, obsession, bombardment, fire, volley, beset, besiege, beleaguer, (defend, forefend, shield, screen)

signal-*n* insignia, banner, flag, colors, streamer, standard, eagle, post, rocket, important, momentous, salient, prominent, memorable, stirring, eventful, (subordinate,inferior, respectable, tolerable)

simple-*adj* mere, sheer, stark, bare, faint, light, slight, scanty, limited, meager, insufficient, sparing, so-so, modest, tender, subtle, inappreciable, unimportant, (extraordinary, important)

sincere-*adj* veracity, truthful, frank, candor, honesty, fidelity, plain dealing, genuineness, scrupulous, honorable, pure, unfeigned, outspoken, undisguised, (sham, pretense, false, forgery)

sink-*v* plunge, dip, souse, duck, dive, plumb, submerge, douse, engulf, bottom, wallow, descent, decline, fall, drop, cadence, subsidence, tumble, (ascent, rise, mount, arise, aspire, climb, clamber)

situation-*n* circumstance, phase, position, posture, attitude, place, point, terms, regime, footing, standing, status, occasion, predicament, event, juncture

skepticism-*n* disbelieve, discredit, doubtful, uncertainty, misgiving, demur, distrust, suspicion, jealousy, qualm, refuse to believe, dissent, hesitate, (believe, confide, assured, positive, satisfied)

sketch-*n* picture, drawing, draught, draft, trace, copy, photograph, image, likeness, icon, portrait, representation, illustration, delineation, depict, personification, (misrepresent, distort, bad)

skim-*v* recapitulation, resume, review, abbreviation, contraction, shorten, compress, abridge, abstract, epitomize, summarize, run over, (dissertation, essay, theme, discourse, memoir)

skittish-*adj* cowardly, fearful, shy, timid, poor spirited, soft, effeminate,

weak-minded, weak,
cower, skulk, sneak, slink,
frightened, dastardly,
(dare, venture, bold,
affront, confront, aweless)
slender-*adj* thin, small,
trifling, narrow, close, fine,
thread-like, finespun,
taper, slim, slight-made,
scanty, emaciated, lean,
meager, delicate, gaunt,
skinny, (thick, broad, wide,
ample, extended)
slink-*v* retreat, turn-tail, fly,
desert, elope, scamper,
sneak, flip, steal away,
decamp, flit, abscond,
levant, skedaddle, escape,
abandon, depart, (pursue,
follow, quest, hunt, seek)
slippery-*adj* dangerous,
precarious, critical, ticklish,
tumble down, threatening,
ominous, alarming,
crumbling, waterlogged,
top-heavy, unsafe,
hazardous, (safe, secure,
sure, shelter)
slow-*adj* idle, drone, droll,
dawdle, mope, truant,
lounge, loaf, indolent, lazy,
slothful, lust, remiss, slack,
inert, torpid, sluggish,
languid, supine, heavy,
dull, leaden, listless, (fast,
hasten, lively, agile)
smash-*v* failure, blunder,
mistake, fault, omission,
miss, oversight, slip, trip,
stumble, claudication,
botchery, scrape, mess,
mishap, collapse, blow,
explosion, misfortune,

(fortunate, attain, secure)
smite-*v* maltreat, abuse, ill-
use, buffet, bruise, scratch,
maul, scourge, violent,
stab, pierce, outrace,
mischief, nocuous,
malignant, noxious,
injurious, deleterious,
(beneficial, valuable,
serviceable)
smother-*v* repress,
suppress, restrain, stifle,
hush, bury, sink, keep
from, withhold, reserve,
ignore, silence, hoodwink,
mystify, puzzle, deceive,
(set right, awaken,
overhear, understand)
snag-*v* hindrance,
obstruction, interruption,
blockade, obstacle,
impediment, knot, bar,
stile, barrier, shackle,
restrain, bolt, cramp,
hamper, (relief, rescue,
help, aid, assist, give a
hand)
sneak-*v* contemptible,
abject, mean, shabby,
little, paltry, dirty, scurvy,
scabby, groveling,
scrubby, rascally, low-
minded, corrupt, venal,
mongrel, dishonest,
(upright, honest, veracious,
honorable)
snub-*v* short, brevity,
abbreviated, curtailment,
retrench, cut short, scrimp,
chop up, hack, hew, clip,
dock, prune, shear, shave,
mow, crop, compact, (long,
span, streak, prolong)

steel-*n* strong, mighty, vigorous, forcible, hard, adamantine, stout, robust, sturdy, hardy, powerful, resistless, impregnable, sovereign, valid, potent, (frail, fragile, shatter, flimsy, unsubstantial, feeble)

step-*n* pace, rate, tread, stride, gait, port, cadence, carriage, velocity, angular velocity, progress, locomotion, journey, voyage, transit, nomadic, motor, erratic, (remain, stay, stand, ride, pause, rest)

stereotype-*n* indication, mark, note, stamp, earmark, label, ticket, docket, dot, spot, score, dash, trace, chalk, print, imprint, engrave, symbolize, typify, represent

stiff-*adj* rigid, hard, stubborn, firm, starched, stark, unbending, unlimber, unyielding, inflexible, tense, indurate, gritty, proof, petrify, crystallization, (soft, pliable, flexible, relax, tender, supple, pliant)

stimulate-*v* excite, provoke, arouse, inspirit, animate, incite, instigate, actuate, encourage, influence, sway, incline, persuade, overcome, engage, invite, procure, (discourage, dampen, hinder, repel)

stock-*v* accumulate, amass, hoard, fund, garner, save, reserve, keep, deposit, stow, stack, load, harvest, heap, collect, preserve, conserve, (spend, expend, use, consume, swallow up)

stoop-*v* low-minded, disgrace, dishonor, demean, degrade, derogate, grovel, sneak, lose caste, sell oneself, dishonest, unscrupulous, fraudulent, (scrupulous, respectful, reputable, candid)

story-*n* narrative, history, memoir, memorials, annals, chronicle, tradition, legend, tale, journal, life, adventures, experiences, confessions, anecdote, work of fiction

stow-*v* place, situate, locate, localize, put, lay, set, seat, station, lodge, quarter, post, install, house, establish, fix, pin, root, graft, plant, insert, (displace, exile, transposition, remove, transfer, banish)

straggle-*v* deviate, stray, sidle, diverge, digress, wander, wind, twist, meander, veer, ramble, rove, drift, adrift, step aside, scent, shift, shunt, wear, draw aside, crook, warp, (align, level, toward)

straight-*adj* rectilinear, direct, even, right, true, in a line, unbent, undeviating, inflexible, align, (deviating, errant, desultory, rambling, stray, curved, arch)

strange-*adj* exceptional, abnormal, irregular, arbitrary, informal, wandering, eccentric, unusual, uncommon, remarkable, noteworthy, monstrous, wonderful, unexpected, (typical, normal, ordinary)

streak-*n* variegated, iridescence, play of colors, spottiness, spectrum, rainbow, stripe, speckle, sprinkle, stipple, maculate, dot, tattoo, inlay, polychromatic

stress-*n* labor, work, toil, travail, manual labor, exertion, effort, strain, trouble, operoseness, drudgery, slavery, flagging, hammering, hardworking, strenuous, (repose, rest, sleep, relax, unbend, slacken)

strict-*adj* exact, accurate, definite, precise, well defined, just right, correct, close, rigorous, religiously, punctual, mathematical, faithful, constant, authentic, (erroneous, untrue, false, fallacious, unsound)

strive-*v* endeavor, attempt, speculation, probation, experiment, tempt, attempt, venture, adventure, try hard, push, exertion, contend, contest,

(tranquil, calm, peaceable, harmony)

stronghold-*n* hold, asylum, refuge, sanctuary, retreat, fastness, keep, last resort, ward, prison, covert, shelter, screen, wing, shield, umbrella, anchor, (attack, assault, charge, aggression)

strut-*v* ostentatious, showy, dashing, pretentious, jaunty, grand, pompous, palatial, high-sounding, splendid, magnificent, sumptuous, theatrical, gaudy, flaunt, (modest, diffident, humble, timid, bashful)

stumble-*v* tumble, trip, titubate, lurch, pitch, swag, topple, tilt, sprawl, plump down, descend, fall, drop, gravitate, slip, slide, settle, decline, set, sink, (climb, clamber, escalade, surmount, tower, soar)

style-*n* tone, tenor, state, condition, category, estate, lot, case, trim, mood, pickle, plight, fashion, light, complexion, character, structure, format, (inconsequential, unconformity, unrelated)

sublime-*adj* height, altitude, elevation, eminence, pitch, loftiness, tallness, stature, prominence, colossus, giant, tower, soar, (low, depressed, underlie, squat, prostrate)

substance-*n* matter, body,

stuff, element, principle,
materialistic, object, article,
thing, something, tangible,
substantial, unspiritual,
sensible, physical,
(immaterial, spiritual,
disembodied, subjective)
subterfuge-n untruth,
evasion, white lie, juggle,
device, plot, maneuver,
strategy, artful dodge,
trickery, deception, shift,
intrigue, contriving,
artificial, (innocence,
candor, sincerity, honest,
guileless)
subvert-v destroy,
demolish, overthrow,
suppression, abolish,
sacrifice, ravage,
devastate, revolution,
incendiarism, deterioration,
ruin, dispel, (flower,
fructify, teem, build, raise,
edify, erect, establish)
succulent-adj eatable,
edible, esculent,
comestible, alimentary,
dietetic, culinary, nutritive,
potable, bibulous, tasteful,
delicacy, gusto, (rank,
tasteless, repulsive)
sudden-adj instantaneous,
abrupt, moment, second,
minute, momentary,
instant, hasty, lightning,
spur of the moment,
(perpetual, eternal,
everlasting, continual,
endless, ceaseless)
suggest-v advice, council,
recommendation,
advocacy, persuasion,

mention, acquaint, instruct,
inform, authorize, inform,
(conceal, suppress,
evasion, silence, mystery)
summary-n short, brief,
curt, compendious,
compact, concise, curtail,
squat, reduce, (long,
lengthy, outstretched,
prolong, extend)
sunshine-n shine, glow,
glitter, glisten, twinkle,
gleam, flare, glare, beam,
shimmer, glimmer, flicker,
sparkle, scintillate, flash,
glance, bright, reflect,
sunny, cloudless, meteoric,
phosphorescent

T

tackle-v undertake, engage,
embark, volunteer,
promise, contract, take
upon one's shoulders,
begin, fasten, tie, ligament,
strap, rigging, standing,
trace, harness, yoke,
bandage, brace, roller
tactic-n game, policy,
execution, manipulation,
treatment, campaign,
career life, course,
conduct, behavior,
carriage, demeanor,
manner, direction,
transact, execute,
dispatch, proceed
tale-n description, account,
statement, report,
specification, particulars,
summary of facts, catalog,
information, fable, parable,

apologue, narrative, novel,
work of fiction, journal,
recital, sketch
talk-*n* speech, locution,
parlance, verbal
intercourse, oral
communication, word of
mouth, oratory, elocution,
rhetoric, recitation, formal
speech, (stammer,
hesitation, impediment,
stutter, falter)
tame-*adj* domesticate,
acclimatize, breed, tend,
break in, train, cage, bridle,
restrain, pastoral, bucolic,
veterinary art, teach,
instruct, edify, school,
tutor, cram, (bewilder,
uncertain, misinform,
deceive, mislead
tangible-*adj* material,
bodily, corporeal, physical,
somatic, sensible,
ponderable, palpable,
substantial, objective,
impersonal, neuter,
unspiritual, (personal,
subjective, spiritualize,
disembody)
task-*n* exercise, curriculum,
explanation, teach,
instruct, edify, fatigue,
weariness, yawning,
drowsiness, lassitude,
tiredness, exhaustion,
sweat, faintness, (restore,
refresh, revive, repair,
relief)
tattler-*n* narrator, scandal-
monger, tale-bearer,
gossip, many-tongued,
rumored, currently,

reported, glad tidings,
eavesdrop, (observe,
swear, hide, close
mouthed)
tear-*v* separate, destroy,
over-turn, nullify, annul,
demolish, crumple up,
sunder, divide, cut up,
carve, dissect, pull,
disintegrate, nip, nib,
cleave, snap, break, (join
secure, inseparable)
tease-*v* annoy, displease,
incommode, discompose,
trouble, disquiet, disturb,
perplex, molest, tire, irk,
vex, mortify, harass, harry,
badger, persecute, harrow,
(please, agreeable,
amusement, charm,
delight)
technical-*adj* artistic,
scientific, businesslike,
talent, ability, ingenuity,
cleverness, endowed,
skillful, experienced,
efficient, qualified, handy,
capable, smart, proficient,
(stupidity, inexperienced,
ignorant)
tell-*v* influence, weight,
pressure, preponderence,
prevalence, sway,
predominance,
ascendancy, dominance,
reign, authority,
(impotence, inertness,
irrelevancy, uninfluential,
unconducing)
temper-*n* pervading,
penetrating, absorbing,
strong, sharp, acute,
cutting, piercing, incisive,

caustic, violent, vehement,
warm, rough, boisterous,
rampant, (moderate,
gentle, mild, cool, sober,
calm)

tempt-v seduce, entice,
allure, captivate, fascinate,
bewitch, carry away,
charm, conciliate, coax,
lure, tantalize, cajole,
deceive, bribe, influence,
prompt, instigate,
(dissuade, discourage,
hinder)

tender-adj offer, proffer,
present, bid, propose,
move, advance, start,
invite, hold out, put
forward, overture, bribe,
give, (refuse, reject,
repulse, rebuff, deny,
decline, nill, repudiate)

tendril-n filament, line, fiber,
fibril, funicle, vein, hair,
capillary, gossamer, wire,
string, thread, packthread,
twine, ribbon, splinter,
yarn, hemp, jute, strand

tenor-n direction, bearing,
course, set, drift, tendency,
incidence, bending,
trending, dip, tack, aim,
collimation, steer, bend,
trend, verge, incline,
(deviation, swerve,
digress, depart, aberration,
sweep)

tenure-n possession,
ownership, occupancy,
monopoly, retention,
sanction, authority,
warranty, charter,
permission, constitution,

security, claimant,
appellant, (infringe,
encroach, exact, relax)

term-n time, duration,
period, stage, space, span,
spell, season, era, limit,
boundary, confine, frontier,
word, vocabulary, name,
nomenclature, verbal,
literal

terrorist-n coward, poltroon,
dastard, sneak, recreant,
weak-minded, effeminacy,
timidity, oppressor, tyrant,
firebrand, incendiary,
anarchist, destroyer,
iconoclast, savage,
(benefactor, savior,
courage)

text-n copy, design, type,
matter, subject, meaning,
signify, convey, imply,
breathe, indicate, bespeak,
expressive, declaratory,
(nonsense, jargon,
gibberish, jabber, absurd,
vague, balderdash, trash)

thankless-adj bitter,
distasteful, uninviting,
unwelcome, undesirable,
obnoxious, unacceptable,
unpopular, distressing,
disheartening, depressing,
(bless, beatify, satisfy,
gratify, thankful, flatter)

thaw-v melt, liquefy, heat,
dissolution, run, dissolve,
resolve, fuse, burn,
combustion, ignition,
inflammation, roast, singe,
incinerate, smelt, boil,
(cool, refrigerate, refresh,
congeal, freeze, chill)

thesis-*n* supposition,
assumption, postulation,
condition, hypothesis,
postulate, theory, proposal,
plan, association of ideas,
topic, proposition,
(perception, image,
sentiment, reflection,
abstract idea)
thick-*adj* dense, solid,
impenetrable, cohesion,
constipation, consistence,
condense, substantial,
lump, massive, (rarefy,
expand, dilate, subtilize,
sponginess, thin, fine,
flimsy, slight)
thin-*adj* insufficient,
inadequate, deficiency,
imperfection, scarcity,
want, need, lack, scanty,
small, stingy, meager,
poor, spare, starve,
stricken, (sufficient, ample,
abundant, enough,
adequate, full)
thorn-*n* point, spike, spine,
needle, pin, prick, spur,
rowel, barb, spit, cusp,
horn, antler, snag, tag,
bristle, nib, tooth, tusk,
spoke, cog, ratchet,
barbed, spurred, (blunt,
obtund, dull)
thoughtless-*adj* negligent,
omission, careless,
inattentive, nonchalance,
insensibility, heedless,
remiss, perfunctory,
unmindful, inconsiderate,
(careful, regardful, prudent,
considerate, provident,
cautious)

thread-*n* pass, perforate,
penetrate, permeate,
enfilade, traverse, journey,
worm, passage, wire,
string, slip, strip, filament,
line, fiber, splinter, ribbon,
soft, fragile, inactivity
threaten-*v* inspiring fear,
alarming, formidable,
perilous, danger,
portentous, fearful, dread,
shocking, terrible, horrid,
ghastly, revolting, awful,
terrorize, startle, (hopeful,
confident, secure,
enthusiastic)
threshold-*n* beginning,
entry, inlet, orifice, mouth,
portal, portico, door, gate,
vestibule, border, edge,
commence, rise, arise,
conceive, initiate, open,
dawn, (end, close,
terminate, conclude, finale,
finish)
thrill-*n* provoke, summon,
raise, rouse, arouse, stir,
fire, kindle, inflame, excite,
stimulate, inspire, infect,
agitate, passion, stun,
astound, electrify,
galvanize, (insensible,
disregard, neglect,
unaffected)
throw-*n* fling, toss,
discharge, shy, propel,
project, cast, pitch, chuck,
jerk, heave, hurl, dart,
lance, tilt, ejaculate, send
forth, expel, shot, (draw,
drag, tug, tow, trail, train,
pull together)
tickle-*v* please, cause

pleasure, delight, gladden, make cheerful, captivate, fascinate, enchant, entrance, enrapture, regale, amuse, stimulate, excite, (irritate, annoy, grieve, vex, displease)

tidy-*adj* orderly, regularity, uniformity, symmetry, methodically, ship shape, routine, arrangement, array, series, neat, spruced, primp, prepared, classified, (disorderly, derange, ruffle, untidy, shapeless)

tight-*adj* firm, fast, joined, close, taut, secure, set, intervolved, drunk, tipsy, intoxicated, inebriation, mellow, groggy, (sobriety, teetotaler, water-drinker, separate, scission, loose)

tilt-*v* obliquity, incline, slope, slant, crooked, leaning, bevel, bias, list, twist, swag, cant, lurch, distorted, bend, recumbent, skew, (parallel, coextension, alongside, straight)

timid-*adj* modest, humble, diffident, timorous, bashful, shy, nervous, skittish, coy, sheepish, shamefaced, blushing, reserved, constrained, demure, quiet, private, (self-satisfied, airs, pretentious)

tinsel-*n* luster, sheen, shimmer, reflection, gloss, spangle, brightness, brilliancy, splendor, lucid,

illuminate, shine, glow, glimmer, sparkle, dazzle, (dark, dim, dingy, gloomy, shady, obscure, black)

title-*n* name, style, baptism, appellation, designation, surname, description, call, term, denominate, entitle, christen, characterize, specify, distinguish, label, (anonymous, nameless, misnomer, pseudonym, alias, nickname)

tolerate-*v* lenient, mild, gentle, soft, indulgent, easy-going, clement, compassion, forbearing, favor, moderation, merciful, spoil, (severe, strict, harsh, domineer, rigid, stern, rigorous, uncompromising)

tone-*n* state, condition, category, estate, lot, case, trim, mood, pickle, plight, temper, aspect, appearance, tenor, turn, guise, fashion, light, complexion, style, character, (circumstantial)

tonic-*n* remedy, help, redress, antidote, prophylactic, antiseptic, corrective, restorative, sedative, cure, physic, medicine, potion, salve, ointment, (poison, leaven, virus, venom, arsenic, fungus, rot, canker)

tool-*n* instrument, organ, implement, utensil, machine, engine, lathe, gin, mill, gear, tackle,

apparatus, appliance,
equipment, harness,
hammer, fittings
top-*n* supreme, superior,
major, greatest, higher,
exceed, distinguished,
vault, important, first-rate,
excellent, unparalleled,
culmination, foremost,
(inferior, smaller, bottom
diminish, short-coming)
topple-*v* unbalanced,
unequal, difference,
uneven, countervail,
disparate, over-balanced,
top-heavy, lop-sided,
inferior, (equal, matched,
reach, balanced, equate,
adjust, accommodate,
level)
torture-*v* punish, chastise,
castigate, cruelty, brutality,
savagery, ferocity,
barbarity, inhumanity,
vivisection, outrage,
persecution, atrocity,
(benevolent, kind, well-
meaning, amiable,
obliging)
total-*n* complete,
integration, entirety,
perfection, entire, whole,
full, thorough, plenary,
undivided, altogether,
beginning to end,
saturated, limit, sufficient,
(deficient, shortcoming,
omit, incomplete)
totter-*v* fluctuate, vary,
waver, flounder, flicker,
flitter, flit, flutter, shift,
shuffle, shake, tremble,
vacillate, wamble, sway,

oscillate, changing,
alternating, mobile, (fixed,
steadfast, firm, immovable,
tethered)
touch-*v* contact, abutment,
osculation, meet, close,
adjoin, graze, coincide,
coexist, adhere, deed, act,
overt act, gesture,
transaction, job, maneuver,
(remote, distant, far off,
away, apart, asunder)
tower-*n* pillar, column,
obelisk, monument,
steeple, spire, minaret,
campaniles, turret, dome,
cupola, pole, pikestaff,
maypole, flagstaff,
mountain, height, (low,
depress, concave, lowland,
underlie)
trace-*v* discover, recognize,
realize, verify, make
certain of, identify, get at,
solve, resolve, unriddle,
unravel, interpret, disclose,
unearth, (obliterate,
extinct, no trace of,
deletion)
trade-*n* commerce, buying
and selling, bargain, sale,
traffic, business, custom,
shopping, commercial
enterprise, speculation,
jobbing, dealing,
transaction, negotiate
tradition-*n* old, ancient,
antique, maturity,
prescription, prime,
primitive, customary,
immemorial, old-fashioned,
time honored, long
standing, (new, novel,

recent, fresh, green,
young, immature, late)
train-v prepare, make
ready, educate, novitiate,
cultivate, mature, evolve,
pioneer, instruct, edify,
tutor, direct, guide, qualify,
drill, practice, explain,
lecture, task, school,
(deceive, conceal,
misrepresent)
trample-v destroy, waste,
dissolve, break-up,
consume, disorganize, fall,
downfall, ruin, crash,
smash, annihilation,
demolish, ravage,
devastate, (produce,
perform, operate,
construct, fabricate)
tranquil-adj calm,
moderate, relax, remission,
mitigation, gentleness,
sedative, assuage,
appease, swag, lull,
soothe, compose, still,
cool, quiet, hush, quell,
sober, (fury, dragon,
demon, tiger, violent)
transcendent-adj super-
excellence, goodness,
superiority, perfect,
complete, immaculate,
spotless, unblemished,
sound, scathless, intact,
harmless, paragon,
(indifferent, middling,
secondary)
transport-v ship, tender,
transit, remove, displace,
relegation, deportation,
conveyance, draft,
carriage, transition, send,

delegate, consign,
relegate, (hold, store,
retain, keep, preserve)
transpose-v exchange,
interchange, reciprocate,
shuffle, castling, barter,
retaliate, commute, mutual,
communicative,
intercurrent, (substitute,
supplant, supersede,
instead of, redeem,
equivalent)
trash-n useless, inefficacy,
futile, inaptitude,
inadequate, insufficient,
unskillfulness,
unproductive, litter,
rubbish, lumber, refuse,
rubble, (useful, value,
worth, fruitful, serviceable,
prolific)
travesty-n imitate, mock,
mimic, ape, simulate,
impersonate, act,
represent, counterfeit,
parody, caricature,
burlesque, plagiarism,
forgery, echo, duplication,
repeat, (originality, unique)
tremor-n agitation, stir,
shake, ripple, jog, jolt, jar,
jerk, shock, succussion,
trepidation, quiver, quaver,
disquiet, perturbation,
commotion, turmoil,
turbulence, fuss, racket,
fits, (calm, quiet,
disentangle)
trenchant-adj strong,
energetic, forcible, active,
intense, deep-dyed,
severe, keen, vivid, sharp,
acute, incisive, brisk,

rousing, irritating, poignant, caustic, corrosive, (inert, inactive, passive, torpid, dull)

trespass-*v* transgression, infringement, transcendence, redundance, surpass, go beyond, over-step, exceed, surmount, encroach, infringe, (default, collapse, extricate, eliminate)

tribute-*n* observe, respectful, deferential, decorous, obsequious, regard, revere, venerate, worship, duty, devotion, salute, inspire, impose, dazzle, (ridicule, disrespectful, irreverent, disparaging)

trickle-*v* ooze, emerge, emanate, issue, pass, pour out, pass off, evacuate, spout, gush, dribble, perspire, vent, filter, filtrate, distill, discharge, extravagate, (absorb, ingest, inhale, swallow, engulf)

trim-*v* equalize, match, balance, cope with, dress, adjust, poise, fit, accommodate, adapt, establish equality, readjust, co-ordinate, (unequal, countervail, advantage, disparate, partial, over balanced)

trip-*n* journey, excursion, expedition, tour, grand tour, circuit, peregrination, discursion, ramble,

pilgrimage, course, ambulation, march, walk, promenade, constitutional, (rest, pause, lull, bivouac)

trouble-*n* difficulty, irksome, laborious, arduous, awkward, unwieldy, unmanageable, impossible, complicated, impracticable, hopeless, embarrassing, perplexing, (easy, facilitate, smooth, submissive)

true-*adv* verity, gospel, authentic, veracity, accuracy, exactness, precise, delicacy, rigor, mathematical, punctuality, plain, honest, sober, naked, real, actual, (mistake, fault, blunder, error, fallacy, untrue)

trump-*n* perfect, faultless, immaculate, spotless, impeccable, sound, superior, transcendence, model, best, inimitable, paragon, superhuman, divine, (bearable, imperfect, below par, indifferent)

trunk-*n* house, stem, tree, stock, stirps, pedigree, lineage, line, family, tribe, sect, race, clan, genealogy, descent, extraction, birth, ancestry, forefathers, patriarchs

truss-*n* support, aid, prop, stand, anvil, stay, shore, skid, rib, bandage, sleeper, stirrup, stilts, shoe, sole, heel, splint, outrigger,

(suspend, hang, sling, hook up, hitch, fasten to, append)

trust-n believe, credit, give faith, credence, esteem, confide, certain, sure, assured, positive, unhesitating, convinced, accredited, persuasive, impressive, (disputable, uncertain, unworthy)

try-v experiment, endeavor, tempt, attempt, venture, adventure, speculate, tempt fortune, assay, contend, contest, strive, struggle, scramble, wrangle

tube-n channel, passage, way, path, pipe, vessel, tubule, canal, gut, fistula, chimney, flue, tap, funnel, gully, tunnel, shaft, alley, mine, (closure, occlusion, blockade, obstruction)

tug-v effort, exertion, strain, pull, stress, throw, stretch, struggle, spell, spurt, labor, work, toil, travail, drudgery, trouble, pains, duty, exert, strive, (repose, rest, slacken, inactive, recline, halt, pause)

tumble-v trip, stumble, titubate, lurch, pitch, swag, topple, tilt, sprawl, plump, descend, dismount, alight, swoop, stoop, titubation, drop, (climb, clamber, surmount, scale, tower, soar, hover, spire)

tumultuous-adj violent, inclemency, vehemence, might, impetuosity, boisterousness, effervescence, turbulence, severity, ferocity, rage, fury, exacerbation, strain, (moderation, relaxation, tranquilize)

turbulence-n disquiet, perturbation, commotion, turmoil, tumult, hubbub, rout, bustle, fuss, racket, spasm, throe, throb, palpitation, convulsion, disturbance, disorder, restlessness

turgid-adj expanded, increase, enlarge, extension, augmentation, amplification, spread, increment, growth, development, pullulating, dilatation, inflation, (condense, lessen, shrink, collapse, atrophy)

turn-v rotate, revolution, gyration, circulation, convolution, whir, vortex, whirlpool, whirligig, roll, axis, axle, spindle, pivot, mandrel, swivel, (vibration, alternation, up and down, fluctuation)

turpitude-n dishonor, disgrace, shame, humiliation, scandal, baseness, vileness, improbity, infamy, tarnish, taint, defilement, pollution, stain, blot, blur, (elevate, ascent, dignify, consecrate, enthrone)

turret-n tower, pillar, column, obelisk,

monument, steeple, spire,
minaret, dome, cupola,
pole, pikestaff, maypole,
flagstaff, top, mast,
skyscraper, (low, debased,
underneath, below, flat,
level)

tutelage-n safe-conduct,
escort, convoy, guard,
shield, defense, guardian
angel, deity, protector,
warden, preserver,
custodian, chaperon,
sentinel, sentry, (danger,
peril, insecurity, jeopardy,
risk)

twaddle-v absurd, jargon,
fustian, exaggeration,
moonshine, stuff, vagary,
tomfoolery, mummery,
nonsensical, preposterous,
egregious, senseless,
quibbling, punning, foolish

twist-v distort, contort,
warp, writhe, deform,
misshape, contortion,
crooked, grimace,
irregular, unsymmetrical,
grotesque, deformed,
misbegotten, (symmetrical,
shapely, uniform, classic,
uniform)

twitch-v traction, draw,
draught, pull, haul, rake,
tow, haulage, lug, trail,
train, take in tow, wrench,
jerk, tousle, tactile, (dart,
propel, project, throw, fling,
cast, pitch, discharge, bolt,
shoot)

type-n form, figure, shape,
conformation, make,
formation, frame,

construction, cut, set,
build, trim, stamp, cast,
mold, fashion, contour,
outline, structure, feature,
lineament, posture, attitude

tyranny-n assume, usurp,
arrogate, domineer, bully,
inflict, wreak, sever, strict,
hard, harsh, rigid, stiff,
stern, rigorous,
uncompromising, (lenient,
tolerant, mild, indulgent,
clement, compassionate,
forbearing)

U

ugly-adj deformity,
inelegance, disfigured,
blemish, squalor, eyesore,
frightful, hideous, odious,
uncanny, forbidding,
repellent, repulsive,
shocking, (form, elegance,
grace, beauty, gorgeous)

ulterior-adj
extraneousness,
extrinsically, foreign, alien,
strange, ultramontane,
excluded, inadmissible,
exceptional, (component,
integral, element,
constituent, ingredient)

ultimatum-n decision,
determination, resolve,
purpose, resolution, with
motive, settled, intent,
undertaking,
predetermination, design,
ambition, (speculation,
venture, stake, gamble,
chance)

unabashed-adj bold,

spirited, daring, audacious, fear, daunt, dread, aweless, undaunted, enterprising, adventurous, ventures, dashing, chivalrous, soldierly, fierce, (courage, bravery, valor, resolute)

unadorned-*adj* simple, plain, homely, ordinary, unaffected, chaste, severe, ungarnished, disarrange, untrimmed, unvarnished, bald, flat, dull, (ornamented, beautified, ornate, rich, gilt)

unanswerable-*adv* categorical, decisive, crucial, demonstrated, proven, deducible, consequential, inferential, following, established, verify, (refutation, answer, disproof, conviction, invalidation)

unassisted-*adv* encumber, stop, prevent, load, burden, lumber, pack, difficulty, dampen, obstruct, stay, bar, bolt, unaided, hinder, block, impede, (assist, aid, rescue, help, contribute, furnish, relief)

unaware-*adv* uninformed, ignore, unexplored, unknown, blind, unconsciousness, shallow, superficial, (aware, cognizant, conscious of, acquainted, versed, learned, instructed, proficient)

unblushing-*adj* dignity, self-respect, pride, haughtiness, vainglory, arrogance, supercilious, disdainful, bumptious, magisterial, imperious, overweening, consequential, (humble, lowly, meek, modest)

unborn-*adv* non-existence, absence, abeyance, nullity, negative, annihilation, extinction, destruction, abrogate, uncreated, perished, exhausted, gone, lost, departed, (real, actual, positive, absolute)

uncertain-*adv* incertitude, doubt, dubiety, hesitation, suspense, perplexity, embarrassment, dilemma, bewilderment, timidity, fear, vacillation, indetermination, vague, obscure, (certain, unerring, infallible)

unclog-*adv* liberate, disengage, release, enlarge, emancipate, enfranchise, discharge, dismiss, deliver, redeem, extricate, acquit, absolve, set free, unfetter, untie, (confine, restraint, hinder, repress)

uncommendable-*adj* dispraise, disapprobation, censure, obloquy, detract, condemnation, ostracize, criticism, sarcasm, insinuation, innuendo, poor, (approval, sanction, advocacy, applause)

undone-v lost, ruined, broken, bankrupt, dead beat, destroy, frustrated, crossed, unhinged, disconcerted, dashed, unattained, uncompleted, (succeed, prosper, triumphant, flushed, well spent

unearthed-v exhume, disinter, autopsy, examination, inhume, lay out, mummify, look, inquire, peer, hunt, leave no stone unturned, seek, search, explore, rummage, ransack, (answer, reply, respond)

unerring-adj unblamed, blameless, above suspicion, irreproachable, venial, harmless, pure, virtuous, innocent, model, paragon, perfection, impeccable, (guilt, misbehave, sinful, fault, failure, atrocity)

uneven-adj diverse, varied, irregular, rough, multifarious, multiform, various kinds, all sorts, not uniform, lop-sided, unequal, different, partial, over-balanced, (even, level, equal, balance, monotony)

unexplored-v hidden, silence, mystery, concealed, darkness, unknown, invisible, impenetrable, undisclosed, unexposed, dormant, unsuspected, (apparent, prominent, flagrant,

notorious, distinct)

unfamiliar-adj unusual, uncommon, rare, remarkable, unexpected, unaccountable, unconventional, unparalleled, newfangled, grotesque, outlandish, (conventional, ordinary, common, usual)

unfit-adj objectionable, unreasonable, unallowable, unjustified, improper, illegal, immoral, wrong, inequitable, partial, unfair, inJustice, (right, fit, impartial, moral, reward, recompense, good, just)

unforeseen-v miscalculation, unexpected, unaware, pounce, abrupt, sudden, startle, instantaneous, surprised, shock, wonder, fall upon, (expect, foreseen, prospective, impending, prepared, count on)

unfortunate-adj unsuccessful, abortive, at fault, inefficient, ineffectual, foiled, defeated, ruined, broken, unattained, uncompleted, frustrated, disconcerted, (successful, prosperous, triumphant, victorious)

unfriendly-adj hostile, inimical, discord, alienation, estrangement, dislike, hate, heartburning, animosity, malevolence, disaffected, (familiarity,

intimacy, fellowship,
friendly, welcome,
harmony)
unguided-v
extemporaneous,
impulsive, improvised,
unprompted, unnatural,
unguarded, spontaneous,
voluntary, flash, spurt,
improvisation,
(predetermined,
aforethought)
unhappy-adj mope, brood,
fret, sulk, pine, yearn,
repine, regret, despair,
refrain from laughter,
depressed, gloomy,
unlively, melancholy,
dismal, somber, (cheering,
inspiriting, jovial, hilarious)
uniform-adj homogeneous,
consistency, conformity,
agreement, regularity,
constancy, routine, even
tenor, monotony,
assimilate, level, smooth,
dress, invariable,
(diversified, varied,
uneven, rough)
union-n combination,
mixture, junction,
unification, synthesis,
incorporation,
amalgamation,
embodiment, coalescence,
fusion, blending,
(decompose, separate,
dissect, unravel)
unique-adj non-conformity,
unconventional, abnormal,
eccentricity, rarity, freak,
individual, originality,
exceptional, exclusive,

eccentric, irregular,
(conform, typical, normal,
formal, ordinary)
unite-v gather, assemble,
collect, convene, draw,
conclave, accumulate,
heap, converge, pile,
pyramid, conglomeration,
muster, meet, join, cluster,
(unassembled. broadcast,
stray, disperse, sow)
unlucky-adj unfortunate, ill-
timed, intrusive,
inopportune, inauspicious,
unfavorable, unsuited,
inexpedient, premature,
unpunctual, (opportune,
timely, well timed,
fortunate, lucky, suitable)

V

vacant-adj absence,
inexistent, nonresidence,
absenteeism, empty, void,
vacuum, truant,
unoccupied, uninhabited,
devoid, deserted, (present,
occupied, inhabited, dwell,
fill, domiciled)
vacate-v depart, cessation,
decampment,
embarkation, outset, start,
removal, exit, egress,
exodus, flight, valediction,
adieu, farewell, good-bye,
abandon, leave, (arrive,
welcome, reception,
return)
vacillate-v unsteady,
changeable, unsteadfast,
fickle, capricious, volatile,
frothy, light, giddy, weak,

feeble-minded, fidgety, tremulous, hesitate, uncertain, (steady, sound, inflexible, hard, resolute)

vacuous-*adv* absent, not present, away, non-resident, gone from home, missing, lost, wanting, omitted, nowhere to be found, nonexistent, empty, void, vacant, untenanted, (fill, pervade, permeate, present)

vagabond-*n* bad man, wrong-doer, worker of iniquity, evil-doer, sinner, bad example, rascal, scoundrel, villain, miscreant, wretch, reptile, viper, serpent, scamp, (model, paragon, hero, saintly)

vagrant-*n* roving, vagrancy, marching, nomad, gadding, flitting, migration, travel, journey, take wing, emigrate, prowl, roam, range, patrol, traverse, wander, (stagnate, stick, pause, anchor)

vague-*adj* indefinite, indistinct, perplexed, confused, undetermined, loose, ambiguous, mysterious, mystic, transcendental, occult, recondite, abstruse, crabbed, (understand, comprehend, grasp)

vain-*adj* vanity, conceit, self-conceit, self-complacency, self-confidence, selfishness,

airs, pretensions, mannerism, egotism, priggish, gaudery, vainglory, elation, (modest, reserved, demure, blushing)

value-*n* price, amount, cost, expense, prime cost, charge, figure, demand, damage, fare, hire, wage, remuneration, dues, duty, toll, tax, impose, tallage, levy, gabelle, excise, assessment, benevolence

vanish-*v* disappear, dissolve, fade, melt away, pass, go, avant, be-gone, leave, no trace, retire from sight, efface, evanescent, missing, lost, gone, (appear, view, vista, spectacle, guise, look, visible)

vary-*v* differ, diverse, heterogeneous, distinguishable, modified, other, another, unequal, not the same, unmatched, distinct, characteristic, (uniform, regular, level, always, without exception)

vast-*adj* great, immense, enormous, extreme, inordinate, excessive, extravagant, exorbitant, outrageous, preposterous, swinging, monstrous, over-grown, (small, diminutive, minute, paltry)

veer-*v* change, alter, vary, wax and wane, modulate, diversify, qualify, tamper with, turn, shift, tack, chop,

shuffle, swerve, warp,
deviate, turn aside, overt,
introvert, resume,
(permanent, stationary)
vehemence-adv feeling,
emotion, excitability,
impetuosity,
boisterousness,
turbulence, impatience,
intolerance, non-enduring,
irritability, agitation,
(serene, calm, placid,
composure, quiet, tranquil)
vein-n tend, contribute,
conducive, lead, dispose,
incline, verge, bend to,
trend, affect, carry,
gravitate, promote,
subservient, instrumental,
nature, temperament,
mood, drift, cast
velocity-n speed, swiftness,
rapidity, expedition,
activity, acceleration,
haste, spurt, rush, dash,
race, lively, gallop, move
quickly, hasten, whisk,
sweep, (retard, relax,
slacken, gentle, easy,
linger)
vent-v divulge, reveal,
break, split, tell, breathe,
utter, allow, acknowledge,
concede, grant, admit,
own, confess, avow,
disguise, transpire, come
to light, (screen, cover,
shade, blinker, veil,
curtain)
ventilate-v gust, blast,
breeze, squall, gale, storm,
tempest, hurricane,
whirlwind, wind, blow, fan,

respire, breathe, waft,
flatulent, issue, bellows,
blow-pipe
venture-n trial, endeavor,
attempt, essay, adventure,
speculation, probation,
experiment, try, strive,
tempt, gamble, bet, risk,
hazard, accidental, (intend,
purpose, design, propose)
verdict-n result, conclusion,
upshot, deduction,
inference, egotism, illation,
estimation, valuation,
appreciation, judicature,
assessment, ponderous,
judgment, (discover, find,
determine, evolve)
verge-n edge, brink, brow,
brim, margin, border, skirt,
rim, flange, side, mouth,
jaws, cops, chaps, lip,
muzzle, threshold,
marginal, conducive, tend,
incline, affect, gravitate
toward, promote
vernacular-n indigenous,
native, domestic,
domiciled, naturalized,
home, indoor, endemic,
interior, intrinsic, closed,
inward, within, (exterior,
outside, surface, skin,
superficial, external)
versatile-adj changeable,
mutable, checkered, ever
changing, inconstant,
unsteady, fluctuate,
restless, agitated, erratic,
fickle, irresolute,
capricious, vagrant,
vibratory, alternating
very-adv fact, reality,

existence, nature, truth,
gospel, authenticity,
veracity, accuracy,
exactness, precise,
unalloyed, regularity,
principal, (error, fallacy,
mistake, fault, blunder,
heresy, deceit)

vessel-n receptacle,
enclosure, recipient,
receiver, reservoir,
compartment, vase,
bushel, barrel, canister, jar,
bottle, basket, hopper,
crate, cradle, bassinet,
hamper, douser, cistern

vexation-n disappointment,
mortification, cold comfort,
regret, repining, taking on,
inquietude, soreness,
heartburning, lamentation,
hypercriticism, malcontent,
(comfort, resignation,
content)

vibrate-v fluctuation,
vacillation, swing, beat,
shake, wag, see-saw,
lurch, dodge, oscillate,
alternate, undulate,
pulsate, beat, dance,
curvet, reel, (fixed,
steadfast, firm, fast,
steady, balanced)

vicious-adj vice, evil-doing,
wickedness, iniquity,
demerit, sin, immorality,
impropriety, indecorum,
scandal, laxity, infirmity,
weakness, frailty,
imperfection, (virtuous,
good, innocent,
meritorious, deserving)

victim-n pigeon, April fool,
laughing stock, flat,
greenhorn, fool, dupe, gull,
gudgeon, cull, deceived,
swallow up, bite,
credulous, mistaken,
(cheat, swindler, thief,
knave, rogue, decoy-duck,
trickster)

view-v see, observe, watch,
attend to, eye, survey,
scan, inspect, glance,
behold, discern, perceive,
discover, distinguish,
recognize, spy,
contemplate, (blind,
hoodwink, dazzle, dim
sighted, wall-eyed)

vigilance-n watchful,
surveillance, vigil, look out,
care, solicitude, heed,
alertness, activity,
attention, prudence,
circumspection, caution,
preparation, accuracy,
(neglect, carelessness,
trifling, omission)

vigor-n healthy, well, sound,
hearty, hale, fresh, green,
whole, florid, flush, hardy,
stanch, staunch, brave,
robust, unscathed, perfect,
excellent, (fever, calenture,
inflammation, ailing,
disease, sick)

villain-n rascal, scoundrel,
miscreant, wretch, reptile,
viper, serpent, urchin,
delinquent, criminal,
malefactor, culprit, thief,
murderer, jail-bird, (good,
paragon, hero, innocent,
good example)

vincible-adj powerless,

impotent, unable,
incapable, incompetent,
inefficient, inept, unfit,
disqualified, harmless,
defenseless, unfortified,
indefensible, pregnable,
(powerful, puissant, potent,
capable)

vinaigrette-*n* fragrance,
aroma, redolence,
perfume, bouquet, sweet
smell, aromatic perfume,
incense, musk,
frankincense, spicy, balmy,
ambrosial, perfumed,
(stench, stink, fetid, strong
smelling, putrid,
suffocating, nidorous)

vindicate-*v* justification,
warrant, exoneration,
exculpation, acquittal,
whitewashing, extenuation,
softening, mitigation, reply,
defence, recrimination,
(accusation, charge,
imputation, slur,
inculpation, exprobration)

vindictive-*adj* resentful,
cantankerous, pugnacious,
perverse, querulous, fiery,
peppery, passionate,
choleric, shrewish, quick,
hot, testy, touchy,
animosity, exasperation,
bitterness

violate-*v* seduction,
defloration, defilement,
abuse, rape, incest, social
evil, adultery, harem,
intrigue, debauch, defile,
rampant, lustful, carnal,
erotic, voluptuous, (pure,
undefiled, modest,

delicate)

viper-*n* snake, serpent, asp,
vermin, beast, poison,
leaven, virus, venom,
arsenic, antimony,
nicotine, demon, sting,
fang, (remedial,
restorative, corrective,
palliative, balsamic,
narcotic)

virgin-*n* new, immaculate,
immaturity, novel, recent,
youth, restore, evergreen,
untried, modern, neoteric,
new born, (old, ancient,
antique, long standing,
prime, primitive)

virile-*adj* strength, power,
energy, force, physical
force, stamina, muscle,
sinew, vitality, athletic,
adamant, steel, iron, oak,
might, stout, robust, (weak,
frail, fragile, languid, poor,
rickety, cranky)

virtual-*adj* inexistence,
negative, blank, missing,
omitted, absent, unreal,
potential, baseless,
unsubstantial, vain,
uncreated, exhausted,
annihilated, gone, lost,
departed, (actual, real,
positive, absolute,
prevalent)

virtue-*n* good, innocent,
meritorious, reserving,
worthy, correct, moral,
righteous, well-intentioned,
creditable, laudable,
commendable,
praiseworthy, admirable,
(vicious, corrupt, atrocity)

W

wade-v gather, learn, acquire, gain, receive, drink in, obtain, collect, knowledge, information, peruse, pore, industrious, studious, (teach, instruct, edify, tutor, enlighten)

waggle-v oscillate, alternate, undulate, wave, rock, swing, pulsate, beat, nod, bob, courtesy, curtsy, play., fluctuate, dance, curvet, reel, quake, shake, flicker, wriggle, roll, toss, pitch, flounder

wait-v put off, defer, delay, lay over, suspend, shift, waive, retard, remand, postpone, adjourn, procrastinate, dally, prolong, protract, knee back, (early, prime, timely, punctual, forward, prompt)

wall-n bar, barrier, turn-stile, gate, portcullis, barricade, defense, breakwater, bulkhead, block, buffer, stopper, dam, weir, drawback, objection, stumbling block, (relief, rescue, lift, aid)

wallop-v strike, punish, chastise, castigate, slap, smack, spank, thump, beat, swing, buffet, thresh, thrash pummel, drum, leather, trounce, baste, belabor, pelt, stone, lapidate, torture

wander-v move, motion, transitional, motor, motive, shifting, mobile, mercurial, unquiet, restless, nomadic, erratic, drift, flow, stream, (remain, stay, stagnate, rest, pause, lull, stop, repose)

want-v desire, wish, fancy, fantasy, need, exigency, mind, inclination, leaning, bent, longing, hankering, inkling, solicitude, anxiety, yearning, coveting, aspiration, (indifferent, cool, unconcerned)

wanton-adj capricious, erratic, eccentric, fitful, hysterical, full of whims, maggoty, inconsistent, fanciful, fantastic, whimsical, crotchety, particular, humorism, freakish, skittish, wayward, contrary, arbitrary

ward-n region, sphere, ground, soil, area, realm, hemisphere, quarter, district, beat, orb, circuit, circle, pale, limit, department, domain, tract, territory, parish, (bound-less, uncircumscribed, extensive)

warehouse-n storehouse, closet, depository, repository, stock, accumulate, hoard, stack, promontory, reservoir, receptacle, amass, collect, harvest, save, reserve, (spend, expend, use, consume, spill)

warn-v discourage, dampen, disincline, indispose, stagger, repel, quench, deprecate, induce, deter, dissuade, obstinate, restrain, keep back, (prompt, persuade, bribe, lure, stimulate)

warrant-n dictate, mandate, caveat, decree, writ, ordination, bull, edict, decretal, dispensation, citation, permit, authorize, admission, grant, empower, (prohibit, forbid, disallow, bar, withhold, shut)

wash-v lavatory, laundry, clean, pure, purification, defecation, lustration, abstersion, ablution, disinfect, fumigate, deodorize, immaculate, (mud, mire, quagmire, sludge, slime, slush)

watch-v observe, attend to, peep, peer, pry, look, witness, contemplate, speculate, cast, discover, distinguish, recognize, spy, behold, demonstrate, (blind, hoodwink, undiscerning, dim sighted)

way-n method, manner, wise, form, mode, fashion, tone, guise, procedure, path, road, route, course, trajectory, orbit, track, beat, means of access, channel, passage, avenue, approach, artery, lane

weak-adj feeble, insipid, illogical, frail, fragile, flimsy, unsubstantial, rickety, cranky, drooping, tottering, broken, lame, withered, shatter,shaken,

crazy, shaky, (strong, might, vigorous, forcible, hard)

wear-v impair, injure, damage, loss, detriment, laceration, outrage, havoc, deteriorate, degenerate, decay, dilapidation, rotten, blight, (improve, refine, rectify, enrich, mellow, elaborate)

weave-v produce, perform, operate, do, make, form, construct, fabricate, frame, contrive, manufacture, forge, twine, entwine, twist, interlace, (destroy, ruin, dilapidation, deteriorate, wreck)

wedge-n fusiform, wedge-shaped, triangular, angular, bent, crooked, firm, fast, close, tight, taut, secure, hinge, tether, pin, nail, rivet, jam, dovetail, (sunder, divide, sever, carve, dissect, detach)

ween-v think, hold, opinion, conceive, trow, fancy, apprehend, embrace, assured, positive, satisfied, confident, nurture, credence, secure, impress, (dispute, fallible, uncertain, untrue, distrust, doubt)

weigh-v influence, tell, have a hold upon, magnetize, bear upon, pervade, prevail, dominate, gain, important, rampant, regnant, reign, (irrelevant, unconducive, impotence, inert, powerless)

Y

yarn-n exaggeration, expansion, hyperbole, stretch, strain, coloring, caricature, extravagance, nonsense, fringe, embroidery, traveler's tale, overestimate, wire, string, thread, twine, cord, rope

yawn-n nod, get sleepy, snooze, nap, dream, sleepy, indolent, lazy, slothful, idle, lust, remiss, slack, inert, sluggish, languid, supine, heavy, dull, leaden, listless, (active, quick, prompt, alert, spry, sharp)

yearling-n infant, babe, child, youth, stripling, youngster, younker, weanling, papoose, bambino, seedling, whipper-snapper, (veteran, old man, seer, patriarch, centenarian, old stager, forefathers)

yearn-v pity, compassion, commiseration, sympathy, tenderness, forbearance, humanity, mercy, clemency, leniency, charity, touched, soften, (unmerciful, uncompassionate, severe, unrelenting)

yeast-n leaven, ferment, barm, light, subtile, airy, imponderable, astatic, weightless, ethereal, sublimated, uncompressed, volatile, buoyant, floating, portable, (heavy, massive, lead, millstone)

yell-v cry, vociferate, raise, shout, roar, bawl, brawl, hop, whoop, bellow, howl, scream, screech, screak, shriek, squeak, squall, whine, pule, pipe, cheer, hoot, grumble, moan, groan

yield-v succumb, submit, bend, resign, defer, submissive, surrender,capitulate, retreat, downtrodden, pliant, undefended, permit, relinquish, sanction, (overpower, struggle, unbending, forbid, refuse)

yoke-n lock, latch, belay, brace, hook, grapple, leash, couple, accouplement, link, bracket, bridge over, span, pin, nail, bolt, hasp, clasp, clamp, (sever, rupture, segregate, breach, rescind, divide)

yokel-n bungler, blunderer, marplot, fumbler, lubber, duffer, awkward, squad, greenhorn, clod, muff, (proficient, expert, adept, connoisseur, veteran)

yokemate-n spouse, consort, husband, wife, better half, mate, helpmate, match, betrothment, promise, (unmarried, bachelor, virgin, single, celibacy)

yonder-adj distant, far-off,

remote, telescopic, distal,
stretching, ulterior,
transmarine, span, stride,
faraway, farther, further,
beyond, far and wide, (near,
close, no great distance,
nigh, within reach)

yore-*adj* formerly, of old, last,
latter, retrospective, ancient,
time immemorial, olden,
forgotten, extinct, gone by,
ancestral, (anticipate,
millennium, advent, look
forward, eventual)

young-*adj* youthful, juvenile,
green, callow, budding,
sappy, beardless, under
age, junior, infant, minor,
pupilage, puberty, prime,
rising generation, (seniority,
elder, longevity, aged,
antiquated, decay)

Z

zany-*adj* fool, idiot,
tomfoolery, wiseacre,
simpleton, witling, donkey,
ass, ninny, nincompoop,
lout, loon, gabby, trifler,
babbler, dullard, doodle,
clod, lack-wit, (authority,
luminary, wise man)

zeal-*adj* quick, prompt, yare,
instant, ready, alert, spry,
sharp, smart, fast, swift,
expeditious, awake,
forward, eager, strenuous,
enterprising, industrious,
diligent, (indolent, lazy,
slothful, idle, remiss)

zealot-*n* bigot, intolerant,
obstinate, immovability,

inflexibility, prejudgement,
opinionist, enthusiast,
tenacious, (changeful, idle,
withdraw from, relinquish)

zealous-*adj* eager,
animated, resolute,
steadfast, vivacious,
diligent, fiery, brisk

zero-*n* nothing, naught,
cipher, none, no one,
nobody, never,
unsubstantial, blank, void,
immaterial, groundless,
nonentity, (substantial,
thing, object, something,
being

zest-*n* pleasure,
gratification, enjoyment,
fruition, delectation, relish,
gusto, satisfaction,
content, well-being,
snugness, comfort,
amusement, happiness,
(concern, grief, sorrow,
distress, affliction, woe)

zigzag-*v* diversion,
digression, departure,
aberration, divergence,
detour, circuit, wander,
vagrant, by-paths and
crooked ways, oblique
motion, deviate,
swerve,(toward, aim, line,
path, road, range)

zone-*n* region, sphere,
clime, climate, meridian,
latitude, territorial, local,
arena, precincts, district,
domain, tract, parish,
province, township, field,
plot, (unlimited space,
wilderness, waste, free
space)